RELIGION AND CULTURE IN THE MIDDLE AGES

Anchorites, Wombs and Tombs

T0083635

Series Editors
Denis Renevey (University of Lausanne)
Diane Watt (Aberystwyth University)

Editorial Board
Miri Rubin (Queen Mary, University of London)
Jean-Claude Schmitt (École des Hautes
Études en Sciences Sociales, Paris)
Fiona Somerset (Duke University)
Christiania Whitehead (University of Warwick)

RELIGION AND CULTURE IN THE MIDDLE AGES

Anchorites, Wombs and Tombs

Intersections of Gender and Enclosure in the Middle Ages

Edited by

LIZ HERBERT McAVOY and MARI HUGHES–EDWARDS

UNIVERSITY OF WALES PRESS
CARDIFF
2005

First published, 2005
Paperback edition, 2009

British Library Cataloguing-in-Publication Data
A catalogue record for this book is available from the British Library.

ISBN 978-0-7083-2200-0

Printed in Wales by Dinefwr Press, Llandybïe

Contents

NOTES ON CONTRIBUTORS

ALEXANDRA BARRATT is Professor in the Department of English, University of Waikato, New Zealand. She has published widely on Middle English women writers and anchoritic writing and her most recent publication, *Anne Bulkeley and Her Book: Fashioning Female Piety in Early Tudor England*, focuses on texts prepared for a female patron.

JOHAN BERGSTRÖM-ALLEN is affiliated to the Université de Lausanne, researching a Ph.D. in the English writings produced by Carmelite Friars in late-medieval England. He lives in York, where he runs the British Province of Carmelites' publishing house, Saint Albert's Press. He is a member of the editorial team of the international journal, *Carmelus*, and is tutor and executive board member of the Carmelite Institute of Britain and Ireland.

SANTHA BHATTACHARJI has taught Old and Middle English for various colleges of Oxford since 1989 and is currently a college lecturer at New College, Oxford. She has published articles on Old English poetry, liturgical topics and the Middle English Mystics, including *The Spirituality of Margery Kempe* (1997) and *Reading the Bible with Gregory the Great* (2001).

SUSANNAH MARY CHEWNING is Associate Professor of English at Union County College, New Jersey. She has published widely on medieval devotional literature and anchoritism. She has edited two volumes of essays, *Intersections of Sexuality and the Divine in Medieval Culture: The Word Made Flesh* (2005) and *The Milieu and Context of the Wooing Group* (2009). Her current research focuses upon gender and sexuality as it is articulated through the early English anchoritic tradition as well as later medieval mysticism and dream vision poetry.

ELIZABETH FREEMAN is Lecturer in medieval European history at the University of Tasmania. Her research focuses on the Cistercian monastic order, particularly the Cistercians in medieval England. Her study of

Cistercian attitudes to the past has been published as *Narratives of a New Order: Cistercian Historical Writing in England, 1150–1220*, Medieval Church Studies, 2 (2002). Her current research focuses on the histories of English Cistercian nuns from the twelfth to the sixteenth centuries.

CATE GUNN teaches medieval literature and religion for the continuing education departments of Essex and Cambridge Universities and for the WEA. Her research has been published as *Ancrene Wisse: From Pastoral Literature to Vernacular Spirituality* (2007).

ROBERT HASENFRATZ is Associate Professor of English and Medieval Studies at the University of Connecticut. He has recently produced a TEAMS edition of *Ancrene Wisse* (2000) and has also taken over the editorship of the journal *Mystics Quarterly*. His primary research interests are in Anglo-Saxon literature, anchoritism, mysticism and textual editing.

REBECCA HAYWARD is currently an adjunct lecturer and tutor in the English Department at the University of Auckland, where she has also held a Post-Doctoral Fellowship. She has recently collaborated with W. R. Barnes on a translation of Goscelin's *Liber confortatorius* (published in *Writing the Wilton Women: Goscelin's Legend of Edith and Liber Confortatorius* (2004), edited by Stephanie Hollis). Her current research interests include anchorites and New Zealand medieval scholars.

LIZ HERBERT MCAVOY is Senior Lecturer in Gender Studies and Medieval Literature at Swansea University. Her research interests lie in medieval anchoritism, female mysticism, medieval women's writing and critical theory, particularly post-structuralist feminist theory. She has published widely in these areas including *Authority and the Female Body in the Writings of Julian of Norwich and Margery Kempe* (2004); ed. *Rhetoric of the Anchorhold: Space, Place and Body within the Discourses of Enclosure* (2008); ed. *A Companion to Julian of Norwich* (2008). She is currently working on a book that examines the intersections of gender and space within representations of the medieval anchorite.

MARI HUGHES-EDWARDS is currently Senior Lecturer in English Literature at Edge Hill University, having taught at the universities of York, Manchester, Liverpool, Salford and Liverpool John Moores.

Originally a medievalist by training, she has research interests in medieval anchoritism, solitude and space, and a monograph entitled *The Ideology of English Anchoritism* is forthcoming with the University of Wales Press. Her research now focuses equally on contemporary British literature and her publications have focused on contemporary poetry, especially on the work of Carol Ann Duffy and Lee Harwood.

CATHERINE INNES-PARKER is Professor of English at the University of Prince Edward Island. She has published widely on *Ancrene Wisse* and its associated texts, and is currently completing an edition of the Wooing Group. Her most recent research involves vernacular passion meditation, focusing particularly on vernacular versions of Bonaventure's *Lignum Vitae*.

KRISTEN MCQUINN graduated with a Master's degree in medieval literature in August 2003 from Arizona State University. She is currently working as an academic counsellor at a local university while pursuing various teaching opportunities. Her most recent research interests include medieval Irish paganism and its connections to Native American shamanism.

ANNEKE B. MULDER-BAKKER taught Medieval History and Medieval Studies at the University of Groningen. She is now Emerita at the University of Leiden. Her publications on historiography, hagiography and gender include *Sanctity and Motherhood* (1995), *De Kluizenaar in de Eik: Gerlach van Houthem en zijn Verering* (1995); ed. with Renée Nip, *The Prime of Their Lives: Wise Old Women in Pre-industrial Europe* (2004); *Lives of the Anchoresses: The Rise of the Urban Recluse in Medieval Europe* (2005); ed. with Jocelyn Wogan-Browne, *Household, Women and Christianities in Late Antiquity and the Middle Ages* (2005); *Mary of Oignies: Mother of Salvation* (2006).

ULRIKE WIETHAUS teaches interdisciplinary courses in the Humanities Program, the Women's Studies Program, the Master of Liberal Studies Program and the Department of Religion at Wake Forest University, North Carolina. She has published widely on medieval mysticism and is currently completing a book-length study of the construction of alterity in medieval Christian mysticism in Western Europe, entitled *Trace of the Other: Medieval Christian Mysticism in Contemporary Context*.

Series Editors' Preface

Religion and Culture in the Middle Ages aims to explore the interface between medieval religion and culture, with as broad an understanding of those terms as possible. It puts to the forefront studies which engage with works that significantly contributed to the shaping of medieval culture. However, it also gives attention to studies dealing with works that reflect and highlight aspects of medieval culture that have been neglected in the past by scholars of the medieval disciplines. For example, devotional works and the practice they infer illuminate our understanding of the medieval subject and its culture in remarkable ways, while studies of the material space designed and inhabited by medieval subjects yield new evidence on the period and the people who shaped it and lived in it. In the larger field of religion and culture, we also want to explore further the roles played by women as authors, readers and owners of books, thereby defining them more precisely as actors in the cultural field. The series as a whole investigates the European Middle Ages, from c.500 to c.1500. Our aim is to explore medieval religion and culture with the tools belonging to such disciplines as, among others, art history, philosophy, theology, history, musicology, the history of medicine, and literature. In particular, we would like to promote interdisciplinary studies, as we believe strongly that our modern understanding of the term applies fascinatingly well to a cultural period marked by a less tight confinement and categorization of its disciplines than the modern period. However, our only criterion is academic excellence, with the belief that the use of a large diversity of critical tools and theoretical approaches enables a deeper understanding of medieval culture. We want the series to reflect this diversity, as we believe that, as a collection of outstanding contributions, it offers a more subtle representation of a period that is marked by paradoxes and contradictions and which necessarily reflects diversity and difference, however difficult it may sometimes have proved for medieval culture to accept these notions.

Acknowledgements

The editors of this volume would like to offer their heartfelt thanks to all its contributors for their cooperation, enthusiasm and patience during its production. They also acknowledge the part played by the department of English at the University of Wales, Aberystwyth, the University of Wales Conference Centre at Gregynog and the British Academy for their generous financial support for the conference in 2002 which initiated this essay collection. Particular thanks are also due to Professor Elaine Treharne from the English department at the University of Leicester for her tireless encouragement and support, both material and moral, whilst the project was coming to fruition We would also like to express our appreciation to the editorial staff and production team of the University of Wales Press for their patient and professional assistance, advice and understanding throughout the editing process and, finally, to friends and family who sustained us through the inevitable highs and lows of its production.

ABBREVIATIONS

BL	British Library
EETS	Early English Text Society
e.s.	Extra Series
MED	Middle English Dictionary
OED	Oxford English Dictionary
o.s.	Original Series
PG	*Patrologia Graeca*, ed. J.-P. Migne (Paris, 1887)
PL	*Patrologia Latina*, ed. J.-P. Migne (Paris, 1841–64)
PRO	Public Record Office
TEAMS	Consortium for the Teaching of the Middle Ages

Foreword

ANNEKE B. MULDER-BAKKER

The research into hermits and anchorites has long been dominated by theologians and church historians. Working from the premises of their own particular discipline, these scholars interpret the source material on anchoritism accordingly, that is from a modern confessional perspective and from a modern dogmatic stance. When researchers from other fields of study, such as cultural historians and literary scholars, consult their textbooks and encyclopedias for an initial introduction to female anchorites or anchoritic spirituality, they read that such women were deeply religious persons who abstained from marital life and motherhood for the sake of their spiritual bridegroom, Christ.[1] Isolated from the outside world, with the door of their cell bolted and the window covered with a black curtain, they lived as if at the gates of heaven, praying day and night in the seclusion of their cells. Such a life, if these accounts are to be believed, was a *Vita angelica* – a life of angels. Immersed in their meditation, so we read, the female anchorite yearned for the moment when the heavenly bridegroom would take her by the hand and lead her into the heavenly bridal chamber. The scholars who wrote these textbooks were, without exception, men whose opinions were formed not only within the discipline of church history, but also by the upper-class ideals of the nineteenth century – the so-called 'Victorian' ideal which saw the 'good' housewife as one who longs for her husband or father in the seclusion of her home. In short, they were unable to contemplate anything diverging from this paradigm. The fact that the sparse information in the extant sources does not seem to support their ideas apparently gave them no second thoughts. As a consequence,

their somewhat narrow views on anchoritic spirituality and their interpretation of its historical sources have tended to direct all research into
the subject during the past generations.

In more recent research, however, 'secular' historians and historical
anthropologists have taken a different approach and come to different,
sometimes almost opposite, findings.[2] Inspired by innovative studies,
such as Peter Brown's 'The rise and function of the holy man in late
Antiquity', French and Italian researchers, starting from a social-
historical perspective, studied the role of hermits and anchorites in historical actuality.[3] Under the leadership of André Vauchez, director of
the École française in Rome, and Sofia Boesch Gajano, founder and
great inspirer of the Italian *Gruppo di ricerca 'Santi e culto dei santi'*, historians, art historians and anthropologists have freed themselves from
the framework of church history and dogma to begin studying
the holy in all its facets from a 'profane' perspective. Research into
anchoritism has found a place in their programme. Sofia Boesch
Gajano herself wrote a pioneering study of Chelidonia, the female successor of Benedict in the cave of Subiaco, showing especially how the
bones and the veneration were subjected to the manipulations of
power politics. Anna Benvenuti Papi inventoried the many recluses in
Florence and Tuscany who lived as in a grave (*velut in sepulchro*), and
Gabriella Zarri did ground-breaking research into a group of living
saints (*Sante Vive*), who won respect at the humanist courts of Italy.
The latter, Zarri maintains, combined mystical ecstasy and the gifts of
prophecy and telepathy with thaumaturgical powers and political influence. They had 'a preference for the mixed life, held to be superior to
the cloistered life if not the contemplative one', along with a 'sense of
having a social and ecclesiastical mission'.[4] This latter study clearly
demonstrates the influence of issues and approaches emanating from
developments within the discipline of Anglo-American Gender Studies,
which provide a highly fruitful route also for the study of anchoritism
in other parts of the western world.

For northern Europe, my own research into female anchorites in the
lands between the Seine and the Elbe shows that in the twelfth and
thirteenth centuries a new ascetic lifestyle was on the rise there – that of
the 'free reclusive' life – in the world but not *of* the world; a life of total
surrender to the love of God without submitting to a fixed rule or an
imposed form of life. In Europe, at least, free recluses, living in their
anchorholds in the hearts of towns, did not lead the isolated existence
that theologians and church historians postulated for them. They were

not penitents who spent their days in seclusion, wallowing in extreme forms of self-castigation, as literary fantasies suggest. Nor were they loners primarily concerned with their own sanctity, a life imagined for them by church reformers. Instead, they seem to have made a clear choice to serve God in a way that included service to their fellow human beings. Unburdened by social obligations, they were free to act as the spirit – the Spirit – moved them. This meant listening to people, instructing them if they lacked knowledge, hearing their confessions, helping them find answers to questions of life and death. But it also meant taking authoritative action against those who behaved immorally.[5]

A reading of any of the extant Middle English anchoritic guides, however, suggests that the anchoritic tradition in England was somewhat different. The sheer number of surviving guides – at least twelve or thirteen – suggests that there was a considerable desire on the part of English recluses for a rule which found its expression in the creation and often the recreation of a corpus of normative literature.[6] Beginning with Goscelin's *Liber confortatorius* (c.1080) and ending with Walter Hilton's late-fourteenth-century *Scale of Perfection*, these guidance writings acknowledge the potential sociability of the recluse, but do not celebrate it. Instead, they posit an anchoritic ideal throughout the Middle Ages which is solitary, secluded and highly individualized. The goal of English medieval anchoritism seems, according to these guidance texts at least, to have been the creation of a safe, solitary space in which the recluse could foster a highly personal relationship with God. Indeed, the high-medieval texts, such as *de Institutione Inclusarum* and *Ancrene Wisse*, actively discourage reclusive sociability. Although the later-medieval guides, such as *Speculum Inclusorum*, Rolle's *Form of Living* and Hilton's *Scale of Perfection*, demonstrate that it has become increasingly acceptable for the recluse to have social contact, it is by no means shown to be the central interest of these writers, or the *raison d'être* of the vocation. Reclusive sociability continues, in England at least, to be constructed in tension with the contemplative ideals of anchoritic life, which demand comparative seclusion and social segregation.

The volume of studies presented here follows on from a conference organized by English Literature scholars. More than scholars on the continent, they stand in a long tradition of historical and literary investigations into medieval anchoritism. Unlike the church-historical work on the continental phenomenon, Rotha Mary Clay's book on *The Hermits and Anchorites of England* already provided a foundation for historical research as long ago as 1914, and it still offers the shoulder of the giant on which the dwarves can stand and look further.[7] Subsequently, Ann Warren supplemented Clay's inventory and studied, especially, the financial relations of anchorites with their often noble patrons.[8] In the last decades, however, British, North American and Australasian scholarship has concentrated mainly on *Ancrene Wisse* and anchoritic spirituality, and investigation has been within the literary context rather than within that of historical practice. As a result, research into the anchoritic life is now largely the domain of literary historians.

Continuing along this literary trajectory, the conveners of the 'Anchorites, Wombs and Tombs' conference brought together with literary scholars a group of international historians with an eye to entering into dialogue with them. Moreover, they also propagated a Gender Studies approach to the research material, a combination which comprised exactly the right initiative at exactly the right moment: the conference itself and the selection of essays included in this volume therefore announce that the time is ripe for a much more international and fully interdisciplinary approach to the subject.

Notes

[1] See for instance the authoritative Hubert Jedin, *Handbuch der Kirchengeschichte*, 7 vols (Freiburg, 1962–79) or the lemmata in well-known encyclopedia, such as: Pierre Doyère, 'Ermites', in *Dictionnaire de Droit Catholique*, 5, pp. 412–29; Pierre Doyère, 'Érémitisme en Occident', in *Dictionnaire de Spiritualité*, 4, i, pp. 953–82; and the very disappointing lemma by M.-C. Chartier, 'Reclus', in *Dictionnaire de Spiritualité*, 13, pp. 221–3. The pioneering volume of studies, *L'Eremitismo in Occidente nei secoli xi e xii*, Atti Mendola, 1962 (Milan, 1965) focuses on (male) hermits in the forest and talks about recluses only in an annex of Jean Hubert, 'Les recluseries urbaines au Moyen Âge', pp. 485–7.

[2] A much more up-to-date introduction from a 'profane' historical perspective is given by Paulette L'Hermite-Leclercq, 'Le reclus dans la ville au bas Moyen Âge', in *Journal des Savants*, 1 (1988), 219–62; 'Les reclus parisiens au bas Moyen Âge', in Georges Jehel et al. (eds), *Villes et sociétés urbaines au Moyen Âge*, Hommage Jacques Heers (Paris, 1994), pp. 223–31; 'La femme, la recluse et la mort', in *Muerte, religiosidad y cultura popular, siglos xiii–xviii* (Zaragosa, 1994), pp. 151–62; 'Reclus et recluses dans la Mouvance des ordres religieux', in *Les Mouvances laïques des Ordres Religieux*, Actes CERCOR (Saint-Étienne, 1996), pp. 201–18. See also my own short lemmata: 'Inklusen' in *Lexikon des Mittelalters*, 5, pp. 424–5, and 'Klause', ibid., p. 1195; Jean Leclercq, 'Solitude and solidarity: medieval

women recluses', in Lillian Thomas Shank and John A. Nichols (eds), *Peace Weavers: Medieval Religious Women*, 2 (Kalamazoo, 1987), pp. 67–83; and Patricia J. F. Rosof, 'The anchoress in the twelfth and thirteenth centuries', in ibid., pp. 123–44.

3   Peter Brown, 'The rise and function of the holy man in late Antiquity', in *Society and the Holy in Late Antiquity* (London, 1982), pp. 103–52. See also Mayr-Harting's study inspired by Peter Brown's approach: Henry Mayr-Harting, 'Functions of a twelfth-century recluse', *History*, 60 (1975), 337–52.

4   André Vauchez, *La Sainteté en Occident aux derniers siècles du moyen âge. D'après les procès de canonisation et les documents hagiographiques* (Rome, 1981); Sofia Boesch Gajano, 'Monastero, città, campagna: il culto di S. Chelidonia a Subiaco tra XII e XVI secolo', in the first volume produced by this group, Sofia Boesch Gajano and Lucia Sebastiani (eds), *Culto dei santi: Istitutioni e classi sociali in età preindustriale* (L'Aquila, 1984), pp. 227–60; Anna Benvenuti Papi, ' "Velut in sepulchro": Cellane e recluse nella tradizione agiografica italiana', in Anna Benvenuti Papi, *'In Castro Poenitentiae.' Santità e società femminile nell' Italia Medievale* (Rome, 1990), pp. 263–314; Gabriella Zarri, *Le sante vive: Profezie di corte e devozione femminile tra '400 e '500* (Turino, 1990); and Gabriella Zarri, 'Living saints: a typology of female sanctity in the early sixteenth century', in Daniel Bornstein and Roberto Rusconi (eds), *Women and Religion in Medieval and Renaissance Italy* (Chicago, 1996), pp. 219–303, which comprises the heart of her book. For France see the studies of Paulette L'Hermite-Leclercq already listed in note 2.

5   Anneke B. Mulder-Bakker, *The Lives of the Anchoresses: The Rise of the Urban Recluse in Medieval Europe* (Philadelphia, 2005); or see my 'Lame Margaret of Magdeburg: the social function of a medieval recluse', *Journal of Medieval History*, 22 (1996), 155–69.

6   Ann K. Warren lists and describes all these English guides as an appendix to her volume on English anchoritism. See her *Anchorites and their Patrons in Medieval England* (Berkeley, 1985), pp. 294–8. Although some of the guides she lists do not seem to have been for anchorites per se but for solitaries who may or may not have lived an anchoritic life, Warren's list is still the closest thing to a comprehensive catalogue of the English texts.

7   Rotha Mary Clay, *The Hermits and Anchorites of England* (London, 1914; repr. Detroit, 1968).

8   Again see Warren, *Anchorites and their Patrons*.

1

Introduction:
Intersections of Time and
Space in Gender and Enclosure

LIZ HERBERT McAVOY AND
MARI HUGHES-EDWARDS

Suddenly she stood up, pushed her long grey hair away from her forehead and without saying a word began shaking the bars of her cell with both hands more furiously than a lioness. The bars held firm. Then she went to fetch from a corner of her cell a big paving-stone which served her as a pillow, and hurled it at the bars so violently that one broke in a shower of sparks. A second blow completed the collapse of the old iron crossbar which blocked the window. Then using both hands she finished breaking and pushing clear the rusty stumps of the bars. There are moments when a woman's hands have superhuman strength.[1]

Until very recently, literary representation of the anchoritic phenomenon frequently tended towards the production of images such as this one, of a bizarre lifestyle chosen by the religious – and eventually reluctant – eccentric who inhabited a dark, mysterious world on the margins of time and space. This account, penned by Victor Hugo in the third decade of the nineteenth century, memorably reconstructs a medieval Parisian woman as a recluse, presenting the enclosed woman as also the madwoman, the frenzied mystic who conflates in one body a whole conglomeration of transcultural and transhistorical fears of the dark, unfathomable alien 'other'. Indeed, far more scholarly examinations of the anchoritic phenomenon than Hugo's dramatic representation for a long time did little to dispel such popular misconception, with their cursory dismissal of the anchoritic phenomenon as a mere footnote to medieval religiosity. The anchorite remained deeply entrenched as an oddity, somebody 'buried alive', prematurely 'entombed', living a punitive life of stark asceticism on the edge of human consciousness and imagination, or else engaged in a relaxed, homely existence, waited on by friends, family or servants.[2] As Anneke B. Mulder-Bakker astutely points out in her foreword to this volume, insight into anchoritic enclosure has also tended to be framed by processes of traditionalist and masculinist intellectual thought, in which issues of gender and its shifting perspectives have had very little part to play. As a result, those more nuanced implications of the phenomenon, which form the focus of the essays collected together here, have tended to escape detailed examination. In many ways, then, this volume constitutes both a response to the one-dimensionality of the large majority of earlier studies of the anchoritic life and a furthering of the rapidly burgeoning interest amongst historians and literary scholars which is currently taking root within academia.[3]

More contemporary insights into late-medieval anchorites, in particular, and their systems of support, are all to a greater or lesser extent indebted to the important research undertaken by Rotha Mary Clay in 1914[4] and by Ann K. Warren in 1985 who, drawing upon many of Clay's earlier findings, examines the role of the anchorite and concomitant support systems from the twelfth through to the early sixteenth century.[5] Although fundamental to most areas of anchoritic studies today, Warren's exemplary work is nevertheless self-confessedly limited in scope, because of what she identifies as a dearth of historical documentation pertaining to anchorites prior to the twelfth century.[6] She also tends to interpret individual anchoritic guidance writings as evidence of general practice and this, as Mari Hughes-Edwards argues in her essay included in this volume, has led to her rigid separation of anchoritic guides into a high-medieval penitential model and a late-medieval contemplative one, an arbitrary division which does not allow for the considerable similarities within the contemplative spiritualities of these two overlapping periods. The working definition of the anchorite which Warren offers is also decidedly narrow and, within her analysis, the late-medieval anchorite tends to be regarded as a synecdoche for the wider phenomenon as a whole. For example, Warren regards the anchorite as a 'solitary recluse' whose life has been dedicated to God and who has embraced an existence of lifelong asceticism. The archetypical anchorite is therefore one who lives in a cell or narrow house attached to a church and who provides for his or her contemporaries a constant reminder of the 'proper focus of Christian existence'.[7] Echoing earlier, more traditionalist approaches, such as that of Jean Leclercq,[8] the medieval anchorite is identified by Warren as being simultaneously 'martyr, viator, penitent, ascetic, mystic, *miles Christi*', who is 'immured, locked up, imprisoned' and who, having become solitary by means of individual choice, now becomes legally solitary in an existence from which there is no retreat until death.[9] Whilst much of this language is potentially reductive, it has a typological usefulness in its identification of some of the roles often played by the medieval recluse. However, it also serves to occlude some of the wider, more nuanced roles played by the anchorite, and the discourse and meanings his/her enclosed state could produce within a wider socio-religious context. Not only that but, as previously suggested, it also has the effect of rendering the late-medieval expression of the anchoritic life as the definitive one, and it is just such an oversight which the essays in this current volume will serve in some measure to redress. Indeed, within the context of Warren's assertion of anchoritism as an issue of personal choice, the volume as a whole aims to demonstrate the myriad ways, both overt and covert, material and discursive, in which that choice was articulated, activated and influenced, not only in specific times and places by specific people, but also within a more general context. It will also reveal that this choice was dependent not only upon epistemic shifts and/or continuities within both culture and religion, but also upon the ways in which attitudes towards gender interacted with these epistemo-logical considerations throughout the entire medieval period.

Of course, any essay collection which claims to concern itself with issues of gender will be indebted to the work undertaken in recent decades by the theorist Judith Butler, who has demonstrated the extent to which gender can be regarded as a private *and* public behavioural performance.[10] According to Butler, what we frequently recognize as an 'ontological' gender emanating from a type of essential 'core' is, in fact, merely a performance of 'acts, gestures, and desire [which] produce the effect of an internal core or substance . . . that suggest, but never reveal, the organizing principle of identity as a cause'.[11] Moreover, such perform-ances tend to traverse both cultures and epistemes, as well as clearly enjoying specific expressions within specific and localized socio-religious cultures. The interaction that arises between expressions of the anchoritic life (which also tended to be equally culturally specific *and* equally transhistorical) and the performances of gender, as identified by Butler, has been almost entirely overlooked to date. Indeed, in this con-text it is worth noting Warren's treatment in her study of the available statistics for the incidences of anchoritic activity in England between the twelfth century and the Reformation, figures which in themselves serve to problematize the type of traditional approaches to the phenomenon which we have been discussing.[12] Whilst demonstrating without question that there was an enormous increase in the number of anchorites during this period and a correspondingly steady increase in the vocation's socio-religious status, Warren notes only in passing – and without interrogation – the implications of late-medieval anchoritism's female bias. Most remarkable, from the twelfth to the sixteenth century, female anchorites consistently outnumbered their male equivalents, sometimes by as many as four to one (in the thirteenth century), dropping eventually to two to one (in the fifteenth century). There is, however, also a high number of anchorites whose sex is not recorded for these periods – something which is recognized as constituting a type of lacuna, and which continues to cause some contemporary scholars to treat the gendered implications of Warren's statistics with extreme caution.[13] Clearly, more research needs to be done into this 'indeterminate' category, but perhaps more pertinent to the objectives of this present volume is the fact that Warren's findings suggest that the majority of women entering the anchorhold throughout the whole period were laywomen, who sought enclosure either upon widowhood, or else as an alternative to the married life. Male anchorites, on the other hand, seem far more likely to have been unmarried priests or other churchmen, who were desirous of moving 'up the ladder' of religious observation upon which they were already positioned.[14]

Remarkable as these statistics and the issues they serve both to reveal and conceal are, Warren has, nevertheless, done very little to analyse their import for reaching an understanding of the complex relationship between gender, power and enclosure which self-evidently existed at this particular point in the later Middle Ages and within the anchoritic phenomenon more generally, from inception to demise. Of course, this is not the purpose of her study; nonetheless, her conclusions about the popularity of the anchoritic life during this time do tend to belie an adherence to traditionalist assumptions about what enclosure may have meant for a man and a woman, something else which this present volume seeks in part to redress. Writing of the enclosed female, for example, Warren concludes, 'it is true that a woman might have wanted to become an anchorite to escape an unattractive marriage, to avoid the dangers of childbirth, to have a private home, because she had no husband, because there was not place for her at the local nunnery'. Of men she writes, 'It is true that a man might have desired to become an anchorite because of the competitions of communal or secular life, because he was poor, because of a desire to have more free time (if only to spend it in virtuous pursuits such as writing or copying manuscripts).'[15] Here, of course, Warren does much to perpetuate the traditional binary of male-active-dominant, female-passive-recessive, which comprised much of the discourse on sex and gender during the Middle Ages, and which has also served to occlude the more complex and heteroglossic interactions between men and women, anchorites and the worldly, which the contributors to this volume uncover.[16] Indeed, the multifarious studies undertaken of women in the towns and countryside by feminist historians in the two decades since Warren published her findings have demonstrated how misleading and frequently erroneous such a representation of women's position in medieval society can be.[17] Yet, if Warren's findings and their identification of a wider gender discrepancy within the anchoritic life are largely accurate, for the gender-minded critic this discrepancy points towards a strong interaction between the anchoritic life and a search for both authority and power. As an ecclesiastic already with access to a level of power and authority, there may well have been less of an imperative towards anchoritic enclosure than for the pious laywoman living extra-institutionally within the wider world.

Fortunately, such issues have been taken up in recent years in a slow proliferation of articles and essays reappraising Warren's findings and offering valuable insights into the gendered nature of the impulse towards and response to anchoritism.[18] Indeed, many of the essays included here are deeply indebted to this body of new research. Much of this work, for example, has focused on what we can learn from anchoritic guides such as *Ancrene Wisse*, and the work of scholars such as Bella Millett, Jocelyn Wogan-Browne, Anne Savage and Nicholas Watson has done much to lay the foundations for a far more open-minded and nuanced look at the ways in which material culture, literary developments, linguistic change and religious practices within the context of the anchorhold are all dependent upon the expediency of a performed gender identity for their shifting expressions and meanings. Likewise, Alexandra Barratt and Elizabeth Robertson have focused on how medical and gynaecological lore seems to have had a marked influence upon how anchoritic women, as opposed to their hagiographers or male equivalents, viewed the connotations of their own enclosure.[19] Indeed, Barratt's contextual essay at the beginning of this volume builds upon her earlier work in this area and cogently demonstrates the multiplicity of ways in which the female anatomy offered up a code of interpretation, which allowed for a gendered deciphering of the physical and metaphysical space of the anchorhold and the anchorite's existential role within it. In this sense, Barratt's essay here is included as a point of departure and sounding-board for the essays of the other contributors to this volume. It serves to identify those aspects of the anchoritic life which may well have led to its being regarded as a feminized – and rarely gender-neutral – phenomenon in much of the extant literature throughout the whole period under scrutiny.

For purposes of chronological and thematic coherence, this volume is divided into three sections. The first of these, 'Enclosure and Discourses of the Desert', traces the origins of anchoritism and maps its consolidation within the religious discourses and practices which it generated in the days of the early Christian Church and into the Anglo-Saxon period in England. The central section, 'Gender and Enclosure: Late Medieval Intersections', concentrates primarily on the uses and functions of gendered discourse within the late-medieval anchoritic or anchorite-associated text. The concluding section, 'Beyond the Tomb: The Question of Audience', traces the trajectory of anchoritic discourse out of the anchorhold and into the world of the laity, demonstrating its wider significance to society beyond enclosure. Ultimately, all of these essays identify and interrogate many of the complex, and always deeply heteroglossic, connotations of the anchoritic life and the many discursive strands produced and promulgated by it throughout the course of the Middle Ages. Above all, the various findings of our contributors suggest that anchoritism was more than a literal and physical way of life; it constituted an intensely malleable discursive entity – indeed, as it continues to do – full of potential for adaptation to suit changing institutional, political, personal and social agendas, from its inception in the early days of Christianity through to its demise at the dawning of the Reformation.

The roots of the anchoritic way of life emanated from the very early days of the Christian Church, when the Christian religion was little more than a threatening and threatened cult, occupying small pockets within the wider context of the Roman Empire.[20] This was a time characterized by persecution, Christian martyrdom and execution, later to be textualized in popular hagiographic accounts of suffering Christ-like bodies, in which burnings, hangings and crucifixion all played a major part in defining the Christian ideal.[21] It is in such accounts, for example,

that we find early saints, like Antony, Paul and Mary the Egyptian, supposedly fleeing the dangers of Palestine and finding both safety and
solace, if not physical comfort, in the inhospitable deserts of northern
Africa.[22] Shoring up this flight into the desert wilderness – an escape
which was both physical and ideological, of course – was a deeply
ingrained affinity with those remote, secluded and abandoned spaces
which hearkened back to the so-called 'wilderness theology' of the
ancient Hebraic scriptures, texts which were also shared by the Christian
Church.[23] According to these accounts, many early patriarchs chosen
by God to lead the Israelites – Moses and Elijah, to name but two –
were subject to long suffering and privation, temptation, loss, longing
and eventual reconciliation, within the frame of the empty desert landscape. Within the narratives of alienation and unification, suffering was
writ large and constituted a necessary stepping-stone on the desert path
between a previous life of sociability and that of ultimate union with
God, via solitary contemplation. In the desert wastes, therefore, could
be achieved the rewards of insight, grace and unity; there would be
received the 'manna' from heaven.

Isolation, separation, spiritual and physical temptation and an empty
arena in which to play out their affects thus formed a central part of
Christian consciousness, both as discourse and within fully realized
individual religious practices. The mytho-historical experiences of the
so-called 'desert fathers' and their urban equivalents, the early Christian
martyrs, were seen as offering a modus operandi for all Christians, and
withdrawal into the desert seems to have had a persistent and subtly
invasive discursive resonance, which developed alongside the more
graphically depicted ascetic discourses of Christian martyrdom.
Entrapped within an alien and reductive landscape, whether desert cave
or urban wall, paradoxically the highest heights of religious contemplation were able to be scaled by the resolute Christian. Ultimately,
stripped of all human artifice and material goods and left with only the
text of an intensely suffering body, both the desert hermit and the urban
martyr seem to have sought and found the closest possible direct communication with God by means of that same body. Ultimately, as the
collective findings of the contributors to this volume will suggest,
hermit and martyr began to conjoin discursively, metamorphosing
eventually into the admixture which we have come to recognize as the
anchorite of later European – and particularly English – tradition.
Initially, then, the discourse of the desert found itself transferred from its
hot, north African origins and superimposed upon any number of other

locations, including bleak and isolated islands, wild, impenetrable forests, perilous, boggy marshlands and the dismal fens of northern Europe, coming finally to rest geographically within the developing urban centres which were springing up throughout England and the rest of Europe during the later Middle Ages.

Unlike many earlier scholars and their audiences, the contributors to this volume choose to differentiate between the terms 'anchorite' and 'hermit'. They also reject the use of the increasingly dated gender-specific term 'anchoress', preferring instead to refer simply to 'female' and 'male' anchorites, unless focusing on a specific usage within a particular text – *Ancrene Wisse*, for example. The word 'anchorite' finds its roots in the Greek term, *anachōrein*, which means 'to withdraw', and it was originally coined to designate the status of a person who had withdrawn from the world to live out a solitary existence, either alone or with other solitaries. A desert solitary could also be *eremitus* (hermit), however, based on the Latin word for desert, *eremus*, thus taking on etymologically the very identity of the geographic location that withdrawal from the world occupied. Even though some of the early sources under discussion in this volume, which were based on the writings of the desert fathers, tend to use them synonymously, this volume retains a sharp differentiation between these two designations of solitary, because of the divergent discourses which came to be attached to each.[24] It is patently clear that, although originating from the same standpoint within an historical context, anchoritism evolved into a spatially fixed and physically restricted vocation, whereas the hermit, equally solitary ideologically, was freer to move about, although a quasi-anchoritic type of solitude could be chosen if desired. Thus the anchoritic life, as opposed to the eremitic, rapidly became imbued with notions of a physically static environment, whilst the hermit was, by definition, peripatetic. Nevertheless, anchoritism never dissociated itself entirely from its desert origins and continued to be shaped by the multiple, associative meanings of a desert existence. It also proliferated its own meanings, however, resulting in the type of literary multivalence with which the essays collected together here are primarily concerned.

Perhaps one of the earliest examples of this type of metamorphosis within the discourse of the desert identifiably emerges in English literature within an Old English account of the life of the English saint, Guthlac, whose construction as a specifically English solitary is examined here by Santha Bhattacharji. By means of an analysis of startlingly gendered imagery within the texts which document his life, Bhattacharji identifies a likely moment of transition between an ideological adherence to desert discourse and the specifically English expressions of the anchoritic life which were to emerge in later centuries. Although extant accounts of the life of Guthlac rely heavily upon the tradition of the 'hairy anchorite' of the desert, as it developed in the writings of Saint Jerome, Athanasius, Sulpicius Severus and others, Guthlac retreats towards the end of his life, not to the desert wildernesses of the source material, but to its specifically English equivalent, the inhospitable Lincolnshire fens, where he proceeds to live out a life of eremitic solitude in a dilapidated hut, built over a partially exposed Anglo-Saxon barrow. Here we have, perhaps for the first time, the caves of the desert fathers being transformed both literally and rhetorically into the nascent English anchorhold of much later tradition. Even more revealing, too, is that the account should culminate in a hitherto unexamined use of what appears to be the first feminization of the concept of enclosure. As Bhattacharji suggests, such a feminization heralds the type of imagistic and exegetical development, already identified by Barratt, of representations of the anchorhold in the later Middle Ages as a womb-like space and of the anchorite, whether male or female, as highly eroticized *sponsa Christi*. As Bhattacharji points out, this development of gynaecentric imagery has hitherto been considered the preserve of the imaginative artistry and interpretative acumen of Bernard of Clairvaux, writing in the twelfth century, rather than part of an earlier impulse towards exegetical feminization within the anchorhold.[25]

Such a merging of the eremitic and the anchoritic in early English literature, however, was not always for the purpose of exegesis. There are clearly other times when we find the discourses interacting, inter-relating – merging, even – for reasons of expedience, be it political, personal, social or religious. It is just such expedience which is argued for by Rebecca Hayward in her highly perceptive examination of Goscelin of Saint-Bertin's eleventh-century *Liber confortatorius*, a type of guide written in epistolary form to his long-term protégée, Eve of Wilton, who had recently been enclosed within an eight-foot anchorhold in Angers. Whilst Eve's newly adopted urban location is clearly not the physically expansive wilderness of eremitic tradition, nevertheless Goscelin's treatment of the physical and metaphysical space in which the newly enclosed Eve finds herself recognizes the expediency of drawing a firm discursive and historical connection between the two. Goscelin's identification of Eve's anchorhold with the desert spaces of her forebears serves to place Eve within a secure tradition, which is both reassuring and authoritative, whilst at the same time emphasizing her own individuality and exceptional spirituality within her local setting. For Goscelin and, we imagine, for Eve also, the anchorhold, far from being a restrictive location, is clearly to be thought of in terms of metaphysical expansiveness according to the precepts of the desert experience of endless wilderness and physical solitude, which is anything *but* static.

Such eremitical discourse and its ability to conjoin the physical and the metaphysical, the material and the figurative, was also crucial to the self-representation of other religious groups during the later Middle Ages, as both Elizabeth Freeman and Johan Bergström-Allen clearly demonstrate in their essays, included within the same section. Freeman's examination of the foundation narratives of male Cistercian houses in England reveals a concerted use of what she terms the 'spatial language' of desert and solitude, which is adopted expediently to represent the institution's self-image as an order 'on the margins'. It is a positionality, however, which relies for its impact upon the Cistercian brethren being able to speak from the very heart of the orthodox Cistercian Order. Conversely, those women who struggled to be accepted as part of the Order, and who were themselves both actively and physically 'marginal', rejected these desert discourses of marginality, fearing, perhaps, their potential for literal interpretation and preferring instead to concentrate on amassing written corroboration of their own *centrality* to the Cistercian Order. Johan Bergström-Allen, meanwhile, focuses on the late-medieval – and similarly expedient – adoption of discourses of the desert as part of the Carmelite Order's own concerted attempt to invoke the authority of its eremitic origins. According to Bergström-Allen, this search for validation is concretized in a Carmelite predisposition for forging close links with female anchorites in the later period, in order to return figuratively and discursively to its origins as a 'desert' order. As solitaries *and* as women, of course, the female anchorites in question were doubly extraordinary and, in turn, were able to transfer that extraordinariness onto the Carmelite monks in their capacity as the female embodiments of what this particular Order regarded as its own 'exceptional' spirituality – that is to say, desert eremiticism. The findings of both Freeman and Bergström-Allen, then, would corroborate those of Bhattacharji and Hayward in demonstrating not only the self-consciousness of male literary employment of eremitic discourse, but that this employment was in itself performative and highly gendered.

The essays collected together in the second section of this volume pick up on this assertion, all directly concerning themselves with the explicit gendering – or conscious attempt at degendering – of the anchoritic experience, as it emerges in a selection of late-medieval texts written by or for anchorites in particular. In this context, Kristen McQuinn usefully builds upon some of the observations of Barratt in her contextual essay by examining the intensive use of gynaecentric, or perhaps more specifically, gynaecological imagery found in fourteenth-century guides for anchorites. Taking as her primary text the Middle English redaction of Aelred of Rievaulx's earlier Latin guide, written in the early thirteenth century for his newly enclosed sister, McQuinn demonstrates the centrality of the feminine and the workings of a highly sexualized female body, in particular, to a late-medieval expression of anchoritic piety, which, as Bhattacharji has suggested, can be read in terms of a trajectory of female-associated imagery with origins in the literature of a much earlier period. In this context, McQuinn examines a movement from enclosure as being primarily a physical phenomenon to its being an experience which can bring about a fuller understanding of more mystical connotations, with the female body as its primary hermeneutic. To this end, McQuinn argues for the mystical encounter within the anchorhold as per se highly gendered and thus constituting a profoundly different experience for men than for women.

It has therefore already become apparent that late-medieval anchoritism was far more than – to coin Warren's own words – simply the embodiment of 'unconscious desires' to escape marriage or obtain social prestige.[26] Indeed, along with Warren, McQuinn acknowledges the firm links between the anchoritic life and mystical expectation,[27] something which is then taken up by Susannah Mary Chewning in an essay which builds upon McQuinn's assertion of the mystical encounter, and the anchoritic mystical encounter in particular, as constituting a profoundly feminine experience. Drawing heavily upon a Kristevan notion of the 'abjection' inherent to the mystical experience, Chewning's examination of the mystical text directed at an anchoritic audience concludes that the mystic is 'always already feminine' and that her power is drawn from the very abjection which simultaneously casts her down and elevates her to union with God. This moment of divine union also forms the focus of Mari Hughes-Edwards's essay, which seeks to remind us that the experience of mystical union itself, something which she terms 'fusion', is in itself gender-neutral, in that it is beyond the body and its attendant gender constructions and performances. Fusion is, Hughes-Edwards argues, frequently feminized at the point of its articulation and its communication to others, but it is not inherently gendered. Hughes-Edwards also reads the significance of the late-medieval growth of anchoritism and the proliferation of anchoritic guides, which also characterized the period, in terms of a reflection of the development of a much more meditational piety which was taking place within the lay sphere, which foreshadows the findings of those essays collected in the final section of this volume.

In keeping with the arguments implicit in most of these essays, anchoritism and its literary representation in the form of anchoritic guides is recognizably a mirror, which reflects back upon the community its own hopes and fears, aspirations, achievements, beliefs and doubts, and particularly those connected with accepted gender boundaries. This is an aspect of the phenomenon of religious enclosure which, in spite of having occasional, albeit cursory, attention paid to it by earlier scholars has not been examined in any depth or complexity prior to this volume. For the first time, in any consistent way, the anchorhold is uncovered here as an intensely multivalent intellectual, spiritual and socially delineated space with a myriad of associations, which always return to the sphere of the surrounding socio-religious culture. In addition to being the crucial physical location wherein the anchorite could embark on the journey towards union with God and the culmination of spiritual perfection, the anchorhold also provided a spiritual and geographic focus for many of those people from wider society who came to ask for advice and spiritual guidance, and who proceeded to read of the works and lives of anchorites, frequently recasting them in their own gendered image as part of a process of identification. Such a recasting of the anchorite in the image of the community has not been restricted to any single place or moment in time. As Ulrike Wiethaus's scrutiny of the historiography connected to the fourteenth-century German mystic, Denys of Ryckel, demonstrates, all traces of the type of feminized response to the mystical experience identified in previous essays in this volume was systematically eradicated by male scholars writing about Denys over the course of seven centuries. Similarly eliminated or occluded was the male mystic's own depiction of a masculine self by the same type of traditionalist scholarship, as identified by Mulder-Bakker in her foreword. As Wiethaus argues, traditional male historiography has always been keen to recast the male mystic in its own image, in an attempt to inscribe upon his body a comfortable and comforting type of epistemological closure, which is dependent upon a whole series of cultural constructions and textual performances of approved masculinity. In turn, this has served to wall up and enclose even the non-anchoritic mystic within superimposed and uninterrogated ideological constraints, reproducing for subsequent generations a type of figurative anchorhold from which the voice of the mystic can no longer be heard.

Those essays included in this central section, therefore, cogently demonstrate the importance to late-medieval anchoritism of interactivity with, and yet simultaneous withdrawal from, community, whether it be a physical community or a literary one. It is clear that, although set apart from the community at large by stone walls and specific ideological precepts, nevertheless the anchorite also lay at the very centre of that same community. The anchorhold was clearly also a communal 'womb' from which would emerge an idealized sense of a community's own reborn potential, both as Christians and as human subjects. In a recent archaeological study of gendered spaces within medieval buildings, Roberta Gilchrist has asserted: 'meanings of space are perceived contextually and . . . assist in establishing and reproducing social order'.[28] In this sense, the late-medieval anchorhold can be read primarily as an arena of both private and public performances which were simultaneously spiritual, physical and frequently highly gendered, reflecting, perhaps, in rarified and hyperbolic form, the fears, desires and aspirations of the society outside at large, whilst at the same time attempting to contain them. The anchorhold, in fact, was not only the invisible arena where these human emotions were staged, but was also the figurative and 'thinking heart', the enclosed and redemptive womb, through which the lifeblood of the communal body which surrounded it flowed.

In the context of this type of performativity and cultural aspiration attached to the anchorhold, the theory regarding the practical logic of everyday action and activity produced by contemporary theorist Pierre Bourdieu has much to offer. According to Bourdieu:

> Every social order systematically takes advantage of the disposition of the body and language to function as depositories of deferred thoughts that can be triggered off at a distance in space and time by the simple effect of re-placing the body in an overall posture which *recalls* the associated thoughts and feelings, in one of the inductive states which, as actors know, give rise to states of mind.[29]

The anchorhold, then, and the 'isolated' body within it, is the place where is staged a forever-repeated performance of communal desire by the anchoritic 'method actor' within, a staging which, along with that of gender identity, serves to repeatedly re-enact, order and confirm the structure of communal thoughts and feelings. As the 'depository of deferred thoughts', which perhaps even includes deferred thoughts of ultimate gender synthesis in the presence of God, the anchorhold is the reification of society's need to marshal rigorously its own socio-religious practices. At the same time, however, because of the invisibility of its interior spaces, it offers the permanent possibility for transgression and change – and the anchorite provides the body upon which this marshalling and transgressive potential is also played out. If, as Bourdieu also asserts, 'symbolic power works partly through the control of other people's bodies . . . that is given by the collectively recognized capacity to act in various ways on deep-rooted linguistic and muscular behaviour',[30] then, far from being, as Warren has asserted, 'separate and separated', the anchoritic space and the body it enclosed were both intrinsic to and inseparable from the surrounding community.

There is nowhere better, then, to witness this heteroglossic interactivity between anchorhold and society at work than in the multiple uses to which specifically anchoritic texts were put within the wider lay community. To this end, all of the remaining essays within this collection focus upon specific texts which have spilled out of their former boundaries of enclosure into the public arena, or else have been re-packaged for reinsertion within the type of discursive anchoritic sphere we have been examining here. Leading on from Hughes-Edwards's recognition of an inexorable sea-change from the asceticism of the high Middle Ages to a more contemplative and meditational mode in the later period (neither of which necessarily excludes the other, however), both Robert Hasenfratz and Cate Gunn take as their focus *Ancrene Wisse*, the anchoritic guide originally written for a group of three female anchorites in the thirteenth century but then revised and adapted for any number of shifting audiences during the centuries which followed. For Hasenfratz, the theory of anchoritic asceticism, which Hughes-Edwards identifies as particularly common to high-medieval guides of this type, is transformed into a type of ascetic symbol for a wider lay audience within the versions of the text which appear during the fourteenth and fifteenth centuries. Indeed, in keeping with Bourdieu's theory of wider social practices being inscribed upon individual bodies, what Hasenfratz identifies is the adaptation and modification of those ascetic practices of individual bodies within the idealized space of the anchorhold to accommodate the different sensibilities of the pious layman and woman living a life outside that environment. This type of movement of anchoritic discourse beyond the 'tomb' is also something on which Cate Gunn focuses in her own study, which documents the relevance of *Ancrene Wisse* to a wide variety of lay audiences during the later period. Indeed, Gunn goes further to suggest a clear and firm link between anchoritism and lay piety, arguing, moreover, that the traditionally accepted demarcations between male and female religious sensibilities were not as clear-cut as previous scholarship has assumed. This is, she argues, clearly demonstrated by the ubiquitous popularity of this supposedly female-oriented text amongst the laity. Like Wiethaus's examination of male historiography, discussed earlier, Gunn's essay breaks open traditional thinking about the encoding of gender within medieval texts, and exposes the potential of the critic to bring his or her own socially conditioned attitudes towards discourses of gender to bear upon those texts. Thus, in many ways Gunn's reading of *Ancrene Wisse* as an inherently unstable text rests as a paradigm for the epistemological shifts and continuities within the discourse of anchoritic enclosure as a whole, and what these actually articulate about the societies upon which they rest.

The essential instability of guidance texts such as *Ancrene Wisse* is further examined by Catherine Innes-Parker, in a close appraisal of the under-examined mid-fifteenth-century text, *The feitis and the passion of oure lord Ihesu Crist*. Written by a woman for a specifically female audience, Innes-Parker's study of this text leads her to conclude that the woman reader/writer of the anchoritic text did not necessarily internalize and reproduce the type of mistrust of female sexuality present in so many of the male-authored texts which have been scrutinized here. Instead, this intensely female-focused text uses the traditional imagery of the female body of the type earlier identified by both Barratt and McQuinn, and redirects it as an expression of woman's unique capacity for union, or, in Hughes-Edwards's terminology, fusion, with Christ. In this late-medieval expression of a specifically female type of anchoritic devotion, the enclosed woman's private prayer is explicitly regarded as a *communal* experience and she is fully encouraged to carry along with her in her contemplation the community which surrounds her. Thus, we see explicitly delineated one of the key facets of the anchoritic phenomenon laid down in this text – the anchorite as tabula rasa, upon which is inscribed the ideal spiritual aspirations of the society of which she is, therefore, a central part. Simultaneously, however, and somewhat paradoxically, she must be removed and necessarily set apart from that same society, in order to become fully subject to its insistent

interpellation of her as 'clean slate', upon which inscription is continually made.[31] Thus, the negativity of the type of misogynistic response
to the female body with which the female anchorite is encouraged to
engage in texts such as *Ancrene Wisse* is eradicated and transformed, in
one place at one time at least, by an anonymous woman writer, whose
text offers a window through which can be glimpsed how fifteenth-
century educated and enclosed women may well have seen themselves
and each other in relation to the wider community, outside the stone
walls surrounding them.

If the *feitis* can be read as an insight into an aspect of female
spirituality – and that of the reclusive female, in particular – the final
essay in this volume demonstrates how anchoritic discourse can be
selectively extracted and then superimposed in order to pull the most
'worldly' of mystical treatises into line with traditional masculinist
thinking about 'appropriate' female behaviour. Within the redacted
version of *The Book of Margery Kempe*, examined here by Liz Herbert
McAvoy, the contemporary ideological climate is seen in an Althusserian
sense to 'recruit' the 'bad subject' retrospectively, so that she actually
appears to 'be' a reflection of that same ideological interpellation.[32] In
this context, McAvoy argues that the original, highly eclectic version of
the *Book* was remodelled in the light of anchoritic discourse and, in
keeping with contemporary lay practices, transformed into a much
reduced and more traditionally contemplative version, and then later
attributed to the anchorhold. Barely a shadow of the original version,
this redaction was also the only witness to Margery Kempe's work until
the rediscovery in 1934 of the manuscript containing the full version.
This brief and anodyne redaction of the colourful, multivocal original
and its redesignation of Margery Kempe as 'ancres' can, therefore, in
many ways stand as a paradigm for much of what this volume attempts
to argue. Just as masculine historiography attempted to reconstruct
Denys of Ryckel in its own image in order to control both image and
memory, and just as the same ideological position has continued to
shape anchoritic studies in its own image until recent times, so this late-
fifteenth-century redactor attempts to bring about closure to Margery
Kempe by encasing her within the heavy weight of ascetic 'historical'
anchoritic discourse, in order to bring her back into line with societal
expectations of where legitimate 'aberrancy' should remain, that is to
say, the idealized and contained location of the anchorhold. As
McAvoy demonstrates, far from being the type of tabula rasa of the
festis construction to which she aspires, whilst living in the world

Margery's unclassifiable persona can act only as cultural *scapegoat* rather than focus of communal aspiration. Once erased from view, however (and arguably from text), her now invisible body can take on the function of the performative; in its literary expression of 'performing the anchoritic', Margery's apparently absent body can carry the whole community along with it on the wings of her 'anchoritic' prayers.

All of the findings collected here, therefore, directly contest the long-accepted assertion, reinforced in many ways by Warren, that the anchorite remained separate and separated from the world at large. Indeed, it emerges that, far from being a mysterious and admired 'other' beyond the boundaries of human culture, the anchorite occupied a position at its very heart, as embodiment of ever-metamorphosing human aspirations and fears. Moreover, these aspirations and fears were always already gendered ones, although not necessarily in traditionally accepted ways: at every turn, at every instant, gender interacted closely with enclosure to produce a myriad of expressions and performances of what has hitherto been regarded as a closed, as well as *enclosed*, institution. What this volume suggests, finally, is that anchorites resist examination merely as an homogeneous 'group whose vocation was the fulfilment of lesser men's [*sic*] dreams'.[33] There were as many expressions of anchoritism and the life of enclosed solitude as there were anchorites and solitaries, and together with those communities, contemporaneous or otherwise, upon which they depended and which depended upon them, they operated within a tightly woven circle of material and spiritual reciprocity, which expressed itself in different ways at different cultural moments. What *does* seem to be common, however, is that the anchorite managed to simultaneously confirm, resist and transcend anxieties and presumptions about gender limitations, and that the community consistently invested in the anchorite their prayers, hopes, vulnerabilities – and their money. Representative of the selfhood of the community in its simultaneous 'sameness' and 'otherness', the anchorhold and its occupant appear to have fulfilled a fundamental role within a society's need to define itself and the individuals who comprised it. The anchorite, like Christ in the stone tomb and as child in Mary's womb, served as a bridge between life and death, between Fall and redemption, between material and metaphysical, and ultimately as agent of reparation between humanity and its God.

Notes

1   Victor Hugo, *Notre Dame de Paris*, trans. Alban Krailsheimer (Oxford and
    New York, 1993), p. 511.

2   The large majority of historical surveys of the medieval religious experience
    written in English have traditionally ignored the figure of the anchorite, or
    else have only mentioned the phenomenon in passing. Even when the
    anchoritic life has been focused on, however briefly, it has often served to
    mislead the reader. The example of Margaret Deanesly is somewhat typical
    of early treatment of the subject. Deanesly places anchoritism in the same
    category as schools and hospitals in *A History of the Medieval Church
    590–1500* (London, 1969), pp. 209–20. Here Deanesly represents the
    anchorite as somewhat homely and comforting, living an unremarkable life
    alongside a group of servants (p. 217). Even Frances Darwin refers to
    anchorites as 'praying automata', in *The English Mediaeval Recluse* (London,
    1944), p. 25.

3   Perhaps the most influential of multidimensional studies of the anchoritic
    life to date include Jocelyn Wogan-Browne (formerly Jocelyn Price),
    ' "Inner" and "outer": conceptualizing the body in *Ancrene Wisse* and
    Aelred's *de Institutione Inclusarum*', in Gregory Kratzmann and James
    Simpson (eds), *Medieval English Religious and Ethical Literature: Essays in
    Honour of G. H. Russell* (Cambridge, 1986), pp. 192–208; Jocelyn Wogan-
    Browne, 'Chaste bodies: frames and experiences', in Sarah Kay and Miri
    Rubin (eds), *Framing Medieval Bodies* (Manchester, 1994), pp. 24–42;
    Catherine Innes-Parker, 'Fragmentation and reconstruction: images of the
    female body in *Ancrene Wisse* and the *Katherine Group*', *Comitatus*, 26
    (1995), 27–52; *Anchoritic Spirituality:* Ancrene Wisse *and Associated Works*,
    trans. and ed. Anne Savage and Nicholas Watson (New York, 1991);
    Nicholas Watson, 'The methods and objectives of thirteenth-century
    anchoritic devotion', in Marion Glasscoe (ed.), *The Medieval Mystical
    Tradition in England*, Exeter Symposium IV, Papers read at Dartington Hall,
    July 1987 (Woodbridge, 1987), pp. 132–53; Elizabeth Robertson, 'The rule
    of the body: the feminine spirituality of the *Ancrene Wisse*', in Julia Bolton
    Holloway, Constance S. Wright and Joan Bechtold (eds), *Equally in God's
    Image: Women in the Middle Ages* (New York, 1990), pp. 109–34 and 'An
    anchorhold of her own: female anchoritic literature in thirteenth-century
    England', in ibid., pp. 170–83; Alexandra Barratt, 'Anchoritic aspects of
    Ancrene Wisse', *Medium Aevum*, 40 (1980), 33–56.

4   Rotha Mary Clay, *The Hermits and Anchorites of England* (London, 1914;
    repr. Detroit, 1968).

5   Ann K. Warren, *Anchorites and their Patrons in Medieval England* (Los
    Angeles and Berkeley, 1985).

6   Ibid., p. 3.

7   Ibid., p. 7.

8   In his discussion of anchorites (as opposed to hermits), Leclercq tends

towards an identification of the anchorite as generically male, fully imbued
with the philosophical leanings of the learned coenobite and dedicated to
'une vie angélique'. Similarly, the anchorite is simultaneously engaged in 'un
"combat singulier" '. For which, see ' "Eremus" et "Eremita": pour l'histoire
du vocabulaire de la vie solitaire', *Collectanea Ordinis Cistercensium
Reformatorum*, 48 (1963), 8–30 (26).

[9]   Warren, *Anchorites and their Patrons*, p. 7.

[10] Judith Butler, *Gender Trouble: Feminism and the Subversion of Identity*
(London and New York, 1990); the theories promulgated here were followed
up to offer a consideration of the categories of both 'gender' and 'sex' in
Bodies that Matter: On the Discursive Limits of 'Sex' (New York and
London, 1993).

[11] Butler, *Gender Trouble*, p. 136.

[12] For a synopsis of the figures, see Warren, *Anchorites and their Patrons*, p. 20,
table 1.

[13] Such reservations were articulated in an unpublished paper, 'Men, masculinity
and the anchoritic life', delivered by E. A. Jones at the University of Wales's
conference 'Anchorites, Wombs and Tombs: Intersections of Gender and
Enclosure' in July 2002. Although it is certainly wise to approach Warren's
statistics with caution, there seems no reason to believe, however, until we
are presented with evidence to the contrary, that the male–female ratio
within this indeterminate group would be significantly different from that of
the groups where sex can be determined. Indeed, it seems likely that the
relation of male-to-female anchorites within this hazy category would reflect
the same trend as in the groups where sex can be determined. This is an area
of anchoritic studies on which Jones is currently working.

[14] Warren, *Anchorites and their Patrons*, p. 22.

[15] Ibid., p. 123.

[16] For a useful overview on attitudes towards sex and gender in the Middle
Ages see Ian Maclean, *The Renaissance Notion of Women: A Study in the
Fortunes of Scholasticism and Medical Science in European Intellectual Life*
(Cambridge, 1980). On sex difference see Joan Cadden, *The Meanings of Sex
Difference in the Middle Ages: Medicine, Science and Culture* (Cambridge,
1993). Also useful in this context is Thomas Laqueur, *Making Sex: Body and
Gender from the Greeks to Freud* (Cambridge, Massachusetts and London,
1990).

[17] See, in particular, Judith Bennett, *Sisters and Workers in the Middle Ages*
(Chicago, 1989); Jocelyn Wogan-Browne, R. Voaden, A. Diamond, Ann
Hutchinson, Carol Meale and Lesley Johnson (eds), *Medieval Women: Texts
and Contexts in Late-Medieval Britain* (Turnhout, 2000); Henrietta Leyser,
Medieval Women: A Social History of Women in England 450–1500 (London,
2002); P. J. P. Goldberg, *Woman is a Worthy Wight: Women in English Society
1200–1500* (Stroud, 1992); Margaret Wade Labarge, *Women in Medieval Life*
(London, 2001); Martha C. Howell, *Women, Production and Patriarchy in
Late-Medieval Cities* (Chicago, 1986); Kim L. Phillips, *Medieval Maidens:
Young Women and Gender in England 1270–1540* (Manchester, 2003);

Stephanie Hollis, *Anglo-Saxon Women and the Church: Sharing a Common Fate* (Woodbridge, 1992); Claire Lees and Gillian R. Overling, *Double Agents: Women and Clerical Culture in Anglo-Saxon England* (Philadelphia, 2001).

[18] See p. 23, n. 3.

[19] See, for example, *Anchoritic Spirituality: Ancrene Wisse and Associated Works*, trans. and ed. Savage and Watson; Wogan-Browne, ' "Inner" and "outer": conceptualizing the body', pp. 192–208; Alexandra Barratt, ' "In the lowest part of our need": Julian and medieval gynecological writing', in Sandra McEntire (ed.), *Julian of Norwich: A Book of Essays* (New York and London, 1998), pp. 240–56; and Elizabeth Robertson, 'Medieval medical views of women and female spirituality in *Ancrene Wisse* and Julian of Norwich's *Showings*', in Linda Lomperis and Sarah Stanbury (eds), *Feminist Approaches to the Body in Medieval Literature* (Philadelphia, 1993), pp. 142–67.

[20] On the early Church see, for example, Ewin R. Goodenough, *The Church in the Roman Empire* (New York, 1970).

[21] On this see, for example, James Howard-Johnston and Paul Antony Hayward (eds), *The Cult of Saints in Late Antiquity and the Early Middle Ages: Essays on the Contribution of Peter Brown* (Oxford, 2002); Lynda L. Coon, *Sacred Fictions: Holy Women and Hagiography in Late Antiquity* (Philadelphia, 1997); for more general attitudes towards the body in early Christianity, see Peter Brown, *The Body and Society: Men, Women and Sexual Renunciation in Early Christianity* (London, 1990).

[22] For an account of some early Christian lives, including that of Antony, see Carolinne White (trans.), *Early Christian Lives* (London, 1998); on Saint Paul see Norman Pittenger, *The Life of Saint Paul* (London, 1970); the *Life of Saint Mary of Egypt*, in translation, can be found in Benedicta Ward, *Harlots of the Desert: A Study of Repentance in Early Monastic Sources* (Oxford, 1987), pp. 35–6.

[23] Leclercq offers a useful overview and analysis of the origins of desert theology, again in ' "Eremus" et "Eremita" '.

[24] Because of a frequent failure to differentiate between the two in a number of early sources, many contemporary scholars prior to Warren's study have tended to follow suit. See, for example, R. W. Southern, *The Making of the Middle Ages* (New Haven, 1953), p. 221. Even R. N. Swanson, writing as late as 1995, tends to categorize anchorites cursorily alongside widows and hermits. See Swanson, *Religion and Devotion in Europe 1215–1515* (Cambridge, 1995), p. 126.

[25] See, for example, Bernard's *Commentary on the Song of Songs* in Bernard of Clairvaux, *Sermones super Cantica Canticorum* in *Opera*, vol. 1, ed. J. Leclercq, C. H. Talbot and H. M. Rochais (Rome, 1957).

[26] Warren, *Anchorites and their Patrons*, p. 123.

[27] Warren refers to the fourteenth century, in particular, as 'less ascetic in its demands and more mystical in its promises', in ibid., p. 40.

[28] Roberta Gilchrist, *Gender and Archaeology: Contesting the Past* (London and New York, 1999), p. 100.

29 Pierre Bourdieu, *The Logic of Practice*, trans. Richard Nice (Cambridge and Stanford, 1990), p. 69.

30 Ibid., p. 69.

31 On the theory of 'interpellation' see Louis Althusser, 'Ideology and ideological state apparatuses', as reproduced in *Literary Theory: An Anthology*, ed. Julie Rivkin and Michael Ryan (Oxford, 1998; various reprints), pp. 294–304.

32 Ibid., pp. 302 and 303.

33 Warren, *Anchorites and their Patrons*, p. 3.

2

Context: Some Reflections on Wombs and Tombs and Inclusive Language

ALEXANDRA BARRATT

In 2002 the *Economist* published an obituary of the British socialist Barbara Castle, who had died at the age of 91. It recalled that Castle had entered Parliament at the time of the 1945 Labour landslide and that, among that government's achievements, 'A welfare system was put in place, promising to take care of everyone "from womb to tomb", as it was put at the time'.[1] It is surprising to find that this familiar expression (not to say cliché) is so recent. The *Oxford English Dictionary* does not record it, although the Supplement has the phrase *womb-to-tomb*, first evidenced as late as 1964, defining it as 'esp. used attrib. to denote procedures, etc., which span a lifetime'. But there seems no reason to doubt the accuracy of the *Economist*'s linguistic information and in retrospect one can see that 'womb to tomb', in the sense of the more common 'from the cradle to the grave', would have to be a relatively recent collocation.

Until relatively recently, *womb* could refer to various parts of the body. Ironically, the only meaning that survives today, 'the organ in the lower body of a woman or female mammal where offspring are conceived and in which they gestate before birth; the uterus', was by no means the predominant meaning in the Middle Ages. So the phrase 'from the womb to the tomb' would not have had for a medieval audience the pungency and appositeness that it has for us. Indeed, it could have been ambiguous or even enigmatic: the *OED* gives the primary meaning of *womb* as 'belly', subdividing it further into 'abdomen' (evidenced from *c.*825 until 1684); 'stomach' (from *c.*950 until 1756); and 'bowels' (*c.*1000 until 1544). Its meaning as 'uterus' comes second: this, too, goes back to c.825, but seems to have been less common during the medieval period than the other meanings. It has, however, been remarkably persistent. Conversely, the names of many other parts of the body – such as *belly*, *bosom*, *bowel*, *flank* and *maw* – could at various times be used to mean 'uterus'.

Two other 'dedicated' words for womb or uterus, both obsolete today but current in the medieval period, are *maris* and *matrice*. *OED* gives examples of *maris* from before 1340 until the fifteenth century, while *matrice* survived somewhat longer, from c.1400 until 1774. Both meant, primarily or exclusively, 'uterus or womb'. A fifteenth-century gynaecological treatise, *The Knowing of Woman's Kind in Childing*, uses all three words.[2] *Womb* appears about twenty times, but with various meanings: the much more specific *matrice* appears about a hundred times, while the rare *marrys/maryce* appears about twenty-nine times in one manuscript, but not at all in the others. *Matrice*, of course, is clearly related to *matrix*, one of whose meanings, evidenced between 1526 and 1840, is 'womb or uterus'. And, finally, *uterus* itself, like a number of anatomical terms borrowed from Latin and Greek, did not come into use until the early modern period: *OED*'s first quotation is dated 1615. *OED* records the figurative use of *womb* from 1593 onwards (undoubtedly there were earlier examples), but even today *uterus* would rarely be used metaphorically.

In *The Knowing of Woman's Kind*, the womb first appears as one of five female sex characteristics. The womb features in the last two:

> The iiij diuersite [difference] ys by-tvene here leggis, for þer have men a yerde with oþer portynavns [penis with other appendage] & þer hathe women an opynynge wyche ys calde in Frenche a bele chose or ellys a wykket [opening] of þe wombe. The v dyuersite is þat in þe body of þe woman be-tvene here navyll & here wyket, for þer hath sche a vessyll þat no man hath, þe wych ys callyde þe maryce.[3]

The text goes on to give a 'clinical' description of the human uterus:

> The matrice ys a vessell made of thyn leddyr, rowgh with-in & playn with-owt & slydynge, thykly fretyde & enterlacyde with small synovys all a-bovt & hath a longe nekk & strayte & [a] large mowthe & a large entre & a plenere euyn schapp lyck [an] vrinall [urine flask], þe bottvm þer-of to þe navyll of þe woman & þe ij sydys to þe ij sydys of þe woman & hit ys par-tyde in-to vij vesellys [divided into seven chambers] of þe wyche iij lyth in

þe party tovarde þe ryȝht syde & iij in þe party tovarde þe lyfte syde & þe vij evyn in þe myddys be-tvene þe navyll & þe wykket.[4]

The womb, then, is shaped like a urine flask, and has seven chambers. Many medieval medical writers accepted this venerable myth, in spite of the contradictory evidence provided by rudimentary human dissection, and the belief was still around in the seventeenth century.[5] It probably arose as an extrapolation from dissection of the sow's uterus which, like that of many other mammals, is bicornate: it has two limbs or 'horns', within which the embryos are spaced at approximately uniform intervals and individually enclosed by chorionic vesicles. This would give a dissector the impression that each occupied its own 'chamber'.[6]

Our text regards the human womb as functional and, indeed, necessary for growing children (preferably male), but it is also troublesome: the transition is swift from 'Heer is taught yow what is þe matrice, and how it lyth' to, literally in the next breath, 'Now vnderstonde the syknesse that deshese it'.[7] Indeed, most of the text is devoted to a discussion of the three 'sicknesses' in women for which the uterus is responsible – childbearing; abnormal movements of the womb up, down or to one side; and menstrual disorders.

After an exposure, however brief, to medieval gynaecological theory one starts to see why the fifth-century author of the canticle *Te Deum Laudamus*, in praising Christ, included the verse 'tu . . . non horruisti virginis uterum' (Thou didst not abhor the Virgin's womb) (*horruisti* literally means 'shuddered at'); for possession of a womb is far from an unmixed blessing. In the learned medical tradition, the womb is one (though only one) marker of female gender, a gender universally regarded as inferior to the male, though different types of writers give different types of reasons. (Woman is the daughter of Eve, or she is cold and moist, rather than hot and dry. Take your pick.) The womb is also the place where children grow (good), but under normal circumstances this happens only as a consequence of sexual activity (not so good). 'Sche þat wol haue no travyll in chyldynge, let kepe here fro þe recevynge of sede of man &, oon my parell, sche schall nevyre drede þe travelynge of chylde', says our text, unsympathetically.[8] Finally, the womb is also a lifelong source of trouble and the primary reason for women's ill-health. One might therefore expect writers outside the medical tradition, such as those focused on in many of the essays in this present volume, to find the womb to be a less than promising, or at least problematic, metaphor.

But, as we know, in spite of its inherent drawbacks it proved too powerful, productive or suggestive a symbol to ignore. *Ancrene Wisse* uses the womb as a metaphor for the anchorhold and, reciprocally, the anchorhold as a metaphor for the womb. Speaking of Christ, the author asks:

Ant nes he him-seolf reclus i Maries wombe? þeos twa þing limpeð to ancre: nearowðe ant bitternesse, for wombe is nearow wununge þer Ure Lauerd wes reclus . . . ʒef ʒe þenne i nearow stude þolieð bitternesse, ʒe beoð his feolahes reclus as he wes i Marie wombe. Beo ʒe ibunden inwið fowr large wahes? Ant he in a nearow cader, i-neilet o rode, i stanene þruh bi-cluset hete feste. Marie wombe ant þis þruh weren his ancre huses.

(And was he not himself a recluse in Mary's womb? These two things belong to the anchoress: narrowness and bitterness. For the womb is a narrow dwelling, where our Lord was a recluse . . . If you then suffer bitterness in a narrow place, you are his fellows, recluse as he was in Mary's womb. Are you imprisoned within four wide walls? And he in a narrow cradle, nailed to the cross, enclosed tight in a stone tomb. Mary's womb and this tomb were his anchorhouses.)[9]

The point of comparison here, or at least the ostensible point, is the womb's cramped nature. But we might also recall the theory of the seven-compartment womb, making it a little like the anchorhold, which often consisted of several rooms.

The twelfth-century Cistercian, Aelred of Rievaulx, whose *de Institutione Inclusarum*, a letter of advice to his sister, was a major source for *Ancrene Wisse*, never explicitly uses the womb–anchorhold metaphor. But we should note his anxieties about the permeability of the solitary's cell:

Cella vertitur in prostibulum, et *dilatato qualibet arte foramine*, aut illa egredietur, aut adulter ingreditur.

(The opening of the cell *must somehow be enlarged* to allow her to pass through or her paramour to enter; what was a cell has now become a brothel.)[10]

But the fifteenth-century Middle English translation of Aelred's text, *The Rule of a Recluse*, influenced, one suspects, by *Ancrene Wisse* (and examined by Kristen McQuinn in this present volume, ch. 7) does introduce an implied association between the womb and 'enclosure'. It twice refers to the unborn Christ as 'enclosed' in the womb',[11] where the Latin omits all reference to the womb, simply reading *claudi* and *clausum*.[12] The Virgin's womb was, of course, very different from that of other women. The late thirteenth-century German mystic, Gertrud the Great of Helfta, had a vision of this virginal womb:

Apparuit quoque immaculatus uterus Virginis gloriosae ad instar purissim[i] crystalli perspicuus, per quam omnia viscera ejus divinitatis medullitus pertransita et repleta refulgebant, velut aurum diversi coloris serico convolutum elucere solet per crystallum. Videbatur etiam puerulus ille floridus, summi Patris unicus, cor Matris virgineae avida delectatione sugere.

(The spotless womb of the glorious Virgin appeared, transparent like the purest crystal; through it all her inner organs, shot through and perfused with his divine nature, shone forth just as gold wrapped in silk of varied colour is accustomed to shine through crystal. She also saw the dewy-fresh little boy, the only child of the highest Father, sucking at the heart of the Virginal Mother with hungry pleasure.)[13]

Possibly this idea of the womb as transparent, 'like the purest crystal', might have been suggested by the comparison of the womb in medical texts to urine bottles, which were, of course, made of glass.

This passage from Gertrud suggests another way in which the anchorhold might be considered to be like the womb: the occupant's physical needs are provided with minimal effort. Like the foetus, the solitary ideally receives just enough to sustain her for one day at a time. The economic bases of the anchoritic life preoccupied medieval writers as much as they do modern historians, for the contemplative ideal meant that, theoretically, the anchorite should have no involvement whatsoever in the secular world. As we know from *de Institutione Inclusarum* and from *Ancrene Wisse*, she must not keep a school, make money from needlework or embroidery, or provide safe-deposit facilities for her neighbours. Even owning a cow was problematic, as the animal might stray and thus embroil its unfortunate owner in awkward dealings with secular society. So she could hardly be financially self-sufficient. Her way of life was costly, in spite of her personal asceticism. There were a number of possible solutions to this dilemma: in late medieval Norwich:

even poor people could have become recluses and lived off the alms of the faithful. Paradoxically the most ambitious attempt to provide them with some kind of regular income came shortly before they disappeared. Robert Jannys, a former mayor who made his will in 1530, wanted each anchorite in the city to have 13d of his money every three months for twenty years.[14]

Thirteen pence a quarter would be just enough to provide the bare necessities.

Some anchorites were more fortunate, financially supported by an endowment so that they would not need to resort to attempts to generate external income. Not everyone, however, thought that a recluse should be fully funded in this way. It is unlikely that Aelred had in mind any permanent provision, however modest, for his own sister: 'prouideat incluse, ut si fieri potest, de labore manuum suarum uiuat: hoc enim perfectius' (if it is possible she should live by the labour of her own hands: this is the more perfect way). But he also recognized that this was often impractical and conceded: 'antequam includatur certas personas quaerat, a quibus singulis diebus quod uni diei sufficiat humiliter recipiat' (she should, before being enclosed in her cell, find someone to provide her with what is necessary for each day. This she may humbly accept).[15]

Several hundred years later, the author of *The Cloud of Unknowing* remarked that if his correspondent is faithful to his life of prayer, God

wol . . . stere oþer men in spirite to ȝeue us oure needful þinges þat longen to þis liif, as mete & cloþes [food and clothes] wiþ alle þeese oþer, ȝif he see þat [we] wil not leue þe werke of his loue for besines aboute hem. & þis I sey in confusion of þeire errour [their mistake], þat seyn þat it is not leueful [desirable] men to sette hem to serue God in contemplatyue liif, bot ȝif þei ben sekir bifore of þeire bodily nessessaryes [previously sure of their bodily requirements]. For þei sey þat God sendeþ þe kow, bot not by þe horne.[16]

Such an approach of simple trust in God was appropriate enough in a Carthusian monk. But to those who endowed anchorholds or left money to anchorites in their wills it might have seemed merely an excuse for hand-to-mouth financial arrangements.

The connections, both overt and implied, between the womb and anchoritic enclosure bear further investigation. A significant sentence precedes the passage already quoted from *Ancrene Wisse*:

for-þi i þe godspel of þe þreo Maries is iwreten þisses weis: . . . þeos Maries, hit seið, þeose bitternesses, weren cuminde to smirien Ure Lauerd . . . Ant nes he him-seolf reclus i Maries wombe?

(Therefore this is written in the gospel about the three Marys . . . 'These Marys', it says, 'these bitternesses, were coming to anoint our Lord' . . . And was he not himself a recluse in Mary's womb?)[17]

Why does mention of the three Marys who came to anoint the body of Jesus for burial make the author think of Christ as a recluse in the Virgin's womb? Medieval writers often work by word-association, and it seems to be the mention of anointing that constitutes the link here. Elsewhere *Ancrene Wisse* refers to the anchorite as 'a smiret ancre ant ancre biburiet, for hwet is ancre hus bute hir burinesse?' (an anointed anchoress, and a buried anchoress – for what is the anchor-house but her grave?);[18] here, 'smiret' must allude to her rite of enclosure. In the ceremony found in the Exeter Pontifical, extreme unction was adminis-tered and the reclusory called a 'sepulchre'; the candidate was sprinkled with dust and the entrance to her cell blocked up, like that of a tomb. (Aelred refers to the door of the reclusory or cell as '*obtruso*', that is, 'blocked' or 'stopped up'.[19]) Anointing was part of other ceremonies and sacraments, notably baptism, confirmation and coronation, but its primary connotation was that of death. And the anchorhold was indeed a tomb: 'Anchorites inhabited a liminal plane between the living and the dead: to be immured in a cell represented a kind of symbolic death.'[20] Nor was this always merely symbolic: excavations in several reclusories have uncovered the remains of those who were presumably its former occupants. The author of *Ancrene Wisse* would certainly have approved: he is notorious for his comment that

hire seolf bihalden hire ahne hwite honden deð hearm moni ancre . . . Ha schulden schrapien euche dei þe eorðe up of hare put þat ha schulien rotien in.

(looking at her own white hands does harm to many anchoresses . . . They should be scraping the earth up every day out of the pit they must rot in!)[21]

Aelred is also clear that the anchorhold is a tomb and the enclosed life a life dead to the world. The recluse, he declares, has chosen '*abscondi desiderans non uideri, et quasi mortua saeculo in spelunca Christo* consepeliri' (to be hidden and unseen, to be dead as it were to the world and buried with Christ in his tomb).[22] Similarly, he exhorts his sister to claim Mary's part, as one who is 'saeculo mortua atque sepulta, surda . . . et muta' (dead and buried to the world . . . deaf . . . and unable to speak).[23] Surprisingly, the Vulgate does not use *spelunca*, the word Aelred uses in association with *consepelire*, to mean 'tomb'. In the New Testament it has its literal meaning of 'cave', although it is closely associated with tombs in John 11: 38: 'Jesus . . . cometh to the sepulchre [of Lazarus]. Now it was a cave; and a stone was laid over it.' (The Church of the Holy Sepulchre in Jerusalem, however, did in fact enclose a cave, in which the body of Jesus was traditionally believed to have rested after the Crucifixion.) Rather than *spelunca*, the gospels of Mark, Luke and John refer to Christ's burial-place as *monumentum*, while Matthew's gospel has *sepulcrum* and is, in fact, the only New Testament book to use the word in any context.

Aelred uses *sepulcrum* metaphorically to refer to the sinner's dead body: 'Non sic impii non sic, quos de corpore quasi de foetenti sepulchro, pessimi spiritus, cum instrumentis infernalibus extrahentes' (Not so is it with the wicked, not so. Evil spirits with the instruments of hell drag them from the body as from a fetid tomb).[24] In the Middle Ages, hooks were used to dismember and remove dead infants from the womb, and Aelred associates the literal womb as much with death as with life. Speaking of his own birth, he reflects that God

> bene utens malo parentum nostrorum creauit nos de carne illorum et inspirauit in nobis spiraculum uitae, discernens nos ab illis qui uel *abortiui proiecti sunt ab utero*, uel qui *inter materna uiscera suffocati*, poenae uidentur concepti non uitae.

> (brought good out of the evil committed by our parents and created us from their flesh, animating us with the breath of life and setting us apart from those who were either *ejected from the womb prematurely* or *stifled within the womb*, conceived, it would seem, for punishment rather than for life.)[25]

On the other hand, we should also remember that in Christian belief baptism is simultaneously death to sin and new birth: not for nothing was oil used at baptism as well as at the hour of death. Indeed, Aelred's use of *consepeliri* [to be buried] echoes the only two Vulgate verses that use the verb, which on both occasions is collocated with *baptismum*: Romans 6: 4 and Colossians 2: 12.[26]

Aelred, therefore, sees the solitary's cell as a metaphor for Christ's tomb. But Christ's tomb in its turn can also function as a metaphor. It provides Gertrud of Helfta with one of her many metaphors for the Divine Heart:

Feria etiam quinta, cum de beata Maria Magdalena legeretur in Evangelio: *Prospexit in monumentum, et vidit duos Angelos*, etc. dixit ad Dominum: 'Ubi est, Domine, monumentum in quod ego prospiciens invenire possim consolationis delectationem?' Tunc Dominus ad vulnus lateris sui ipsam obtendit. Ad quod dum se inclinare deintus quasi in vice duorum Angelorum, intellexit haec duo sibi dicta . . .

(Also on Thursday, when 'She looked into the tomb, and saw two angels' and so on was being read in the Gospel about Mary Magdalene, [Gertrud] said to the Lord: 'Where, Lord, is the tomb into which I could look and find delight of consolation?' Then the Lord placed her at the wound in his side. While she was bending down, as if in the place of the two angels from within she perceived these two sentences spoken to her . . .)[27]

Modern readers, such as McQuinn in her essay included here, are inclined to see such medieval representations of the Divine Heart, especially when they emanate from the pens of women mystics, as occluded images for the womb, so yet again, albeit by a circuitous route, we come full circle from tomb to womb.

In a final digression I want briefly to explore another metaphor for the anchoritic life which is neither womb nor tomb but has associations with both: that of the prison. In Shakespeare's *The Winter's Tale*, Paulina equates the womb with a prison:

> The child was prisoner to the womb, and is
> By law and process of great nature thence
> Freed and enfranchised . . . (II. ii)

Julian of Norwich writes of her anchorhold (though it is also possible that she is simply referring to this earthly life), 'This place is prison, and this life is penance.'[28] There is one reference in *Ancrene Wisse* that indubitably equates the anchorhold and the prison: 'in-to an ancre-hus, in-to godes prisun' (into an anchor-house and into God's prison)[29] and two that are more ambiguous: 'we beoð all i prisun her' (we are all in prison here)[30] and 'with-ute cwitance of þis prisun nis nan inume' (without clearance no one is taken up out of this prison).[31] We might well query the significance of this. Is not the equivalence between an anchoritic and a prison cell self-evident? But *cell* does not acquire the meaning 'madhouse or prison cell' until the eighteenth century. Nonetheless there is, I believe, a genuine medieval association between enclosure and prisons. The Latin nouns *inclusus* and *inclusa*, two of the commonest words for a recluse, derive from the verb *includere*, 'to enclose'. This word appears in the Vulgate New Testament only twice, in Acts 26: 10 and Luke 3: 20; on both occasions it means to incarcerate, specifically in prison.[32]

But the enclosure sought by the recluse does not have to be quite as literal as is suggested by such metaphors of confinement as prison, womb or tomb. True enclosure was surely a state of mind. Perhaps Gertrud of Helfta can throw some light on why anyone would want to pursue this solitary vocation. Whether she was a Benedictine or a Cistercian nun (there is some dispute), she was certainly a coenobite and lived the community life. She could, however, achieve the effect of enclosure by other means: specifically, by sickness or physical weakness, which would isolate her from her sisters. On many occasions she received revelations in a liturgical context, not while singing the office in choir but, while too sick to participate, observing the performance of the liturgy – just as a recluse might do through her 'squint'. A passage in her revelations throws light on the role that this recurrent motif of sickness and physical weakness played in her own life and, perhaps, in the lives of many other devout or visionary women. On Palm Sunday, her amanuensis records:

post prandium . . . nimium lassata membra repausatura lectulo se reposuisset, non tamen ut dormiret, sed ut se a tumultibus crebrius se visitantium abstraheret, ait ad Dominum: 'Ecce, Domine . . . tibi soli amatori meo intendere desiderio, ut tu loquaris animae meae.' . . . Et cum ista adverteret quod homines parcerent ne eam inquietarent, putantes eam dormire, requisivit a Domino utrum eis dicere deberet quod non dormiret, ne impedirentur facere quicquid vellent.

(after the midday meal . . . she had laid her exhausted limbs on her bed to rest, not however that she should sleep but so that she might withdraw from the disturbance of too frequent visitors, she said to the Lord: 'Look, Lord . . . I desire to concentrate on you alone, my lover, that you may speak to my soul.' . . . And when that woman noticed that people were leaving her alone so as not to disturb her, thinking that she was asleep, she asked the Lord whether she ought to tell them that she was not asleep, so as not to prevent them from doing whatever they wanted.)[33]

This vividly evokes the strains and hazards of religious life in community in the Middle Ages – and the strategies to which even the most holy might resort. The anchoritic life undoubtedly had its hardships, but it also possessed advantages. Images of tomb and prison largely convey the negative, ascetic side of enclosure: the metaphor of the womb, which protects and nurtures as much as it confines, foregrounds a more optimistic view.

Notes

1 *Economist*, 11 May 2002, 84.
2 *The Knowing of Woman's Kind in Childing*, ed. Alexandra Barratt, Medieval Women: Texts and Contexts, 4 (Turnhout, 2001).
3 *The Knowing of Woman's Kind*, p. 44.
4 Ibid., p. 44.
5 *Medieval Embryology in the Vernacular: The Case of* De Spermate, ed. Päivi Pahta (Helsinki, 1998), pp. 38–40.
6 B. M. Patten, *The Embryology of the Pig* (Philadelphia, 1948), p. 7, fig. 2, and p. 101, figs 52 and 53.
7 *The Knowing of Woman's Kind*, p. 47.
8 Ibid., p. 50.
9 *The English Text of the Ancrene Riwle: Ancrene Wisse: Edited from MS. Corpus Christi College Cambridge 402*, by J. R. R. Tolkien, EETS o.s. 249 (London, New York and Toronto, 1962), pp. 192–3. The corresponding translation of every quotation from *Ancrene Wisse* is taken from *Anchoritic Spirituality*: Ancrene Wisse *and Associated Works*, trans. and intro. Anne Savage and Nicholas Watson (New York and Mahwah, 1991), here at p. 186.
10 *de Institutione Inclusarum*, in *Aelredi Rievallensis Opera Omnia: 1 Opera Ascetica*, ed. A. Hoste and C. H. Talbot (Turnhout, 1971), p. 638 (my emphasis). All subsequent quotations from *de Institutione Inclusarum* are from this edition. The corresponding translation is taken from 'A Rule of Life for a Recluse', trans. Mary Paul Macpherson, in *Aelred of Rievaulx: Treatises: The Pastoral Prayer*, intro. David Knowles (Spencer, M. A., 1971), here at p. 47.
11 *Aelred of Rievaulx's de Institutione Inclusarum: Two English Versions*, ed. John Ayto and Alexandra Barratt, EETS o.s. 287 (Oxford, 1984), p. 18, lines 707–8 and 716.
12 *de Institutione*, p. 663.
13 *Legatus Divinae Pietatis*, 4, 3, in *Revelationes Gertrudianae ac Mechtildianae*, ed. Monks of Solesmes (Paris, 1875), 1, p. 300; the translation is my own.
14 Norman P. Tanner, *The Church in Late Medieval Norwich* (Toronto, 1984), p. 131.
15 *de Institutione*, p. 639; Macpherson, pp. 47–8.

[16] *The Cloud of Unknowing*, ed. Phyllis Hodgson, EETS o.s. 213 (London, New York and Toronto, 1944, repr. 1973), p. 57.

[17] *Ancrene Wisse*, p. 192; Savage and Watson, p. 186.

[18] *Ancrene Wisse*, p. 58; Savage and Watson, p. 54.

[19] *de Institutione*, p. 638.

[20] Roberta Gilchrist, *Contemplation and Action: The Other Monasticism* (London and New York, 1995), p. 190.

[21] *Ancrene Wisse*, p. 62; Savage and Watson, pp. 91–2.

[22] *de Institutione*, p. 648; Macpherson, p. 62.

[23] *de Institutione*, p. 660; Macpherson, p. 75.

[24] *de Institutione*, p. 678; Macpherson, p. 98.

[25] *de Institutione*, p. 673 (my emphasis); Macpherson, pp. 92–3.

[26] 'For we are buried together with him by baptism into death' (Romans 6: 4) and 'Buried with him in baptism' (Colossians 2: 12).

[27] *Legatus Divinae Pietatis*, 4, 31, in *Revelationes Gertrudianae*, 1, p. 393 (again, the translation is my own). Compare also *The Shewings of Julian of Norwich*, ed. Georgia Ronan Crampton, TEAMS (Kalamazoo, 1994), pp. 69–70.

[28] *The Shewings*, p. 146.

[29] *Ancrene Wisse*, p. 57; Savage and Watson, p. 54.

[30] *Ancrene Wisse*, p. 66; Savage and Watson, p. 63.

[31] *Ancrene Wisse*, p. 67; Savage and Watson, p. 63.

[32] 'Many of the saints did [Paul] shut up in prison', and '[Herod] . . . shut up John in prison'.

[33] *Legatus Divinae Pietatis*, 4, 23, in *Revelationes Gertrudianae*, 1, p. 372.

I

Enclosure and Discourses of the Desert

3

Guthlac A and *Guthlac B*: Changing Metaphors

SANTHA BHATTACHARJI

The life of the Anglo-Saxon hermit Guthlac (673–714) comes down to us primarily in the Latin prose biography by Felix of Crowland.[1] It is also the focus of two poems in Old English, which follow each other in the late tenth-century *Exeter Book*,[2] though both may actually have been composed earlier, possibly before 900.[3] Both poems are assumed to derive ultimately from Felix's Latin *Vita Guthlaci*, since they give us no substantially different information about the saint.[4] *Guthlac A*, the longer poem at 818 lines, gives us a complete biography from birth, focusing on the heroic character of Guthlac's strenuous eremitical life. Closure for this narrative is provided by a triumphant picture of Guthlac's soul being borne to heaven in the arms of angels (lines 781–2). In contrast, *Guthlac B*, shorter at 561 lines as it stands, although unfinished,[5] focuses almost entirely on the saint's final illness and death.

In this second poem, the heroic figure has become death's passive and exhausted prey, described as 'adlwerigne' (wearied by sickness) (line 1008); he is shot at and wounded by arrows of disease; the sudden illness enters him ('him faeringa adl in gewod') (lines 939–40). This language of penetration culminates in an unexpected image of the saint as a treasure-chest, whose lock is opened by the 'searocægum' (cunning keys) of death (lines 956, 1029 and 1144). 'Hoard' and 'treasure' are widespread terms in Old English poetry, but, surprisingly, they rarely occur in association with the verb *unlocan* (to unlock),[6] as they do here in each of three key passages within the poem:

> wæs se bancofa
> adle onæled, inbendum fæst
> lichord onlocen. (lines 954–6)

(The bone-chest was consumed by disease, the treasure-hoard of his body, made fast by inner bonds, was unlocked.)

> Ic wille secgan þæt me sar gehran,
> wærc in gewod in ðisse wonnan niht,
> lichord onleac. (lines 1027–9)

(I will state that in this dark night pain seized me, agony entered into me and unlocked my body's treasure-hoard.)

> Com se þæs þe him in gesonc
> hat, heortan neah, hildescurun,
> flacor flanþracu, feorhhord onleac
> searocægum gesoht. (lines 1141–5)

(The seventh day arrived for men since the flickering storm of arrows sank into him in battle-showers, hot, near the heart, and unlocked the treasure-hoard of his life, sought it with cunning keys.)

In this chapter, I will argue that this is a striking and unusual image for death, and one which carries deeply gendered overtones. Indeed, the other principal associations of 'treasure-chest' with the idea of unlocking in Old English poetry occur, as we shall see, in two obscene riddles within the *Exeter Book*, riddles 44 and 90.[7] In these riddles, the key plays an active, masculine role as it seeks to unlock the feminized treasure-chest. By association, in *Guthlac B*, the passivity of the hermit confronted by death seems to cast him in a suggestively female role. This image has not been much discussed by previous scholars,[8] as *Guthlac B* is usually dismissed as slavishly following Felix's *Vita*, whose content it replicates closely as regards events. In order to establish the unconventionality of the image, therefore, I shall first outline the more traditional ways of describing the hermit life and their influence on Felix's *Vita* and on *Guthlac A*, looking in particular at their gender overtones. I shall then return to *Guthlac B* and the function of the treasure-chest image within it, arguing that it is both a key image in the text and also heralds an important shift in the language used to describe the hermit experience.

Any attempt to write the biography of a hermit presents the author with a fundamental paradox: how to describe the events of a life which seeks to have none. Once a hermit has established a place of stability and solitude, ideally he or she disappears from the world and has nothing to record. Consequently, every biography of a hermit is a largely interpretative tract, seeking key words and metaphors whereby to bring out the significance of this apparently pointless life. Metaphor, in particular, is used of necessity where the achievements of a life are largely internal, in an unseen spiritual realm. When we look at the evolving tradition of hermit biography which influences Felix, the kind of themes we see emerging include the following: victory over basic human drives and temptations; spiritual vision; divinely infused wisdom; a gentleness which attracts animals and damaged human beings alike; a role as counsellor and teacher. These themes emerge in the texts that Felix, as an eighth-century Anglo-Saxon monk, was most likely to know:[9] Athanasius' *Life of Antony*, in the Latin version of Evagrius of Antioch;[10] Jerome's life of *Paul the Hermit*;[11] Sulpicius Severus' *Life of St Martin*;[12] Gregory's account of Saint Benedict in Book II of the *Dialogues*;[13] and within England, Aldhelm's *de Virginitate*[14] and Bede's prose *Life of St Cuthbert*.[15] Most of these texts use very similar rhetorical devices to structure the text. They often begin with a claim to eye-witness sources, as in Athanasius' preface to his *Life of Antony* and in the prologue to Gregory the Great's account of Benedict (which does not necessarily imply that the sources have no basis in fact).[16] They also frequently end in a standardized manner. Thus Sulpicius' *Life of St Martin* and Felix's *Life of Guthlac* culminate in almost identical peror-ations, describing the hermit's general eloquence and particular gift for solving the problems of Scripture.[17] However, each text usually also includes one major, controlling metaphor, which serves to pinpoint the overall emphasis of that particular work. This metaphor may occur only once or twice in the text, but is so placed that its summing-up function emerges clearly, even if there are other thematic strands in the work.

In general, these dominant metaphors create a very masculinized discourse on sanctity, while the lesser strands can have more potential as feminizing agents – something which is seldom exploited, however. For example, all these saints (with the exception of Guthlac himself) are, to a certain extent, presented as the *puer senex* (wise child): they are gentle, studious boys, mature beyond their years, who dislike violence and coarseness. Although there is the potential here for a degree of feminization of these saints, the opposition established tends to be

between the violence of the passions and the peacefulness of the spirit.
Thus these men can be seen as 'spiritual', as opposed to 'carnal', men.
In Benedict's case, for example, the 'wise child' evolves into the grown
man who chooses the true wisdom of simplicity, abandoning his studies
in so doing. In his Prologue, Gregory sums this up as: 'Recessit igitur
scienter nescius et sapienter indoctus' (He withdrew, knowledgeably
ignorant and wisely unlearned).[18]

Most often, however, the controlling metaphor is that of warfare: the
saint is a warrior of God, engaged in spiritual combat against the Devil.
We find this language repeatedly in Athanasius' *Life of Antony*, which,
as the earliest of the texts considered here, becomes in some ways
normative. Antony not only fights against demons (chs 5–15, 51–3), but
gets the better of the wisest men of Alexandria in theological and
philosophical debate (chs 73–80). Jerome, however, counters this
interpretation of the eremitical calling in his *Life of Paul the Hermit*,
where Paul of Thebes is depicted as a gentle, humble man, forgotten by
all, whose intercession slowly redeems the strange creatures of the
desert. Nevertheless, the controlling metaphor is still one of masculine
achievement: as he is about to die, he says to Antony: 'Peracto cursu
superest mihi corona iustitiae' (There remains for me a crown of
righteousness now that I have run the course),[19] using the language of
athletic competition also found in the Pauline epistles (2 Tim. 4: 7–8).

The influence of this masculinized discourse can be seen even in
apparently unlikely contexts. Thus, a gentle, healing, animal-loving saint
such as Cuthbert is also described by Bede in heavy warrior vocabulary,
specifically at the point when he embarks on the hermit life. We are told
that he first lives on the outskirts of the monastery: 'At cum ibidem
aliquandiu solitarius cum hoste inuisibili orando ac ieiunando certaret,
tandem maiora praesumens, longiquiorem ac remotiorem ab hominibus
locum certaminis petiit' (But when he had fought there for some time as
a solitary against the invisible foe, by prayer and fasting, at last aiming
at greater things, he sought a place of combat further away and more
remote from men).[20] Cuthbert therefore goes to the island of Inner
Farne, where no one had dared set foot because of the 'phantasias
daemonum' (phantoms of demons), but when he as 'miles Christi'
(soldier of Christ) entered it, 'fugatus est hostis' (the enemy was put to
flight).[21] Bede maintains this vocabulary even in his more meditative
verse *Life of Cuthbert*: when he gives up the duties of bishop to return
to his hermitage on Inner Farne at the end of his life, the verse Life
explains: 'Malebat Satanae tetricis pulsarier armis' (he preferred to be

assaulted by the dismal weapons of Satan).[22] Similarly, Aldhelm's *de Virginitate* also makes striking use of this warrior discourse. Aldhelm gives a series of brief lives of both male and female virgins, using the same warrior imagery for both. For example, Eugenia, he says, runs away from home and 'non muliebriter quaesitura rasis cincinnorum criniculis sub tonsura masculini sexus contra iura naturae sanctorum coetibus aggregatur et militonum Christi cateruis . . . adsciscitur' (not like a woman, but against the laws of nature, with her curling locks shaved off, in the short crop of the masculine sex, she was joined to the ranks of the saints and . . . was recruited to the troops of Christ's army).[23] Moreover, if a saint is already a soldier, as is Martin of Tours, this military imagery intensifies: upon leaving the army, for example, he declares: 'Patere ut nunc militem Deo . . . Christi ego miles sum: pugnare mihi non licet' (allow me now to fight for God . . . I am a soldier of Christ: I am not allowed to fight).[24]

When we turn to Felix's *Vita Guthlaci*, we find that Guthlac himself starts life as a successful warlord and freebooter, and, in his case, his very name means 'reward of war'. This is reinterpreted by Felix to mean that he would be divinely rewarded for his struggle against the vices.[25] Felix addressed his *Vita* to King Aelfwald of East Anglia, who reigned from 713 to 749, and the text seems to have been written somewhere between 730 and 740, that is, around twenty years after Guthlac's death. Since the hermit died in 714, around the age of forty, this is well within living memory of him, and Felix lists the eyewitnesses whom he gives as his main sources, even claiming to reproduce what they told him in the very order in which they narrated it.[26] While this might signal a biography marked by freshness and authentic-sounding detail, this opening actually serves to set Felix's text within the literary conventions on hermits discussed above.

The main facts of Guthlac's life, as outlined by Felix, are that, after nine years as a bloodthirsty warrior, having reached the age of 24, he became oppressed by the obvious mortality of human beings, particularly within the warrior lifestyle. He therefore resolved to change his life, and entered the double monastery of Repton, at that time ruled by an abbess. Two years later, having learnt to read and gained familiarity with the Scriptures and the Liturgy, he withdrew to a hermitage at Crowland in the Lincolnshire fens. There he built a hut over a partly exposed grave-barrow, and thereafter lived a solitary life until his death, fifteen years later. Nevertheless, he was visited by many people for advice and counsel, including King Athelbald of Mercia.[27] His fifteen years of solitude were marked by attacks from the demons. Here we see Felix's debt to Athanasius: the hermit is repeatedly referred to as 'miles Christi' (soldier of Christ), fighting against the 'antiquus hostis prolis humanae' (the ancient enemy of the human race).[28] However, the emphases are slightly different from what we might expect. Like Antony, Guthlac remembers his family obligations and yearns for human company, but sexual temptation is not dwelt on. Rather, he is tempted to despair because of his past crimes. Thus, we see demons with large yellow heads, filthy beards and horses' teeth seeping into his cell through every nook and cranny, and carrying him off to the place reserved for him in Hell, from which he is later rescued by Saint Bartholomew.[29]

When it comes to Guthlac's death, Felix closely models the sequence of events on Bede's account of Cuthbert's end.[30] In both, the hermit is suddenly stricken by disease on a Wednesday, and dies on a Wednesday; a disciple comes to the hermit's window and finds him sighing and speaking with difficulty; the hermit admits to being ill with more than his usual bodily weaknesses, and foretells his death. At some point both men give instructions about their burial, and also utter their final, inspired, spiritual instruction. There are differences of emphasis, however. Bede's Cuthbert is still suffering the onslaught of the Devil: in the five days when his illness is at its worst and he can barely nibble an onion for moisture, he is attacked more fiercely than at any time in his life 'antiqui hostis acriori certamine' (by a still fiercer contest with the ancient foe).[31]

Felix, however, shows a striking element of independence in presenting a more joyful slant to the experience of death, with Guthlac preparing himself for his departure in a triumphant spirit. The theme of resurrection is emphasized by the saint's struggling to rise from his sickbed to celebrate the rites of Easter Day, at the exact midpoint of his week-long illness, which Felix has shortened from Bede's three weeks. In the work as a whole, however, the controlling metaphor remains the warrior one, even though Felix takes over some of the delightful animal stories associated with Cuthbert; for instance, birds fly to Guthlac's hands, and swallows nest in his hut.[32] Felix draws the two strands together by taking this special bond with nature as a sign of triumph in the spiritual battle: the birds flock to him after he has fought off the demonic temptations to despair.[33]

The first Old English poem, *Guthlac A*, replicates this masculinized discourse by drawing heavily on the warrior imagery, intensified by all the overtones of Anglo-Saxon heroic poetic diction. Indeed, there is some debate as to how much or how little the poem is copying the prose Life, since the vernacular poet could be spontaneously reconstituting the warrior imagery from within his own cultural tradition, which might well respond particularly warmly to a saint who could be seen as a Germanic warrior-hero. The words *cempa* and *oretta* for 'warrior' occur repeatedly,[34] and much Grendel-like vocabulary is used for Guthlac's spiritual foes, who 'wæron hy reowe to ræsanne / gifrum grapum' (lines 406–407) (were fierce in attacking with greedy clutches).[35]

Guthlac B, for its part, has attracted little attention, precisely because the language is less interestingly heroic. However, set against a background of heavily masculinized discourse, with hermits as triumphant spiritual warriors, any shift towards more feminized overtones is worthy of note. While we do get a few instances of the warrior terms *cempa* and *oretta* in *Guthlac B*,[36] these form a preamble describing Guthlac's hermit life, before moving on to the substance of the poem, which centres on his death. However, in this text it is the unconventional image of unlocking the treasure-chest which provides the controlling metaphor. In fact, this image occurs in three key places, as I suggested earlier: the first, when the poet shifts his focus from a description of Guthlac's style of life, in which he waited for deliverance from this world, to announcing that this deliverance was about to come; the second, when Guthlac announces his impending death to his disciple; the third, on the morning of the actual day of death. Guthlac's passive endurance as the flickering arrow of disease enters him serves the theological purpose of the poet, which is to present a Christian meditation on death as the looked-for release from this world and departure for heaven. The poet signals the novelty and unexpectedness of this Christian view of death by heralding the arrival of Guthlac's final illness with the word 'bliss':

> Hyght wæs geniwad
> blis in breostum; wæs se bancofa
> adle onæled. (lines 953–5)

(Hope was renewed, bliss in the breast; the bone-chest was consumed by disease.)

In her doctoral thesis on the Guthlac texts, Jane Crawford has argued strongly in favour of both the literary merits of *Guthlac B* and the notable coherence of its disquisition on death. Taking from Felix a

comment on the mortality that afflicts every member of the race of
Adam, the poet develops this into the most sustained treatment of the
poculum mortis (the drink of death) in Old English literature, referring
to the apple of paradise as 'þone bitran drync þone Eue fyrn Adame
geaf' (the bitter drink that Eve gave the sons of Adam) (lines 868–9).[37]
The body as treasure-chest of life takes on striking theological
resonance in this context, with mortality trying to unlock the chest and
steal the treasure. Crawford does not comment on this particular
metaphor, but Elizabeth Tyler discusses it at length.[38] While the body
as a treasure-chest is a common enough image, she argues that this poet
reconcretizes and vivifies it in a masterly way. She also draws attention
to the difference between willing and unwilling prey, contrasting the
imagery in *Guthlac B* with the more conventional image of fate 'seeking'
a warrior's life, as in *Beowulf*, lines 2419–24.

Thus, I would argue that once we have a cooperative and willing
treasure-chest and an approaching key, further overtones come into
play: the male saint is playing the female role in a drama resembling the
sexual act. These resonances are given legitimacy by the occurrence
within the same manuscript (the *Exeter Book*) of a handful of obscene
riddles, including two on the image of the 'key': riddles 44 and 90.

Riddle 44, a straightforwardly bawdy poem, serves chiefly to establish the masculine function of the key:

> Wrætlic hongað bi weres þeo
> frean under sceate foran is þyrel
> bið stiþ ond heard stede hafað godne.
> þonne se esne his agen hrægl
> ofer cneo hefeð wile þæt cuþe hol
> mid his hangellan heafde gretan
> þæt he efelang ær oft gefylde.

(A strange thing hangs by a man's thigh, under the lord's clothes. In front
is a hole; it is stiff and hard; it is fixed in a good place. When the man lifts
his own garment above the knee, he desires to greet with the head of his
hanging object the well-known hole which it, when of equal length, has
often previously filled.)[39]

Riddle 90, however, develops the key image in ways more relevant to
this poem:

Min heafod is homere geþuren
searopila wund sworfen feole
oft ic begine þæt me ongean sticað
þonne ic hnitan sceal hringum gyrded
hearde wið heardum hindan þyrel
forð ascufan þæt mines frean
modwynne freoþað middelnihtum.
hwilum ic under bæc bregde nebbe
hyrde þæs hordes þonne min hlaford wile
lafe þicgan þara þe he of life het
wælcræfte awrecan willum sinum.

(My head is beaten by a hammer, wounded by sharp tools, polished with a file. Often I open what is fixed opposite me when, girded with rings, I must push hard against what is hard; pierced from behind, I shove forth that which protects my lord's joy in the middle of the night. Sometimes I draw back, with my beak, the treasure's guardian, when my lord wishes to receive the inheritance of those whom, at his own wish, he has commanded to be exiled from life by the work of slaughter.)[40]

Here we have the treasure itself as a source of joy for its owner, who has gained this treasure both by inheritance and conquest. In a Christian context, this opening of the treasure-chest is to be desired not just by the owner but also by the chest, since the treasure of the soul is thereby released into the hands of its true owner, God. In addition, the riddle serves to remind us of the intense physicality of the attack of death on the individual, and so gathers up one of the central points in the whole discourse of hermit life as a battle: the battleground is localized in the hermit's actual body, as we saw with Cuthbert dying of disease. In *Guthlac B*, therefore, the frailty of the worn-out and dying saint prompts a change of poetic metaphor which, while serving the broader purpose of emphasizing the desirability of death, crosses, however tentatively, the sex/gender divide.

In the light of late-medieval discourse concerning hermits this is a significant development. Later discourse, heavily indebted to the language of the Song of Songs in the Bible and to the *Homilies on the Song of Songs* of Bernard of Clairvaux,[41] establishes any Christian hermit, male or female, in the role of the Bride awaiting her Bridegroom. This language arises in the context of the much greater emotional intensity of late medieval devotion. However, emotional intensity in itself does not automatically lead to a more feminized discourse. The affectivity of the later Middle Ages is often traced back to Anselm of Canterbury's seminal *Prayers and Meditations*, in which the reader is exhorted not to read a prayer from end to end, but to dip into it and read only enough 'ad excitandam mentem' (to stir up the mind) towards certain feelings.[42] Anselm addresses these prayers to Countess Mathilda of Tuscany, but they reflect clearly his own masculine monastic tradition.[43] In this, the psalms are the chief vehicles of emotion, and the meditating monk is encouraged to identify with King David, to whom they were ascribed, sharing his emotions of grief, despair, rejoicing or trust. Consequently, in Anselm's text there is much emphasis on stirring up fear of judgement, self-abasement and contrition, as well as thanksgiving for pardon and salvation. These emphases are, of course, as appropriate to a male as to a female supplicant.

The feminization of discourse seems to arise when this affectivity is taken over by Saint Bernard and applied by him to an already ancient spiritual literary tradition within Christianity: that of commenting allegorically on the Song of Songs in the Bible, which consists of a lyrical evocation of sexual desire between a man and a woman. This tradition goes back at least as far as Origen in the third century AD,[44] and early Latin commentaries include those by Ambrose and Gregory the Great.[45] The importance of Gregory's commentary is that it forged, in Latin, a spiritual vocabulary of longing, desiring, seeking and waiting, followed by exultation at the fleeting moments of contact with the lover, and finally the bliss of union. Many of these feelings are described in terms of wounding and sickness: the bride 'desiderio aestuat' (burns with desire);[46] the words of preachers 'majori amore sagittant' (pierce [her] with arrows of greater love).[47] As we have seen, however, this alternative vocabulary did not find its way into early-medieval discourse about the eremetic life. We can thus appreciate Bernard's innovative boldness in taking this text as the basis for his long sequence of homilies, addressed specifically to his monks, particularly as the newly founded Cistercian Order consciously looked back to the hermit tradition of the desert fathers – something on which Elizabeth Freeman focuses in her essay in this volume (ch. 5). By using the affective tradition initiated by Anselm, Bernard produced a minutely detailed meditation on every nuance of the Bride's feelings, applying her experiences to the steps of the spiritual life. Bernard himself came from the knightly class[48] and strongly supported the new military orders, such as the Templars;[49] his choice, therefore, of aligning himself and his monks so closely with the female figure within the Song of Songs is the more unexpected, since the pre-existing warrior vocabulary might be assumed to resonate with them more strongly. Thanks to the rapid expansion of the Cistercian Order and Bernard's own enormous personal influence, both within and outside it, his *Homilies on the Song of Songs* soon established this new, feminized vocabulary as a norm, in which nearly all later-medieval devotion, whether aimed at the laity or monastics, came to be written. This also included writings for and by male hermits. A striking example in England, for instance, is provided by the fourteenth-century Monk of Farne, one of the long line of hermits who occupied Inner Farne in succession to Saint Cuthbert.[50] In his *Meditations*, we find the wide knowledge of the whole Bible and of the Fathers that we might expect from someone who was for many years, we suspect, a monk of Durham Abbey; but he also draws increasingly on Bernardine language,[51] particularly in his long meditation addressed to Christ.

This chapter argues that perhaps Bernard's focus on the Bride was so readily received precisely because a more feminized discourse was already emerging. In *Guthlac B*, we see it taking shape in response to the theological demands of this particular poet's interpretation of the Christian eremitical life. The poem *Guthlac B*, written possibly before the year 900, shows us the dim beginnings of this more feminized discourse.

Notes

[1]   Bertram Colgrave (ed.), *Felix's Life of St Guthlac* (Cambridge, 1956; repr. with English translation, 1985). In this chapter, all translations from any text are my own. Apart from the Latin *Vita*, a block of four chapters (chs 28–32, warning against excessive fasting) excerpted from an Old English translation now lost, make up the last homily in the Vercelli Codex: see *The Vercelli Book*, ed. Celia Sisam, Early English Manuscripts in Facsimile, 19 (Copenhagen, 1976), Homily 23, ff. 133v–135v; *The Vercelli Homilies and Related Texts*, ed. D. G. Scragg, EETS o.s. 300 (Oxford, 1992), pp. 383–92. For date and language of the Old English translation from which the homily is excerpted, see Jane Roberts, 'The Old English prose translation of Felix's *Vita Sancti Guthlaci*', in P. E. Szarmach (ed.), *Studies in Earlier Old English Prose* (Albany, NY, 1986), pp. 363–79. A different, complete, Old English translation of the *Vita* dates from the eleventh century: see Roberts, ibid., p. 369. For the dating of the Vercelli homilies in general, see Scragg, *Vercelli Homilies*, xxxviii–xlii.

[2]   Jane Roberts (ed.), *The Guthlac Poems of the Exeter Book* (Oxford, 1979). For a text with facing translation, see Israel Gollancz (ed. and trans.), *The*

Exeter Book, Part I: Poems I–VIII, EETS o.s. 104 (London, 1895), pp. 104–89.

3 For the dating of the two poems, see Roberts, *Guthlac Poems*, pp. 63–71, particularly at pp. 70–1. For a full description of the *Exeter Book*, see the facsimile edition: R. Chambers, M. Forster, R. Flower (eds), *The Exeter Book of Old English Poetry* (London, 1933).

4 For a summary of the extensive debate on the indebtedness of the poems to Felix, see Roberts, *Guthlac Poems*, pp. 19–29.

5 The lines of the two poems are always numbered consecutively. For the complicated history of the line numbering, see Jane Crawford, 'Guthlac: an edition of the Old English prose life together with the poems in the *Exeter Book*' (unpublished D.Phil. thesis, Oxford, 1967), 664–6. For the possibility that *Azarias* (on the Song of the Three Children in the Furnace), another *Exeter Book* poem, is the ending of *Guthlac B*, see R. T. Farrell (ed.), *Daniel and Azarias*, Methuen's Old English Library (London, 1974), pp. 39–40.

6 Elizabeth Tyler, 'The collocation of words for treasure in Old English verse' (unpublished D.Phil. thesis, Oxford, 1994), 236–9.

7 W. S. Mackie (ed.), *The Exeter Book, Part II*, EETS o.s. 194 (London, 1934), pp. 140–1, pp. 232–3 (text with facing translation).

8 For example, Greenfield quotes it but does not discuss it: S. B. Greenfield, 'The Christian saint as hero', in S. B. Greenfield and D. G. Calder (eds), *A New Critical History of Old English Literature* (New York and London, 1986), p. 178.

9 Colgrave, *Felix's Life*, pp. 16–17.

10 For Athanasius' Greek text, see *PG*, 26, cols 835–976, which reprints the edition by Bernard de Montfaucon (Paris, 1698). For an English translation of the Greek text, see R. C. Gregg (trans.), *Athanasius's Life of Antony* (New York, 1980). For Evagrius of Antioch's Latin version, see G. J. M. Bartelink (ed.), *Vite dei Santi*, vol. 1 (Milan, 1974). For an English translation of Evagrius, see Carolinne White (trans.), *Early Christian Lives* (London, 1998), pp. 3–70.

11 Jerome, *Vita S. Pauli Primi Eremitae, PL*, 23, cols 18–28.

12 Sulpice Sévère, *Vie de Saint Martin*, ed. J. Fontaine, vol. 1, Sources Chrétiennes, 133 (Paris, 1967), pp. 248–316.

13 Gregoire le Grand, *Dialogues*, ed. A. de Vogüé, vol. 2, Sources Chrétiennes, 251 (Paris, 1979), pp. 126–49.

14 *Aldhelmi Malmesbiriensis Prosa de Virginitate*, ed. Scott Gwara, Corpus Christianorum series Latina CXXIV A (Turnhout, 2001).

15 Bertram Colgrave (ed. and trans.), *Two Lives of Saint Cuthbert* (Cambridge, 1985), pp. 142–307.

16 Grégoire, *Dialogues*, 2, p. 126.

17 Sévère, *Saint Martin*, p. 310, cap. 25.6; cf. Colgrave, *Felix's Life*, p. 162.

18 Gregoire, *Dialogues*, 2, p. 126.

19 Jerome, *Vita S. Pauli, PL*, 23: 26.

20 Colgrave, *Two Lives*, p. 214.

21 Ibid., p. 214.

[22] Bede's verse *Life of Cuthbert, PL*, 94, cols 575–96, at col. 590, ch. 33, line 5.

[23] *Aldhelmi de Virginitate*, ch. XLIV, pp. 621–31, at p. 623.

[24] Sévère, *Saint Martin*, p. 260, cap. 4.2.

[25] Colgrave, *Felix's Life*, p. 79.

[26] Ibid., pp. 60–4.

[27] Ibid., pp. 80–94, 126–150.

[28] Ibid., p. 73; cf. pp. 90, 96.

[29] Ibid., pp. 100–8.

[30] Ibid., pp. 150–60; cf. Colgrave, *Two Lives*, pp. 270–84.

[31] Colgrave, *Two Lives*, p. 274.

[32] See chiefly the *Anonymous Life of Cuthbert* (by a monk of Lindisfarne): see Colgrave, *Two Lives*, pp. 78–86, 100–2; cf. Bede, ibid., pp. 188–90, 220–4; cf. Colgrave, *Felix's Life*, pp. 116–26.

[33] Colgrave, *Felix's Life*, p. 120.

[34] *Guthlac A*, lines 91, 153, 180, 324.

[35] *Guthlac A*, line 407; cf. *Beowulf*, lines 765, 1542.

[36] *Guthlac B*, lines 889, 901.

[37] Crawford, 'Guthlac: an edition', 41–7.

[38] Tyler, 'The collocation of words', 239–48.

[39] Mackie, *Exeter Book*, p. 140 (my translation).

[40] Ibid., p. 232 (my translation).

[41] Bernard of Clairvaux, *Sermones in Cantica, PL*, 183, cols 785–1198.

[42] *S. Anselmi Cantuariensis archiepiscopi Opera Omnia*, ed. F. S. Schmitt, vol. 3 (Edinburgh, 1946), pp. 3–91, at p. 3; St Anselm, *Prayers and Meditations*, trans. Benedicta Ward (Harmondsworth, 1973), p. 89.

[43] *Anselmi Opera Omnia*, vol. 3, p. 4; *Prayers and Meditations*, p. 90. He wrote 'at the request of several brothers'.

[44] Origen, *Commentary on the Song of Songs, PG*, 13, cols 37–216. Origen, *The Song of Songs*, trans. R. P. Lawson, Ancient Christian Writers, 26 (London, 1957).

[45] Ambrose, *Commentarius in Cantica Canticorum, PL*, 15, cols 1851–1961; Gregoire le Grand, *Expositio super Cantica Canticorum, PL*, 79, cols 471–548.

[46] Ibid., 79, col. 502.

[47] Ibid., 79, col. 521.

[48] *Vita Bernardi, PL*, 185, cols 225–643, at 227.

[49] See Bernard, *Liber ad milites Templi de laude novae militiae, PL*, 182, cols 941–73.

[50] See 'A Benedictine of Stanbrook' (trans.), *The Monk of Farne*, with Introduction and Notes by [David] Hugh Farmer (Baltimore, 1961). For the Latin text, see Durham Cathedral Library MS B. IV. 34, ff. 6–75v.; [David] Hugh Farmer (ed.), 'The meditations of the Monk of Farne', in *Studia Anselmiana 41: Analecta Monastica series IV* (Rome, 1957), 141–245.

[51] *Monk of Farne*, Meditation I, chs 20, 25, 60–2, 87.

4

Representations of the Anchoritic Life in Goscelin of Saint-Bertin's *Liber confortatorius*

REBECCA HAYWARD

First-time readers of Goscelin of Saint-Bertin's *Liber confortatorius* can be forgiven for thinking that they have stumbled upon a love letter. The work is addressed by the monk to his former spiritual friend, Eve, who had been a nun at Wilton but departed to become a recluse in Angers without telling Goscelin of her plans.[1] It was written in about 1082. Goscelin relates the story of their friendship in terms that seem startlingly affectionate to modern readers. For him, however, it seems that his emphasis on the love of Christ is sufficient justification that it was *caritas*, not *eros*, that they shared in their friendship.[2] Only once does he admit consciousness that a third party might think that the tensions of heterosexual desire had entered into their spiritual friendship, when he writes in the Prologue: 'Absint a puro susurrio sibilantes insidie, nequam oculus, uafer digitus, uentilator et cachinnator impurus' (May hissing calumny, the wicked eye, the artful finger, the impure gossip-monger and cackler be far from our pure whispering).[3] Although the whole book is structured as a letter to Eve, he is aware that others will read it, too.

The book does function as a kind of love letter to Eve, but not in the conventional sense. After Goscelin has explained, with some vagueness, the circumstances of their friendship and has expressed his distress at her decision to leave without consulting him, he takes it upon himself to counsel her in her new life. The result, however, is markedly different from the guides for female anchorites we see in later periods. Gopa Roy has explored some of the changes in the extant spiritual guides for women between the eleventh and thirteenth centuries, and concludes that the later period was characterized by less flexibility and a firmer establishment of male authority over female religious.[4] Instead of pre-scribing Eve's daily routine and activities, Goscelin concentrates on her intellectual development; he had, after all, been her teacher since she was a child at Wilton. He encourages her to locate herself within Christian temporal and spatial paradigms. Although, like later writers of guides for female anchorites, he does exhort her to curb the instincts of her body and mind to fit within the preordained structures of Christian life, the lack of misogyny in his assumptions about her spiritual potential is a striking feature of his work.

Goscelin uses his description of the personal encounters he and Eve had at Wilton to locate his text within precise terms of time and space. When he discusses her life as a recluse, something he can only imagine, as he remains in England while she is in Angers, he sets her life within the context of human history, pagan and Christian, and the divine plan. The site of her cell becomes a term in a set of contrasts between the cell and the rest of the world, and the rest of the world and the kingdom of heaven. Ultimately, in Goscelin's view, the time she passes in the restricted space of the cell will allow her to enter the limitless abundance, temporal and spatial, of heaven. In this chapter, I will discuss Goscelin's use of the history of the anchoritic life, which he drew from a letter of Jerome's to a young woman, Eustochium. I will then consider how Goscelin suggests that Eve place herself within temporal and spatial perspectives. Finally, I will examine the way in which Goscelin's narrative about an anchorite, near the end of the text, offers an analogue to the Fall, with a significant change in emphasis of the distribution of blame between the sexes.

In his consideration of human history, Goscelin discusses those pagans who have embraced asceticism as a way of life, ranging from classical philosophers to the Brahmins.[5] Then he offers Eve a history of anchoritism, adapted from Jerome's *Letter 22, To Eustochium*.[6] Eustochium, Paula's daughter, was one of the Roman women with whom Jerome corresponded. She remained a virgin and lived in her home as a holy woman. Later, she and her mother followed Jerome and first Paula, then Eustochium, became head of the convent in Bethlehem. Jerome's text offers Goscelin an important model of a male educator and exhorter writing to a young holy woman, but Goscelin's own work has a very different tone from that of Jerome. Jerome writes to Eustochium as a family friend, and playfully recounts the different ways of describing their relationship by the multiple terms he uses to address her: 'filia, domina, conserva, germana' (daughter, lady, fellow servant, sister).[7] Goscelin's connection with Eve is more fraught. He uses the term 'daughter' to describe their past relation, but now describes their respective positions as those of a lady and her servant. He also exhorts her to be a masculine warrior for the Lord, and to accept himself as her passive and feminized encourager.

Jerome offers Eustochium information about coenobitic monks and anchorites in Egypt, with a primarily educative purpose, although he does also wish to exhort and inspire her in her own spiritual vocation.[8] He defines anchorites as those who go alone into the desert, and take only bread and salt. In a brief historical note, he says that Paul was the founder of this way of life, and that Antony made it famous. Jerome himself wrote the *Life of Paul the First Hermit*, in which Antony, who believes himself to be the first hermit, is sent to look for Paul.[9] When he meets him, he acknowledges Paul's superior sanctity. The *Life of St Antony* had been written earlier by Athanasius, as Santha Bhattacharji outlined in the previous chapter.[10] Jerome also points out in this section of *Letter 22* that, if earlier times are considered, John the Baptist was the first to go out into the desert and adopt this lifestyle, and he refers to a description by Jeremiah of the benefits experienced by the man who has been solitary from his youth.[11] In this way, recent history is supplemented with references from both the Hebrew Scriptures and the New Testament to support this way of life. He offers to give Eustochium more information about this way of life, if she would like it.

Goscelin's account of the history of anchoritism draws on Jerome's in a way that, as well as informing Eve, specifically encourages her to locate herself within anchoritic traditions: 'Erat lucerna ardens et lucens[12] Iohannes precursor Domini, clamans in deserto ut uox precedens uerbum Dei: "Dirigite uiam Domini."[13] In eius familia tu cepisti censeri anachorita' (John, the precursor of the Lord, was a burning and shining light, calling in the wilderness as a voice preceding the Word of God: 'Make straight the way of the Lord.' In his household you have begun to be enrolled as an anchorite).[14] The hymn that Goscelin inserts at this point describes John's privations and the great honour that he received thereby. Goscelin normally uses the metaphor of the household to describe monastic life, such as his relationship to the community of Saint Bertin or Eve's relationship to that of Wilton. This account offers Eve, then, a new imagined community, based upon the ideals of anchoritism.

Goscelin gives a description of Paul's life, drawn from the *Life of Paul the First Hermit*:

Post hunc Paulus heremita, diuina attollens uexilla, unicus homo in mundo ultra sexaginta annos solitudinem pertulit, ab omni genere sequestratus humano. Hunc palma uestiuit et aluit, fons concauis uolis potauit. Camelinam togam probitas non fugit, sed regni celestis heres paupertas non habuit.

(After him [John the Baptist] Paul the Hermit, raising high the divine banners, a man alone in the world, endured solitude for more than sixty years, sequestered from the whole human race. The palm clothed and fed him; the spring gave drink to his cupped hands. Goodness does not fly from camel's hair clothing, but the poverty that was heir to the kingdom of heaven did not have any.)[15]

As is fitting for the first hermit of the Christian era, Goscelin stresses the extremity of Paul's deprivations, with the implication that Eve's trials are not so severe.

Goscelin adds to Jerome's account of anchoritic history in *Letter 22* the story of Mary of Egypt, which dates from the sixth century and which, Jane Stevenson argues, was based in part on Jerome's *Life of Paul the First Hermit*.[16] Goscelin is clearly eager to offer Eve a female anchoritic role-model.[17] Even more than in the account of Paul's trials, Goscelin stresses the physical suffering that Mary endured:

Omnia flagrantis solis spicula, omnia brume pila, omnis aeris intemperies, longarum dierum ardores, profundarum noctium tempestates, nudo corpore nudo tulit uertice . . . Caput serpentis contriuit, bene nuda cum nudo luctata, et de Eve uictore palmata.

(She bore all the shafts of the burning sun, all the weapons of winter, all the excesses of weather, the burning of long days, the storms of dark nights with a naked body and a bare head . . . She crushed the head of the serpent, appropriately naked in her struggle with his nakedness, and winning a robe of triumph from the victor over Eve.)[18]

What Goscelin does not report here from the original is the extent to which this Mary had succumbed to the 'victor over Eve' before her triumph; her sexual sins are graphically described in her *Life*.[19] Goscelin stresses her exemplary repentance through physical endurance, not her sin, and with the reference to her crushing the head of the serpent associates her with her namesake, the Virgin Mary, rather than with Eve's own namesake.[20]

Goscelin's focus, then, is on the extreme abstinence of Paul and Mary, and Mary's penitence. He does not relate the elements in both stories that savour of the fabulous and miraculous. Although Jerome makes a strong truth-claim for the story of Paul the Hermit, he includes marvellous motifs, such as Antony's encounters with a centaur, a satyr and a she-wolf on his way to Paul, the miraculous loaf of bread brought by a raven to feed both holy men, Paul having received a half-loaf every day throughout his time in the wilderness,[21] and the appearance of two lions to dig Paul's grave for Antony after Paul's death. The story of Mary of Egypt has fewer marvels, but includes bread that lasts for years in the wilderness, a miraculously fast journey undertaken by Mary just before her death and a lion to dig her grave, one of the elements that leads Jane Stevenson to see it as drawing from Jerome's narrative. These wonders are typical of the 'hairy anchorite' tradition, stories about a recluse who has spent an extremely long time in the wilderness, to which these stories are linked.[22] The message that Goscelin wants to emphasize to Eve, however, is that she can follow their example and see her own life as an anchorite in the context of their endeavours. The narratives themselves contain hints of a tradition of anchoritism. In the Prologue to the *Life of Paul*, Jerome says that when people consider who the first monk to live in the desert was, some say Elijah and John, but because of their significance they can be separated from more recent anchorites, such as Paul and Antony.[23] Later in the text, Antony claims that in meeting Paul he has seen Elijah and John in the desert.[24] Mary of Egypt visits the church of John the Baptist and takes Mass before she begins her time in the desert.[25]

Having given this historical background in book 3, Goscelin confronts the physical circumstances of Eve's life and draws his spiritual exhortations from them. Firstly he discusses the associations of her cell. Her 'little cell of eight feet' is compared to Noah's ark, which saved eight souls, and to a house of refuge.[26] Goscelin repeatedly contrasts the safety of her ascetic way of life with the dangers of his own, tossed as he is by the tempests of the world. He claims in book 1, as part of his complaint about her departure, to long for just such another little cell, although his would need to be attached to a large church, where he could fast, read, pray and produce writings for the glory of God.[27] The only works he expects Eve to produce are letters to him.

To counter the possibility that external stimulus to sin may still be a problem even in the cell, in book 3 he instructs her: 'Absint detrahentium conciliabula, sepi aurem tuam spinis in custodia timorata. Celle, lingue et aurium fenestre a fabulis et uaniloquiis, immo maliloquiis, sint obserate' (Let there be no gatherings of detractors; hedge your ear with thorns and guard it devoutly. May the windows of your cell, tongue and ear be closed against stories and idle talk, or rather malign talk).[28] Jerome exhorts Eustochium to remain in her room, saying that the door of her heart should be open to Christ and closed to the Devil. Her 'windows' should be open so that she, like Daniel, may see the city of God, but closed to the possibility of the entry of death (through sin). He also tells her not to talk to roving clerics or worldly women.[29] Goscelin heightens the metaphor by making a strong association between Eve's cell and her body.

Goscelin admits in book 3, however, that Eve's cell may seem small and that this may cause her to feel confined. As a remedy to this, he evokes the extensiveness of the world and then explains that although her cell now seems small when compared to the world, that same world will seem even smaller when the full size of heaven is known.[30] Not only does he describe the world's natural features, but he also gives her a picture of the basic structure of the world, a sphere divided into five zones, with one cold zone at either end, and two temperate ones, divided by a fiery zone that prevents anyone from travelling between the two.[31] This global perspective gives his claims for the size of heaven the largest possible comparison.

Goscelin employs a similar device when he discusses time, acknowledging that as a young woman she may be frightened by the prospect of a long life in the cell. He tells her to treat every day as if it were her last, and not to think ahead.[32] To this end he recommends that she fill her time with prayer and reading, including meditations on the passion of Christ. In a paper at the Kalamazoo conference in 2002, Monika Otter argued that Goscelin's own allusive and digressive style is designed to give Eve a model for the meditative process. She described Goscelin's image of the richly decorated tabernacle as a metaphor for the space of the cell.[33] Earlier in book 2 he discusses the amount of time that has elapsed since the beginning of the world, 6,000 years, to put into perspective the length of eternity for both the blessed and the damned.[34] Both this digression on the length of time and the sense of a historical tradition of anchorites put the use of Eve's own time in context.[35]

Thus, the safe, patrolled space of the cell and the time that Eve spends there, if used correctly, will ensure her salvation. In addition to the description of the tabernacle, Goscelin attempts to create a sense of spaciousness within the cell in book 3 by listing all the domestic offices

that can be considered to be contained in it.[36] He argues that, although
her domain is small, she derives more security and freedom from it than
Octavian Augustus had from his whole empire. In his dramatic climax
to book 4, when he reveals lavish imagery about the end of time and the
joys of heaven, he says that Eve may see her cell from heaven as a royal
palace. He does not pursue this image, preferring to concentrate on his
comparison of Wilton to the new Jerusalem.[37] Yet this inclusion of the
cell as a potential locus of transformation is the logical development of
this chain of spatial imagery in the text.

But there is one final fear that Goscelin has: that Eve may pass her
life in her cell and yet lose her chance of salvation, because she becomes
proud of her holiness. Having made anchoritism such an important
theme in the work, in book 4, which deals with pride, he uses stories
about anchorites to call this fact urgently to her mind. Firstly, he
returns to the narratives of Paul the Hermit and Mary of Egypt that he
used as part of his roll-call of the founders of the anchoritic life, but this
time he focuses on the perspective of the witnesses and the spiritual
lessons that both needed to learn:

> Beatus Antonius, cum inter excellentissima meritorum preconia et miracu-
> lorum insignia, unicum se uel primum heremitam in mundo estimaret,
> diuina uoce iussus est Paulum querere, quem et priorem et meliorem in-
> ueniret se. Zozimas ab infantia in centenarium Christi militia emeritus, cog-
> itans tandem nullum uixisse sanctius, omnem uite canonem nullum implesse
> perfectius, hoc responsum accepit celitus: 'O Zozima, bene quidem ut
> homo decertasti; sed nunquam maius quam modo certamen incidisti, quo
> oporteat glorianti conscientie ut intimo aduersario reluctari.' Sic superna
> iussione egressus de sua cognatione, inuenit peccatricem, cui se cum mundo
> non auderet comparare.

> (When St Antony, among most excellent matter for praise in his merits and
> signs of miracles, judged himself to be the best or the first hermit in the
> world, he was ordered by a divine voice to seek Paul, whom he would find
> to be his predecessor and better than himself. Zozimas, a veteran in the
> war-service of Christ from infancy to his hundredth year, finally thinking
> that no one had lived more holily, no one had filled every rule of life more
> perfectly, received this response from heaven: 'O Zozimas, indeed you have
> fought well, for a man; but never have you met with a greater contest than
> lately, in which you must struggle with a boastful conscience as with an
> inner enemy.' So by the heavenly command he left his monastic family, and
> he found the sinful woman, to whom he did not dare to compare himself as
> well as the world.)[38]

Eve, then, is invited to associate herself with men whose holiness was so beyond question that their chief danger was in spiritual pride.

In addition to extensive reference to well-attested textual traditions about anchorites, Goscelin includes further stories about anchorites, the origins of which have not been identified.[39] The story of 'Saint Alexander' is a previously unnoticed example of the 'hairy anchorite' tradition. Alexander, an anchorite in a deserted location, is tricked by the Devil in the guise of a monk into accepting a baby foster-daughter. When the girl grows up, he has sex with her and makes her pregnant, and then, at the suggestion of the Devil, kills her to avoid scandal. He fends off the triumphant Devil by calling upon Christ, and stands for fifteen years with his hands in a tree as penance. Eventually, the girl's father, a king, comes to the place and is shown his daughter's grave. Her body is found to be uncorrupted, and when a rod is placed in her fingers she makes a gesture of forgiveness towards Alexander. The king establishes a monastery in the place and thus all three are saved, because the Devil's plan was foiled.

Goscelin's concern is that Eve, like Alexander, should avoid the spiritual danger of pride and rely upon God's mercy. Yet it is surely no coincidence that the story, with its wilderness location, the Devil's presence and the supernatural delivery of the girl, is so resonant of the Fall. It seems likely that, while at the level of narrative the story is designed to fit with the spiritual lessons learned by Antony and Zozimas in their encounters with Paul and Mary, its explosive subject-matter, in a text so loaded with reference to the strained friendship between a male and a female religious, introduces a strong theme of male guilt. This seems to deflect the facile misogyny that blamed women for the entry of sin into the world because of the fault of Eve.[40] Because of the circumstances of the story, the young woman is wholly innocent, and the invocation of Christ allows all to end in heaven. That Goscelin does this in a text for a woman called Eve must surely be a calculated move.

Goscelin's gift to Eve, then, is not only an attempt to encourage her to place herself within the traditions and structures of anchoritism, since that is the life she has chosen. He also draws out the elements of the traditions that could be read in non-misogynistic ways, and offers an analogue of the Fall which, far from blaming the woman, reconfigures her as an innocent victim of male lust and an instrument of forgiveness and salvation. His wider agenda is to ensure that he and Eve will be enabled to continue their friendship in heaven, and he argues that Eve's salvation will be beneficial to him as well, as she will be able to pray for him. However, we have no idea what Eve's response was to this careful incorporation of themes and stories of anchoritism into his book of exhortation, which is also to such a large degree an appeal for the continuation of their friendship.

Notes

[1] C. H. Talbot (ed.), 'The *Liber confortatorius* of Goscelin of Saint Bertin', *Analecta monastica*, series 3, *Studia Anselmiana*, fasc. 37 (Rome, 1955), pp. 1–117. Quotations are from this edition, checked against British Library MS Sloane 3103, and referred to hereafter as *Liber*. Translations are from the version by W. R. Barnes and myself in Stephanie Hollis (ed.), *Writing the Wilton Women: Goscelin's Legend of Edith and Liber confortatorius*, Medieval Women: Texts and Contexts, 9 (Turnhout, 2004). Page numbers from this edition will appear in parentheses. Thanks to Stephanie Hollis, W. R. Barnes, Michael Wright and the editors of this volume and participants at the conference 'Anchorites, Wombs and Tombs: Intersections of Gender and Enclosure in the Middle Ages', University of Wales Conference Centre, Gregynog, 5–7 July 2002, for comments on this material. For discussion of the *Liber confortatorius*, see A. Wilmart, 'Ève et Goscelin (I)', *Revue Bénédictine*, 46 (1934), 414–38; 'Ève et Goscelin (II)', *Revue Bénédictine*, 50 (1938), 42–83; Gopa Roy, ' "Sharpen your mind with the whetstone of books": the female recluse as reader in Goscelin's *Liber confortatorius*, Aelred of Rievaulx's *de Institutione Inclusarum* and the *Ancrene Wisse*', in Lesley Smith and Jane H. M. Taylor (eds), *Women, the Book and the Godly* (Cambridge, 1995), pp. 113–22; Irene van Rossum, '*Adest meliori parte*: A portrait of monastic friendship in exile in Goscelin's *Liber confortatorius*' (unpublished D.Phil. dissertation, University of York, November 1999); see also the forthcoming studies by W. R. Barnes, Stephanie Hollis and myself in *Writing the Wilton Women*.

[2] Goscelin also uses the word *dilectio* to describe it. This word is appropriate for warm personal affection without sexual overtones.

[3] *Liber*, p. 26 (99).

[4] Roy, 'The female recluse as reader', p. 122.

[5] *Liber*, pp. 73–4.

[6] *PL*, 22, cols 394–425. Translation in *The Letters of St Jerome*, trans. Charles Christopher Mierow (London, 1963), 1, pp. 134–79.

[7] *Letter 22*, 26, col. 411; Mierow, *Letters of St Jerome*, p. 159.

[8] *Letter 22*, 36, col. 421.

[9] *PL*, 23, cols 17–30. Translation as 'The life of Paul of Thebes' in *Early Christian Lives*, trans. Carolinne White (London, 1998), pp. 75–84.

[10] *PL* 73, cols 125–94. Translation in White, *Early Christian Lives*, pp. 7–70. Goscelin recommends that Eve read this work (p. 80).

[11] Lamentations 3: 27–8.

[12] John 5: 35.

[13] John 1: 23.

[14] *Liber*, p. 75 (157–8).

[15] Ibid. (158).

[16] 'The holy sinner: the life of Mary of Egypt', in *The Legend of Mary of Egypt in Medieval Insular Hagiography*, ed. Erich Poppe and Bianca Ross (Blackrock, Co. Dublin, 1996), pp. 19–50 (pp. 29–30). Stevenson cites F. Delmas as having first made this observation. The Latin text and translation of Paul of Naples's ninth-century version of Mary's life can be found in Hugh Magennis, *The Old English Life of Saint Mary of Egypt* (Exeter, 2002), pp. 140–209. Magennis characterizes Jane Stevenson's Latin edition and translation in Poppe and Ross as 'not reliable' (p. 3).

[17] The author of *Ancrene Wisse*, in his section on the history of the anchoritic life, mentions the figures discussed here, but not Mary of Egypt. Instead, he uses Syncletica and Sarah as examples of anchoritic women. See *The English Text of the Ancrene Riwle: Ancrene Wisse: Edited from MS. Corpus Christi College Cambridge 402*, by J. R. R. Tolkien, EETS o.s. 249 (London, New York and Toronto, 1962), pp. 81–5, esp. p. 84. See also p. 10.

[18] *Liber*, pp. 75–6 (158).

[19] Benedicta Ward considers Mary's life from a theological perspective, together with several other stories of sinful women who are converted, in her book *Harlots of the Desert: A Study of Repentance in Early Monastic Sources* (Kalamazoo, 1987).

[20] In Genesis 3: 15, God tells the serpent that the woman will crush its head. This was widely taken in the Middle Ages as a reference to the power of the Virgin Mary. Goscelin also refers in the *Liber confortatorius* to the dream of Perpetua in which she treads on a dragon (p. 50).

[21] White, *Early Christian Lives*, notes that Elijah was fed by ravens: 3 Kings 17: 4–6 (p. 212, n. 14).

[22] For scholarship on the 'hairy anchorite' tradition, see Charles Allyn Williams, 'Oriental affinities of the legend of the Hairy Anchorite', Part I, *University of Illinois Studies in Language and Literature*, 10 (1925), 1–56; Part II, *University of Illinois Studies in Language and Literature*, 11 (1926), 57–139. Williams treats all three figures in Part II: see 87–93 for Antony, 93–100 for Paul and 107–10 for Mary of Egypt.

[23] *Life of Paul*, 1, col. 17.

[24] Ibid., 13, col. 27.

[25] Magennis, *Life of Mary of Egypt*, pp. 182–5.

[26] *Liber*, pp. 72 and 78.

[27] Ibid., p. 34.

[28] Ibid., p. 80 (163).

[29] *Letter 22*, 26, cols 28–9, 411–16; cf. Daniel 6: 10 and Jeremiah 9: 21. The similarity of Jerome's advice to Goscelin's is noted by Talbot, the editor of the text (p. 80, n. 74), and Roy, 'The female recluse as reader', pp. 114–15.

[30] Cf. *Life of Antony*, 15, col. 135, in which Antony tells the monks that the world is small compared to the infinite size of the heavens. Cf. also Cicero's *Dream of Scipio (De Republica VI)*, in Cicero, *On Friendship and the Dream of Scipio*, ed. and trans. J. G. F. Powell (Warminster, 1990), pp. 142–5. Thanks to W. R. Barnes for this suggestion.

[31] *Liber*, pp. 85–6.

[32] Ibid., p. 70.

[33] Monika Otter, 'Paint your tent from within: *acedia* and the pictorial imagination in Goscelin's *Liber confortatorius*', 37th International Congress on Medieval Studies, Western Michigan University, Kalamazoo, MI, 2–5 May 2002.

[34] *Liber*, p. 48.

[35] Cf. *Life of Antony*, 15, col. 135, where Antony comments on the brevity of the span of human existence in comparison with eternity.

[36] *Liber*, p. 78.

[37] Ibid., pp. 114–15.

[38] Ibid., pp. 105–6 (193).

[39] Goscelin claims oral testimony for Alexander's story (pp. 104–5) and also the story in book 2 of Brihtric, an illiterate recluse. He is firstly almost tricked by the Devil into abandoning his one constant prayer. He then becomes an example of adherence to the place of enclosure when he refuses to leave his cell, despite that fact that it is part of a castle that is being attacked and set on fire at the time (pp. 67–8).

[40] For example, Jerome says in *Letter 22*, 21, col. 408, 'Mors per Evam: vita per Mariam' (Death came through Eve, life through Mary). See Mierow, *Letters of St Jerome*, p. 154.

5

Male and Female Cistercians and their Gendered Experiences of the Margins, the Wilderness and the Periphery

ELIZABETH FREEMAN

The textbook view of the medieval Cistercians is that they were a monastic order with a particular fondness for the margins. Browsing through introductory surveys one will read that Cistercian abbeys were hidden away in valleys and isolated places, and one will probably also read Walter Map's provocative comments that the Cistercians actually created these isolated places in the first instance, via a concerted practice of depopulation.[1] Prompted by a variety of surviving sources and scholarly priorities, research on Cistercian isolation has taken many forms.[2] Theological studies have produced insights into the emotional, conceptual and spiritual meanings of withdrawal while, on the other hand, economic and geographic investigations have suggested that the Cistercians were fully integrated into local economies and social networks and were in fact never as isolated as they claimed to be. Regardless of their varied conclusions on the matter, all these studies are linked by their dedication to investigating medieval Cistercian history in terms of both the theory and practice of physical isolation.

However, despite such a strong focus on spatial debates, Cistercian scholars have yet to tackle the ways in which retreat, isolation and the so-called quest for the desert were (or were not) gendered activities. Here the weight of past scholarship seems to have worked against new interpretations. The 'grand narrative' of medieval Cistercian history has always been written as a purely male enterprise. Even today, the two authoritative Cistercian histories for English-language researchers feature nuns only in separate chapters at the conclusions of the relevant books.[3] This reflects and perpetuates an approach in which Cistercian nuns are marginalized in the scholarship today, just as they were marginalized in the past. Among commentators on Cistercian history, developments in Cistercian monks' histories have been taken as the norm, with nuns' histories either interpreted as unfortunate falls from otherwise glorious ideals or, just as often, simply ignored because they do not fit into the accepted teleological framework of Cistercian development.

In this chapter I argue that the medieval Cistercians provide an excellent case-study for identifying how marginalization can be a gendered process and, especially, for how it can bring advantages to some groups and limitations to others. Due to the multiplicity and ambiguity of Cistercian attitudes to the periphery, dominant groups such as Cistercian monks were able to exploit the politics of marginalization, ironically, as a means of maintaining their institutional centrality. Less institutionally secure groups such as nuns were forced into a particularly disadvantageous kind of marginalization. Critically, however, the fact that the male centre 'needed' the female margin (that is, the male institutional hierarchy can be dominant only if it defines itself in reference to another group which it creates as subordinate) provided a window of opportunity for nuns who wished to assert Cistercian affiliation, and hence take small steps from the margins to the centre of the monastic order. In marginalizing a certain sub-group, then, the institutional hierarchy also furnishes that sub-group with the desire and, indeed, means of resisting such marginalization, hence resulting in a complex interdependence between the centre and margin. Monastic case-studies from thirteenth-century England demonstrate this codependent relationship particularly well.

The male houses in question are the abbeys of Fountains and Kirkstall in Yorkshire. The sources are the foundation histories produced in the abbeys themselves in approximately 1210–20.[4] These are narrative histories which describe the initial hardships the monks experienced when establishing the houses in the 1130s and 1140s, and which then proceed to describe the great spiritual, territorial and liturgical successes that the houses currently enjoy at the time of writing in the early 1200s.

The Fountains history opens with a standard introduction in which it promises to describe its foundation: 'quo auctore vel ordine [illa mater] nostra sancta, scilicet Fontanensis ecclesia . . . suae fundationis sumpserit originem' (by whose authority and in what way our holy mother, the church of Fountains . . . was first founded).[5] In addition, the Narratio will describe the growth of the Order: '[qualiter illa vin]ea

Domini benedicta in loco horroris et [vastae] solitudinis sic creverit, sic se dilataverit, extendens palmites suos usque ad mare et propagines [suas ad ex]teras nationes' (in what way that vine, blessed by God, grew in a place of horror and vast solitude, and spread itself abroad, stretching out its branches as far as the sea, and its shoots to the outer nations).[6] And indeed the history does go on to describe this monastic expansion, informing the readers of the early history of Fountains and also referring to the daughter houses that Fountains in turn established. The key section is the reference to the 'place of horror and vast solitude'. According to the foundation history, this place is where Fountains was initially implanted. Another location is the desert (*eremus* and similar terms) – a physical term of marginalization that appears in both the Fountains and Kirkstall histories. According to the Fountains text, one of the reasons the monks founded the abbey in the first place was to satisfy their urge for the desert.[7] At Kirkstall, there is a similar description of place and, importantly, this description of place also occurs at the start of the story. The history betrays a persistent need to equate physical and territorial experience with spiritual and institutional experience. From the outset, whatever happens to the land foreshadows what happens to the community overall. As described in the Kirkstall *Fundacio*, the monks first arrive in a region which is 'locum nemorosum et frugibus infecundum, locum bonis fere destitutum' (a wooded place, useless for crops, a place almost destitute of good things).[8] The monks must pick up their axes, cut down the woods and turn up the fallow ground. Finally, they make the place habitable, bring the thickets under control and cultivate the soil so that it flourishes with crops. And, then, in a direct cause-and-effect relationship between land and institutional success, the house also flourishes, not with crops but this time with monastic recruits.

In all their brevity, these anecdotes distil the very essence of the two male communities' relationships with the Cistercian centre. At the literal level the foundation histories refer to the houses as physically and geographically marginal. But there is more here than the literal. To begin, we know that the Cistercians did not really settle wild and solitary places at all. The Kirkstall history actually concedes that the monks had established themselves on the site of a local parish and had, in fact, openly expelled the parishioners.[9] The monks were by no means in the actual physical margins, yet clearly the solitude and desert were worth claiming. This was not a literal or physical claim but instead an allegorical claim.

The power of this allegorical argument makes sense once we appreciate the Cistercians' devotion to the Deuteronomy reference concerning the place of horror and vast solitude, 'in loco horroris et vastae solitudinis'.[10] By the 1200s Cistercian monks had united themselves into a cohesive textual community, in part thanks to the shared meanings that were conjured up by such popular texts as this Deuteronomy verse. By invoking this Old Testament verse Cistercian authors offered their Cistercian audiences a shorthand or metonymic means of pinpointing a core quality of Cistercian identity. Monks in the Cistercian house at Fountains in England, or the Cistercian house at Clairvaux in France, or the Cistercian house at Eberbach in Germany – monks in all these sites, and more, produced texts which employed this image from Deuteronomy.[11] Significantly, the most influential Cistercian use of the phrase was in reference to the original house at Cîteaux, where it appeared in one of the Order's official constitutional documents, the *Exordium Cistercii* from the 1130s.[12] Thus, when other houses invoked the 'in loco horroris' reference they were using a communal shorthand to assert that their own house was equivalent in orthodoxy to the Order's key house, Cîteaux, in the Burgundian heartland.

The same applied with the desert, another image bursting with communal meaning for Cistercians. Two things are significant here. First, the shared meanings come wrapped in the form of spatial language – vast solitude, desert. Second, the meaning towards which these spatial terms point is always a meaning of orthodoxy and authorization. Fountains describes itself using the spatial language of 'in loco horroris' that Cîteaux and Clairvaux had used, therefore it claims its place as an English equivalent of these great houses. Meanwhile, Kirkstall describes itself using the same language that Cîteaux had used, adopting the spatial imagery of the desert to insert itself, textually, into authoritative Cistercian history. This ensures that Kirkstall is far from the margins but, instead, is equated through language and motif with the very centre of the Cistercian Order. Thus, in these foundation histories the margin always signifies culture. This is its strength. The allegorical meanings and communal history of the desert and solitude meant that when the Fountains and Kirkstall foundation histories invoked these ostensibly marginalizing terms they were, in fact, invoking a known Cistercian tradition of the precise opposite, namely, institutional orthodoxy.

This is quite different from the ways in which Cistercian women related to the margins. The women's examples come from the diocese of Lincoln, approximately two generations later, in around 1270. The documents here are not foundation histories but, instead, deeds and cartularies (both featuring incorporated letters) from the women's houses themselves. The *raison d'être* of these documents is to state that the female communities are 'of the Cistercian Order'. The immediate prompt behind the documents was financial. The local sheriff was collecting tithes for Henry III, following the pope's granting of this additional tithe to the king in 1266. This led in the late 1260s to a handful of houses of religious women making a joint claim that they were Cistercian, the relevant point being that Cistercians were traditionally exempt from certain tithes.[13] Over time, the parties to the claim changed, with the full number including the nuns of Stixwould, Greenfield, Gokewell, Legbourne, Nun Cotham, St Michael's outside Stamford, Fosse and Heynings.

The surviving sources allow us to trace the different spheres in which the debate over Cistercian affiliation was enacted. Monastic, royal, papal and episcopal parties all played a role, and all convey their respective views on the question of whether or not female houses should be counted in a given monastic order. Sometimes the female houses banded together to make a joint claim for their Cistercian status, and sometimes one of the houses made the claim on its own (Stamford). There are thus two families of documents – Stamford's correspondence with the bishops, archbishops and king, and the other houses and their correspondence with these same authorities. Sometimes the houses appealed to the bishop of Lincoln, but then they anticipated alternative possibilities by also appealing to the archbishop of York. Somehow the communities managed to gain Henry III's support and he agreed to their Cistercian affiliation, as did his successor, Edward I. But the nuns did not succeed in convincing the abbot of Cîteaux that they were Cistercian, and in fact the reason the letters were continually written over several years is that the sheriffs collecting the taxes also did not accept that these houses were members of the Cistercian Order, and thereby exempt from tithes. Clearly, then, these letters provide evidence that in medieval England different parties defined institutional religious membership in different ways.

These events happened in the late 1260s and early 1270s, but for the women's houses the issue carried meaning long beyond this time. The events were important enough for one of the participant houses (Nun Cotham) to record the letters in its cartulary, not long after the event.[14] In the late thirteenth century, another house (St Michael's, Stamford) somehow collected six letters stating its Cistercian affiliation (where these letters were previously kept is unknown), then had these letters copied into one document and endorsed, via an *inspeximus* from the bishop of Lincoln's official.[15] Sometime in the fifteenth century the community had the same *inspeximus* document endorsed again. Evidently, two centuries later the nuns considered this proof of their Cistercian status to be somehow useful or necessary. The dossier therefore had a double life, being consulted by the Stamford nuns in both the thirteenth and fifteenth centuries. On both occasions the texts provided evidence of membership, of a transposition away from the margins into the centre, away from ill-defined status into membership of the institution that was the official Cistercian Order.

This evidence took a specific linguistic form. The documents that the female communities chose to have created and then kept all have a particular form, quite different from that of the men's documents. We read Henry III telling the sheriff of Lincoln not to collect the tithes, since houses of the Cistercian Order are exempt and the houses in question are indeed 'of the Cistercian Order'.[16] The bishop of Lincoln agrees: '[M]oniales . . . ordinem Cisterciensem profitentur et observancias tenent ipsius' (These nuns profess themselves to be of the Cistercian Order and they maintain the observances of that same order).[17] This same bishop also writes another letter, this time referring to one of the houses only, Stamford, and likewise he accepts that the prioress and convent 'de ordine sunt Cisterciensis' (are of the Cistercian Order).[18] Finally, the Stamford community included a further letter in the *inspeximus* document, this one from the Cistercian abbot at Kirkstall, who agreed that the nuns had indeed been 'secundum ordinem Cistercii erudite' (instructed according to the Cistercian Order).[19]

Other documents indicate that in the fifteenth and sixteenth centuries Stamford once again took energetic steps to have its affiliation recognized as Cistercian.[20] The point at issues seems to have been the specific terminology; in each instance, documents were produced which specifically stated that the house was 'of the Cistercian Order'. Nowhere here is there any reference to spatial phrases or to the desert and Deuteronomy references that are so prevalent in the textual productions from male houses. Of course, one might object that this metaphoric language of deserts and solitude was not appropriate for a letter or cartulary, that it was simply far more customary for the Cistercians to include these biblical passages in their foundation histories rather than in their cartularies. But this simply leads to the next question of why it was that genre and archives were gendered. Why did male Cistercians write and keep foundation histories, whereas female communities favoured letters and cartularies and spent their textual energy commissioning documents, asking other people to endorse these documents, and preserving documents that so plaintively tried to 'prove' their Cistercian memership?

To appreciate the differences in male and female document production we need to examine the peculiarities of female Cistercian history in England. The history of Cistercian nuns in England was, without doubt, different from the history of Cistercian nuns on the continent, although perhaps less different than scholars have previously believed. Traditional arguments have it that there were only two 'official' Cistercian nunneries in England, whereas on the continent there were hundreds.[21] Instead of official houses, the English scene was allegedly characterized by around twenty-five so-called 'Cistercian' convents. The modern definition of these unofficial female communities is that they were houses which claimed a Cistercian identity, yet for which the Cistercian statutes provide no evidence of formal incorporation. In this chapter I have deliberately focused on these unofficial communities – houses like Stamford, Stixwould, Nun Cotham and so on. According to the premise of the modern definition, these houses most certainly were 'unofficial'. After all, the abbot of the Cistercian headquarters at Cîteaux actually wrote a letter denying these houses' affiliation.[22] Following this, it has not been difficult for modern scholars to find what they have been looking for. The axiomatic belief in a highly bureaucratic, documentary and centralized Cistercian Order has in fact preceded all analysis, and has left researchers no option but to say that these female houses could never have been Cistercian.

Fortunately, some scholars have begun pointing out that explicit mentions in legislative sources should not be the sole criterion of monastic affiliation or non-affiliation.[23] Indeed, many male houses would fail on this count, such is the partiality of the surviving legislative record. But this just prompts the next question – why did female communities go to the trouble of asserting Cistercian membership, why go to such trouble repeatedly, whereas male houses do not seem to have needed to take these steps? Here I return to the model of the margins and the centre. It is clear that, despite the statements of the self-proclaimed hierarchy, institutional life does take place on the margins, just as much as it occurs at the centre. In the case of the Cistercians, we can learn so much about what it meant to be a member of this organization precisely from activities that took place 'beyond the pale'. From the nuns' position on the margins, there must have been some benefits in being members of the Order (financial advantages and, possibly, exemption from episcopal visitation being two attractions, not to mention access to the wealth of shared corporate memory that membership of a consolidated textual community could bring). But, more than this, the female communities were producing these documents *for* someone. They were initiating and preserving documents which would constitute sufficient evidence according to the criteria of someone else. So here we necessarily must look at the defining centre. An institutional centre, somewhere, wanted and needed this linguistic, definitional evidence and it demanded that very specific terminology be employed (the nuns must be defined, precisely, as 'of the order'). Here we cannot deny that names and definitions are important. They are the means by which a group is no longer confined to the periphery but is instead immersed within the Cistercian Order and free to partake of the rewards of that order.

We can see now why the women's houses do not use the language of wilderness and desert, why they do not use these particular expressions to present their self-identity. The language of Deuteronomy and horror and solitude was certainly liberating, but it was liberating only for Cistercian men. In principle the desert and vast solitude was a universal positive of Christianity, available to both male and female. But in the Cistercian context, in England, in practice, the desert's benefits were gendered and these benefits were not a realistic goal for women to aspire to. Before the women's communities could use a play on words to argue for their metaphorical distance from culture they needed to insert themselves within this culture at a practical level. This takes us to the premise behind renunciation. One can renounce only when one possesses in the first place. The male monks could use language and metaphor to renounce the centre and claim their metaphorical place on the margins precisely because, in more structural and systematic terms, they did possess and define that culture. But for the female houses there was no point claiming to live on the margins, and this is because in practical terms they actually were on the margins. At the most basic level, they could not even count on being recognized as members of the organization. This is why they had to focus on the literal meanings of words. This is why the main phrases in their documents were simply the most basic (we are 'of the order'), while the monks could employ metaphorical imagery of vines and deserts and valleys.

There are implications here for how we understand Cistercian nuns more broadly. Scholarship on medieval Cistercian women has always been framed in terms of the continental context.[24] For instance, many commentators see the urban context of the Low Countries and the rise of the beguines as essential backgrounds to the history of Cistercian nuns. But while this approach has its advantages, it will never permit us to include the English nuns within this grand Cistercian narrative. Surely, in England the relevant contextual background is not so much that of the beguines but, rather, a wider regular and non-regular world which spans Benedictines, Gilbertines, Fontevraudines, hermits and anchorites, to name a few. Following the evidence I have presented here with Stamford and the other houses, it is clear that in England there was ambiguity as to the precise institutional status of female communities within this span from Benedictine to Cistercian and beyond. But it is also clear that distinctions could be made and were made. Some medieval people did think it was possible to be an English Cistercian nun, and hence modern scholars have an opportunity here to expand our previously limited notion of what constituted the Cistercian Order. By stressing that English female Cistercian life was actually at its most vibrant when it was unofficial and, indeed, marginalized, I hereby endorse the newly developing school of Cistercian scholarship which sees the Cistercians as far messier and more localized (more 'bottom up', rather than 'top down') than the traditional historiography has suggested.

Following on from the preceding points, it is logical to wonder why it was that the male houses did not need to confirm their institutional status, as had the nuns in the 1270s. The answer to this is that in fact the monks did take steps to establish their institutional identity; however, this movement took place much earlier, in around 1120–50. It was during these decades that Bernard of Clairvaux and others wrote regularly about the Cistercian *ordo*, describing and occasionally defining what they thought it was that characterized this emergent monastic custom. Not surprisingly, in a new monastic experiment, initial views and definitions of the *ordo* varied.[25] However, by the late twelfth century, certainly, there was an institutional and administrative organization which was called 'the Cistercian Order' and of which it was possible to detect whether or not a male house was a member. Following this, I would argue that the male foundation histories of *c.*1200 were able to indulge in the luxury of metaphoric marginalization precisely because the hard work of thrashing out the meaning of this Cistercian *ordo* and the criteria for membership had already taken place. But the female houses (particularly in England) did not enjoy this clear position of incorporation. The English nuns therefore needed to reopen debate over what the Cistercian *ordo* meant and how one could determine which communities were members. Here we find that the margin and the centre are closer than we might imagine. On the one hand marginalized, the nuns were, on the other hand, engaged in a practice of identity creation via textual production that was not dissimilar to the practice of male Cistercians in the century before. This similarity of practice offers promising opportunities for future research. By highlighting these nuns' similarity to 'official' Cistercian history, we can in fact create space for Cistercian nuns in a new, more complete, narrative of Cistercian history.

The way to envisage this new Cistercian history is to remember that the periphery and institutional centre are integrally related. Each in turn constitutes and is constituted by the other, and we can fully comprehend one only when we examine the other. This has bearing beyond the arena of Cistercian history. In terms of broader points about the intersections of gender and enclosure, the lesson of these Cistercian case-studies is that intersections do occur, even where the evidence seems to suggest parallel tracks. Foundation histories from early-thirteenth-century male houses may seem to have little in common with deeds and cartularies from late-thirteenth-century female houses. But if we move behind the texts to the cultural world that made these texts possible and, indeed, necessary, then we can see that the same issue is at stake here, represented by its presence in the male texts and by its absence in the female texts. Completely separate textual results have been produced, but the social logic behind them is the same – that is, authority, Cistercian orthodoxy and centrality. As historians, we need to make ourselves see these less obvious intersections, make ourselves see that the most important historical force, the one which binds together otherwise disparate case-studies, is often lurking offstage, away from and prior to our documents.

Notes

[1] Walter Map, *De nugis curialium. Courtiers' Trifles*, ed. and trans. Montague Rhodes James, rev. C. N. L. Brooke and R. A. B. Mynors (Oxford, 1983), Dist. I, chap. 25.
[2] See, for example, Jean-Baptiste Auberger, *L'Unanimité Cistercienne primitive: mythe ou réalité?* (Achel, Belgium, 1986), pp. 87–133; Constance Brittain Bouchard, *Holy Entrepreneurs: Cistercian Knights and Economic*

Exchange in Twelfth-Century Burgundy (Ithaca, NY, and London, 1991); Robert A. Donkin, 'Settlement and depopulation on Cistercian estates during the twelfth and thirteenth centuries, especially in Yorkshire', *Bulletin of the Institute of Historical Research*, 33 (1960), 141–65.

3   David H. Williams, *The Cistercians in the Early Middle Ages* (Leominster, 1998); Louis J. Lekai, *The Cistercians: Ideals and Reality* (Kent, OH, 1977).

4   For detailed studies of the two histories, see my *Narratives of a New Order: Cistercian Historical Writing in England, 1150–1220* (Turnhout, 2002), chs 4 and 5.

5   Hugh of Kirkstall, *Narratio de fundatione Fontanis monasterii*, in John Richard Walbran (ed.), *Memorials of the Abbey of St Mary of Fountains*, 1, Surtees Society, 42 (Durham, 1862), pp. 1–129 (p. 1).

6   *Narratio*, p. 2.

7   Ibid., pp. 5–6.

8   *Fundacio abbathie de Kyrkestall*, in E. Kitson Clark (ed. and trans.), *Miscellanea*, Publications of the Thoresby Society, 4 (Leeds, 1893), pp. 173–208 (p. 179).

9   *Fundacio*, p. 175.

10   Deuteronomy 32: 10.

11   For references see Auberger, *L'Unanimité Cistercienne primitive*, pp. 119–24.

12   *Exordium Cistercii*, 1, in Chrysogonus Waddell (ed.), *Narrative and Legislative Texts from Early Cîteaux* (Brecht, 1999), p. 400.

13   On the complex tithe claim and counter-claim, see Coburn V. Graves, 'English Cistercian nuns in Lincolnshire', *Speculum*, 54 (1979), 492–9, and Linda Rasmussen, 'Order, order! Determining order in medieval English nunneries', in Linda Rasmussen, Valerie Spear and Dianne Tillotson (eds), *Our Medieval Heritage: Essays in Honour of John Tillotson for his 60th Birthday* (Cardiff, 2002), pp. 30–49 (pp. 33–7).

14   Oxford, Bodleian MS, Top. Lincs. d. 1, fols 42r, 43v–44r.

15   PRO E 326/11356, 1270s *inspeximus* by the bishop of Lincoln's official of six letters from St Michael's nunnery, Stamford, concerning exemption from tithes, with fifteenth-century endorsement. The letters survive only in this deed – the originals are lost.

16   Henry wrote several letters to this effect, to various recipients, once referring to the 'team-application' from Greenfield, Nun Cotham et al., and later referring to Stamford alone and Stixwould alone. On the multiple houses, see the two letters (one undated, one 22 October 1269) incorporated into the Nun Cotham cartulary, fol. 43v. On Stamford, see Henry's letter to the sheriff of Lincoln, 20 October 1271, in the Stamford deed of PRO E 326/11356. On Stixwould, see the letter of 12 December 1270, incorporated into the Nun Cotham cartulary, fol. 44r.

17   Written by Richard Gravesend, Bishop of Lincoln, on 17 July 1269, regarding Greenfield, Nun Cotham, Legbourne, Fosse and Gokewell; Nun Cotham cartulary, fol. 43v.

18   On 19 April 1269 Richard Gravesend wrote to the archdeacon of Lincoln, concerning Stamford alone. Referring also to earlier correspondence concerning

other houses, he stated 'quod dilecte in Christo filie priorissa et conventus Sancti Michaelis extra Stanford de ordine sunt Cisterciensis, sicut alie pro quibus vos nuper scripsimus'; PRO E 326/11356.

[19] Letter of the abbot of Kirkstall and prior of 'Parco' (Healaugh Park), *conservatores privilegiorum* of the Cistercian nunnery of Nunnappleton, 15 June 1270, writing of the nuns at St Michael's, Stamford; PRO E 326/11356.

[20] See later PRO documents: E 326/10567 from 1447; E 135/6/48 from 1512; E 326/6819 from 1528; E 326/10568 from 1528.

[21] For England as a special case, see Graves, 'English Cistercian nuns in Lincolnshire', and John A. Nichols, 'Cistercian nuns in twelfth and thirteenth century England', in John A. Nichols and Lillian Thomas Shank (eds), *Hidden Springs: Cistercian Monastic Women* (Kalamazoo, 1995), pp. 49–61.

[22] *Calendar of Close Rolls*, vol. 14, 1268–72, ann. 1270, p. 301.

[23] See Constance H. Berman, 'Were there twelfth-century Cistercian nuns?', *Church History*, 68 (1999), 824–64.

[24] As evidenced in Brigitte Degler-Spengler's ground-breaking work, 'The incorporation of Cistercian nuns into the Order in the twelfth and thirteenth centuries', in John A. Nichols and Lillian Thomas Shank (eds), *Hidden Springs: Cistercian Monastic Women* (Kalamazoo, 1995), pp. 85–134.

[25] Michael Casey, 'Bernard and the crisis at Morimond: did the Order exist in 1124?', *Cistercian Studies Quarterly*, 38 (2003), 119–75, responding to Constance H. Berman's *The Cistercian Evolution: The Invention of a Religious Order in Twelfth-Century Europe* (Philadelphia, 2000).

6

The Whitefriars' Return to Carmel

JOHAN BERGSTRÖM-ALLEN

Twenty years ago, Ann K. Warren pointed out in the introduction to *Anchorites and their Patrons in Medieval England* the usefulness of 'detailed exploration of anchoritism in a local setting'.[1] Whilst anchoritic studies have flourished in recent years, the study of anchorites within a specific geographic locale, or social or religious community, remains a fertile field of research yet to be thoroughly ploughed.

This chapter focuses upon the religious community of the Order of Carmelites ('Whitefriars'), which provided noteworthy spiritual direction for anchorites in later medieval England. It will argue that Carmelites regarded anchorites as engaging in a 'discourse of the desert' that had strong parallels to the early spirituality of their Order. The chapter highlights one particular example: the relationship between an English Whitefriar, Richard Misyn, and a fifteenth-century recluse in York, Margaret Heslington. Their association, known only through Misyn's translation of theological literature, demonstrates the strong spiritual and social bonds that existed between Carmelites and anchorites, but also highlights questions of gender politics and contemporary ecclesiastical concerns about policing the solitary life. Before examining Misyn and Heslington's relationship, however, it is worth reviewing the early history and spirituality of the Carmelites, since the Order has suffered more than most from the oversight of modern scholarship.[2]

The anonymous traditional hymn 'Laudemus omnes Virginem', which opens the Office of Readings in the modern Carmelite breviary for the Feast of All Carmelite Saints, recalls the Order's origins as a community of hermits gathered upon Mount Carmel in Palestine:

Come, let us praise the Virgin Queen
Who called her sons from earthly strife
To Carmel, ever since the scene
Of silent eremitic life.[3]

These 'silent hermits' emerge from legend into history sometime
between 1206 and 1214, when they requested a *formula vitae* from
Albert Avogadro, the Latin Patriarch of Jerusalem.[4] This *formula vitae*
stipulated that each hermit was to live in prayerful contemplation
(ch. 7), occupying a single cell (ch. 3) in a community alongside other
solitaries (chs 1 and 9).[5] This guiding text of the somewhat paradoxical
'community of solitaries' remained a dynamic expression of the Order's
self-identity, even after conflicts between Crusaders and Saracens
forced the hermits on Carmel to migrate west, in 1238.

From that date, or possibly even earlier, these Carmelite solitaries
established hermitage-communities across Europe. The first established
in England, at Hulne (Northumberland) and Aylesford (Kent) in 1242,
eventually gave rise to almost forty houses across the province, which
approached a thousand friars at its height. England became the largest
of the Order's twelve medieval provinces.[6] It was in England that the
first general chapter was held, and at this gathering in 1247 the
Carmelites decided to petition Pope Innocent IV to adapt their
Albertine *formula* into a *regula*, suitable for friars rather than hermits.
This response to the twelfth-century 'evangelical awakening' radically
transformed the Carmelite modus vivendi from eremitic solitude to
coenobitic mendicancy.[7] Rural hermitages gave way to friaries in
Europe's urban centres, where the Carmelites could gain income and
recruits, and minister to the growing populace.

Conventional historiography has seen the Carmelites' development
from a gathering of hermits to a community of friars as a smooth progression. However, the transformation – though necessary and fruitful –
was not without spiritual difficulties. Despite adopting the *Vita
Apostolica* by papal sanction, many Carmelites still regarded themselves
as contemplative desert hermits, as witnessed by the *Rubrica Prima*, a
text introducing the Carmelite Constitutions of 1281. The *Rubrica
Prima*, written to provide novices with a simple answer to any who
questioned the Order's origins, emphasized the reclusive nature of
Carmelites as 'true lovers of solitude'.[8] The document instructed young
friars that they were the hermit descendants of the prophets Elijah and
Elisha (and thus the oldest of the Church's orders), a privilege confirmed

by the Chancellor of Cambridge University at a *determinatio* in 1375.[9] The figure of Elijah was of great importance to the Order as a prototype of their solitary life, Jacques de Vitry (Bishop of Acre 1216–28) noting in his *History of Jerusalem* that men, 'in imitation of the holy anchorite the prophet Elijah, led solitary lives on Mount Carmel'.[10]

Like the Carmelites, anchorites can be traced back to Elijah and the desert hermits of antiquity.[11] Of course, hermits and anchorites – though closely connected – are vocations not to be confused, as pointed out in the introduction to this volume.[12] Nevertheless, it is clear from this brief and selective survey of Carmelite history that enclosure and solitude were key concepts in the Order's development; a subsequent interest in the solitary life of anchoritism might well be expected, and was manifested in a particular relationship between a friar and a female anchorite in fifteenth-century York.[13]

The friar in question is Richard Misyn, O. Carm. (d. 1462).[14] Misyn's *conventus nativus* where he joined the Order was at Lincoln. His further studies were conducted at the Carmelite *studium* in York,[15] then the second city of England, where Episcopal registers inform us that he was ordained acolyte and subdeacon in 1419, and deacon two years later.[16] He proceeded to university, possibly Oxford (within Lincoln diocese), before returning to his filial house. In Lincoln, Misyn translated into English the Latin treatise *de Emendatio Vitae*[17] by the celebrated Yorkshire hermit Richard Rolle of Hampole (*c.*1290–1349).[18] Misyn's translation, entitled *mendynge of lyfe*, is preserved in three manuscripts,[19] and is dated by the colophon in each to 1434. Each manuscript of the *mendynge* includes another text translated by Misyn a year later, Rolle's *Incendium Amoris* or *fyer of lufe*.

Misyn's translation of the *fyer* is prefaced with a prologue, in which both he and his addressee are almost entirely anonymous:

> At þe reuerence of oure lorde Ihesu criste, to þe askynge of þi desyre, Syster Margarete, couetynge a-sethe [reconciliation] to make, for encrece also of gostely comforth to þe & mo, þat curiuste of latyn vnderstandes noght, I, emonge lettyrd men sympellest, and in lyfynge vnthriftyest, þis wark has takyn to translacion of lattyn to englysch, for edificacyon of many saules.[20]

Not until the Latin colophon of the translation's second book do we learn the identity of the translator and his intended recipient:

Explicit liber de Incendio Amoris, Ricardi Hampole heremite, translatus in Anglicum instancijs domine Margarete Heslyngton, recluse, per fratrem Ricardum Misyn, sacre theologie bachalaureum, tunc Priorem Lyncolniensem, ordinis carmelitarum, Anno domini M.CCCCXXXV. in festo translacionis sancti Martini Episcopi, quod est iiij nonas Iulij, per dictum fratrem Ricardum Misyn scriptum & correctum.

(Here ends the Book of the Fire of Love, of Richard Hampole, hermit, translated into English at the instigation of Dame Margaret Heslington, recluse, by friar Richard Misyn, Bachelor of Theology, at that time Prior of Lincoln, of the Order of Carmelites, in 1435, on the feast of the translation of St Martin, Bishop, that is, the 4th nones of July, written and corrected by the said friar Richard Misyn.)[21]

The colophon identifies the recipient of the translation, 'Syster Margarete', as 'recluse', that is to say, an anchorite, but gives no further information about her. However, more can be deduced about this solitary from other sources. The proximity of York to the village of Heslington (now the site of the city's university) hints at a northern provenance, and York was certainly a fruitful centre of fourteenth- and fifteenth-century anchoritism.[22] York city records supplement Heslington's biography. A 'Dom. Isab. Heslyngton, reclusa' is listed as being admitted to the celebrated York Guild of Corpus Christi in 1429/30.[23] It was not unusual for anchorites to be members of guilds, who sometimes patronized them,[24] and the surname, date and title of 'recluse' indicate that she is surely the anchorite Misyn knew. Just as Julian of Norwich took her name from the church of St Julian, Isabel was probably Heslington's baptismal name, 'Margaret' deriving from the church to which she was anchored. Testamentary records reveal that until her death in 1439 (just four years after receiving Misyn's translations), Heslington received the generous bequests of several York citizens, as one in a succession of anchorites living in the churchyard of St Margaret's, Walmgate, located within a few hundred yards of the Carmelite convent.[25]

At the time of Heslington's entry into the Guild of Corpus Christi, Richard Misyn was probably lecturing at the York *studium*. He was himself granted membership into the Guild two decades after Heslington's death, whilst a suffragan bishop in the city.[26] Since Misyn did not join the Guild until after Heslington's death, it is hard to know whether the organization helped to foster the relationship between them. However, their mutual membership reveals something of the milieu in which the friar and the anchorite lived. The Guild admitted only clergy and laity of good character,[27] and especially men and women of social and intellectual distinction, including leading book-owners of the Diocese of York; merchants, abbots, bishops and royalty.[28] Many anchorites were from these governing classes, and Heslington's membership of the Guild might suggest financial as much as spiritual capital. Given the expense of book production in the Middle Ages, it is even possible that Heslington paid Misyn for his translation, thus reviving the practice among the early mendicants of earning income from 'manual' labour.[29]

Heslington must have been a powerful patron to have commissioned work from such a high-ranking cleric, and the opening sentence of Misyn's prologue suggests that the anchorite played a dynamic role in the translation of the *Incendium*. I agree with Felicity Riddy that 'we should not assume that women were merely passive recipients of books, or that they could not have taken the initiative in the process of translating from Latin into the vernacular . . . In the relation between the male clerks and their women readers it must often have been difficult to tell who followed and who led.'[30] Heslington's example would suggest this was as true for female anchorites as it was for female readers/listeners in general.

Misyn apparently wrote for Heslington in response 'to þe askynge of þi desyre',[31] and since works of anchoritic guidance 'seem to have been genuine responses to requests for such a guide',[32] it seems likely that this was not a literary device. However, Rolle's *Incendium* is not a traditional guide for female anchorites, and Heslington's request for a copy demonstrates that she was interested in the contemporary spirituality of Yorkshire rather than in anchoritic texts already available.[33]

It seems natural that this Yorkshire eremitic spirituality should have appealed to an anchorite such as Heslington, given that the *Emendatio* and *Incendium* both vehemently praise the solitary life. There is no evidence that the original *Incendium* was ever targeted at women – its Latin would largely preclude this. Nevertheless, Rolle's repetitive insistence on the desirability of death would have special resonance for Heslington, whose immurement ceremony probably echoed the funeral rite.[34] Furthermore, Misyn's translation of the *Incendium* into English at a woman's request disempowered some of the patriarchal aspects of the text. In this context, Rolle's statement that 'an olde wyfe of goddis lufe is more expert, & les of wardly likynge, þen þe grete devin, whos stody is vayne'[35] takes on new gynaecentric significance. In some respects Rolle's texts would seem to appeal more naturally to an anchorite than to a Carmelite. Rolle's teachings pre-dated fourteenth-century developments in the theology of the 'Mixed Life', and his praise of the contemplative vocation does not seem to accept any integration with the active, as favoured by the friars. Heslington's withdrawal thus concurs more with Rolle's description of the solitary life than with Misyn's. Yet Misyn's desire for the status of solitary is plain in his self-labelling as 'hermit'.[36] Though 'Hermits of Mount Carmel' was dropped from the Order's official title before 1435,[37] Misyn applied it to himself in the colophons, perhaps reflecting his self-perception as both a solitary and a peripatetic friar.

There are indications within the text that Misyn did not undertake the task of translation without trepidation. In Misyn's dedicatory epistle, the Carmelite warned his audience not to stray beyond the bounds of church teaching, 'for drede þou erre, namely in slyke þinges þat touches þe .xij. artikils of þi fayth, als of þe holy Trinite, & oþer dyuers, als in þis holy boke filouynge is to oure lernynge connyngly writtyn'.[38] Perhaps aware that some of Rolle's writings had been appropriated by the Lollards, Misyn feared that his own translations of the *Emendatio* and *Incendium* might be regarded as heretical interpolations. He thus declared that 'to reforme I make protestacyon, with entent no þinge to wryte ne say agayns þe faith or determinacion of holy kyrk, god to wytnes'.[39]

Misyn's apologia can be accounted for by the climate of censorship and control that existed in fifteenth-century England. Following the 1407/9 *Constitutions* of Archbishop Thomas Arundel, writing in English could be perceived as evidence of seditious leanings. Article 6 restricted the production of literature, and 'any vernacular religious work produced from the 1380s on . . . was liable to be treated with circumspection by orthodox readers'.[40] It is perhaps for this reason that Misyn translated for Heslington texts which pre-dated the time of Wyclif.

Carmelites in late-medieval England were generally renowned for their orthodoxy.[41] Yet they seem to have been surprisingly pragmatic in their promotion of the vernacular. Just as Alan of Lynn's Bible discussions with Margery Kempe must have involved the vernacular,[42] so Misyn believed that the translation of Rolle's Latin text was of benefit to Heslington and others 'þat curiuste of latyn vnderstandes noght'.[43] Presumably Misyn had confidence in Heslington's orthodoxy, though Lollard anchorites were not unheard of.[44] However, whilst the *fyer* was not a coterie text, Misyn's prologue shows that he anticipated the translation circulating to readers beyond Heslington's anchorhold; Misyn wrote his *fyer* for 'all redars', and 'for edificacyon of many saules'.[45] How he anticipated the text being transmitted beyond an enclosed space is an intriguing question, and, though not one that can be considered here at length, it is worth remarking that palaeographic dating of the extant Misyn manuscripts suggests that they were copied within a decade of Heslington's death.

In order to put Misyn's relationship with Heslington into the context of the Carmelite community's interest in anchoritism, we must return to the fact of the Order's enduring preoccupation with solitude and the desire of some Whitefriars in late-medieval England to 'return to Carmel'. A few years before Misyn translated Rolle, a text was rediscovered in the Carmelite Order that called for a return to desert solitude. In his letter, *Ignea Sagitta* (*The Flaming Arrow*), Nicholas the Frenchman, prior general of the Order from 1266–71, called for a return to the primitive traditions of Mount Carmel, rejecting the cities in favour of the desert.[46] Written in 1272, this text was lost for many years but recirculated within the Order from about 1411.[47] About a decade later, the Order produced records about the quasi-mythical prior general, Saint Simon Stock, a visionary and recluse, and the revived interest in him is symptomatic of the Order's quest for reclusive exemplars.[48] The simultaneous promotion of the *Ignea Sagitta* and the dissemination of the 'Ribot collection' (a set of texts describing the life of the Order from its supposed Old Testament and anchoritic beginnings),[49] may have been formative during Misyn's novitiate. As Valerie Edden observes of the Order's literary output in the fifteenth century, 'the body of writing in which Carmelite friars reflected on their own history and identity suggests a spirituality much indebted to the memory of those hermits'.[50] It is further significant that Misyn's translations were written only two to three years after the Carmelite Rule was again mitigated. Pope Eugenius IV's bull *Romani Pontifices Providentia* (1432) relaxed regulations on enclosure, allowing Whitefriars to vacate their cells and wander around the convent freely when not occupied in communal duty. In this context, Rolle's criticisms of 'rynnars aboute, þat ar sclaunderes of hermyts',[51] and *girovagi* who 'trow þame-self be þe warld may ryn & be contemplatyf'[52] might have had uncomfortable echoes for a Carmelite translator.

Roberta Gilchrist observes that as monastic orders declined from the fourteenth century onwards, the contemplatives in the cities – friars and anchorites – became increasingly popular.[53] By the early fifteenth century, however, Carmelite communities were beginning to decline. Scholastic output, at which the Carmelites had excelled in the previous decades, began to diminish.[54] Yet, concurrently, anchorites continued to flourish, and Carmelites in England encouraged a new expression of their reclusive ideals that was lived in anchorholds, rather than friaries. In order to put Misyn's relationship with Heslington in a wider context of Carmelite interaction with anchorites, therefore, it would be helpful to highlight a few of the other such relationships that existed in England and on the continent in the middle to late medieval period.

One of the earliest known female Carmelite recluses was 'blessed' Jane (or Joan) of Toulouse (d. 1286).[55] The antiquarian John Bale (1495–1563), a source of much (if biased) information about the medieval province, claimed that Jane was affiliated to the Order as a tertiary, demonstrating that female solitaries lived according to the direction and possibly even the Rule of Carmelites. Thus, Misyn's provision of a 'rewl of lyfynge'[56] for Heslington could likewise be seen as extending to her 'honorary membership' of the Order.

Whilst Jane of Toulouse was an anchorite who was offered some kind of affiliation to the Carmelite Order, in the case of Thomas Scrope (alias Bradley), we find a Carmelite friar who rejected community life in favour of the anchorhold. From 1425 Scrope spent approximately twenty years as an anchorite at the Carmelite friary in Norwich.[57] In his study of medieval religious life in that city, Norman Tanner regards the Carmelite-associated anchorites as representing 'an interesting return to the original traditions' of the Order.[58] The Norwich friary provided shelter for female anchorites as well, including a contemporary of Margaret Heslington, Emma Stapleton, who lived under the spiritual direction of the Whitefriars from 1421.[59] Dame Emma was veiled by the prior provincial Thomas Netter (d. 1430),[60] rather than the local bishop, and, if this was the norm for female anchorites associated with the Carmelite Order, it would account for why neither Stapleton nor Heslington appear in bishops' registers (the Carmelites operating as they did largely beyond episcopal control).[61] Moreover, the Carmelite provincial appointed the most able friars as Stapleton's counsellors: none less than the prior, sub-prior and three other highly educated members of the convent, including a former Master of the Carmelite School of Theology at Paris.[62] Thus, anchorites under Carmelite guidance seem to have flourished in academic centres where the Order had *studia* (Jane at Toulouse, Stapleton at Norwich and Heslington at

York) and both Stapleton and Heslington were contemporary anchorites, whose spiritual progression was encouraged by educated and senior members of the Carmelite Order. Of course, enclosure meant these highly educated Carmelites could monitor an anchorite's religious sentiments. It was far easier for the Carmelites to regulate Stapleton and Heslington than to control Margery Kempe, for example, who regularly consulted the Carmelites of Lynn, where Bale informs us another anchorite, Joan Catfeld, was living under Carmelite direction in 1421. Bale, whose travels in England were restricted largely to the south-east, also records Carmelite anchorites in Cambridge, Ipswich and Northampton.

The fact that Carmelites so often gave spiritual guidance to anchorites suggests that the latter were valued additions to the contemplative community, and not only because of the financial benefits of supporting aristocratic recluses. Both mendicants and anchorites relied upon the generosity of others to support their 'deserts' within the urban environment. The relationship between anchorites and Carmelites was symbiotic; the friars provided the recluse with spiritual direction, and through prayer he or she sustained them by adding to the Order's 'spiritual treasury' of grace.

Thus, the full significance of Misyn's relationship with Heslington becomes more apparent within the anchoritic climate, and is evidence of the Carmelites' ongoing concern to reconcile an active apostolate with their identity as solitary contemplatives. Whilst the life of the Carmelites as a 'community of solitaries' was continually evolving, Misyn was keen to instruct another – outside the convent, but perhaps within the Order's confraternity – in the benefits of the solitary life. Encouraging the anchoritic way of life allowed semi-monastic mendicants such as Misyn to live anchoritic spirituality by proxy. Maybe Misyn perceived in Heslington some imitation of the heroism and holiness of the early desert hermits, and saw in her manner of life some type of return to Carmel.[63]

Notes

[1] Ann K. Warren, *Anchorites and their Patrons in Medieval England* (Berkeley, 1985), p. 4.
[2] The major history of the Carmelite Order is Joachim Smet's four-volume study *The Carmelites: A History of the Brothers of Our Lady of Mount*

Carmel (Rome, rev. edn 1976–88). Useful reading on the Order's distinctive spirituality includes Bernard McGinn, 'The role of the Carmelites in the history of Western mysticism', in Kevin Culligan and Regis Jordan (eds), *Carmel and Contemplation: Transforming Human Consciousness* (Washington DC, 2000), pp. 25–50; Keith J. Egan, 'The spirituality of the Carmelites', in Jill Raitt (ed.), *Christian Spirituality: High Middle Ages and Reformation* (London, 1987), pp. 50–62; Wilfrid McGreal, *At the Fountain of Elijah: The Carmelite Tradition* (London, 1999). On the Order's legendary history, see Fr. Richard Copsey, 'Establishment, identity and papal approval: the Carmelite Order's creation of its legendary History', *Carmelus*, 47 (Rome, 2000), 41–53; Andrew Jotischky, *The Carmelites and Antiquity: Mendicants and their Pasts in the Middle Ages* (Oxford, 2002).

3   *Proper of the Liturgy of the Hours of the Order of the Brothers of the Blessed Virgin Mary of Mount Carmel and of the Order of Discalced Carmelites* (Rome, 1993), p. 337.

4   Vincenzo Mosca, *Alberto Patriarca di Gerusalemme: Tempo, Vita, Opera* (Rome, 1996).

5   The Carmelite Rule, probably the least known of all medieval texts of guidance on the religious life, has been frequently edited in modern times: Bede Edwards, *The Rule of Saint Albert*, Vinea Carmeli, 1 (Faversham, 1973); Joseph Chalmers, 'Appendix two: the Rule of Saint Albert' in *Mary the Contemplative* (Rome, 2001), pp. 89–93; Kees Waaijman, *The Mystical Space of Carmel: A Commentary on the Carmelite Rule*, trans. John Vriend (Leuven, 1999).

6   On the history of the Province, see Patrick Fitzgerald-Lombard (ed.), *Carmel in Britain*, 2 vols (Rome, 1992); Richard Copsey, *Carmel in Britain 3: The Hermits from Mount Carmel* (Faversham, Kent, 2004); Keith J. Egan, 'The establishment and early development of the Carmelite Order in England' (unpublished Ph.D. thesis, Cambridge University, 1965); Valerie Edden, 'The mantle of Elijah: Carmelite spirituality in England in the fourteenth century', in Marion Glasscoe (ed.), *The Medieval Mystical Tradition, England, Ireland and Wales*, Exeter Symposium VI (Cambridge, 1999), pp. 67–83.

7   On the conversion see C. H. Lawrence, *The Friars: The Impact of the Early Mendicant Movement on Western Society* (London, 1994), p. 100, and *Medieval Monasticism: Forms of Religious Life in Western Europe in the Middle Ages* (London, 3rd edn, 2001), p. 274.

8   'Dicimus enim veritati testimonium perhibentes quod a tempore helye et helisei prophetarum montem carmeli devote inhabitancium, sancti patres tam veteris quam novi testamenti eiusdem montis solitudinem pro contemplatione celestium tamquam veri amatores.' Adrian Staring, *Medieval Carmelite Heritage* (Rome, 1989), pp. 40–1. (We say that, on the evidence of trustworthy witnesses, that from the time of the prophets Elijah and Elisha, the holy fathers of both the Old and New Testaments, have lived devotedly on Mount Carmel, true lovers of the solitude of that mountain for the contemplation of heavenly things). Translated by Richard Copsey in *Early Carmelite Documents* (private printing).

9 'We, John Dunwich, Chancellor of the University of Cambridge, having heard the arguments and allegations, having read and examined all the privileges, together with the chronicles and ancient writings, we state, judge and declare that the Order of the brothers of the blessed Mary of Mount Carmel is in common and particular law confirmed, and especially decorated with the title of the glorious Virgin, blessed Mary, Mother of God, and that the brothers appear to us from the chronicles and other ancient writings to be the imitators and successors of the holy prophets Elijah and Elisha.' Excerpt translated by Copsey in *Early Carmelite Documents*. On the dispute between the Carmelites and the Dominicans which led to the *determinatio*, see J. P. H. Clark, 'A defence of the Carmelite Order by John Hornby, O. Carm., A.D. 1374', *Carmelus*, 32 (1985), 73–98.

10 Jacques de Vitry, *The History of Jerusalem*, ch. 27, quoted in Joachim Smet, *The Carmelites*, 1, p. 3.

11 Selected reading on the development of the solitary life in medieval England includes Rotha Mary Clay, *The Hermits and Anchorites of England* (London, 1914); Warren, *Anchorites and their Patrons in Medieval England*; Roberta Gilchrist, *Contemplation and Action: The Other Monasticism* (London, 1995), pp. 157–208; Grace M. Jantzen, *Julian of Norwich* (London, 1987), pp. 28–50; Joan M. Nuth, *God's Lovers in an Age of Anxiety: The Medieval English Mystics* (London, 2001), pp. 19–22; Charles Kingsley, *The Hermits* (London, 1890).

12 See also Johan Bergström-Allen, 'Looking behind to see ahead: finding a future from the early Carmelites', *Assumpta*, 46, 4 (2003), 13–27.

13 The rest of this chapter is largely based upon my Master's research, ' "Heremitam et Ordinis Carmelitarum": a study of the vernacular theological literature produced by medieval English Whitefriars, particularly Richard Misyn, O. Carm.' (unpublished M.Phil. thesis, University of Oxford, 2002). On the context of religious life in the medieval city of York, see ibid., 181, n. 99.

14 I am grateful to Richard Copsey for providing me with his biography of Misyn, written for the *New Dictionary of National Biography*.

15 The most helpful and authoritative works on the York Carmelites to date are listed by Copsey in Fitzgerald-Lombard's *Carmel in Britain*, 1, p. 250. See also Copsey's *Chronology of the Medieval Carmelite Priory at York* (http://www.carmelite.org/chronology/york.htm); Barrie Dobson, 'Mendicant ideal and practice in late medieval York', in P. V. Addyman and V. E. Black (eds), *Archaeological Papers from York Presented to M. W. Barley* (York Archaeological Trust, 1984), pp. 109–22; Angelo Raine, *Mediaeval York: A Topographical Survey based on Original Sources* (London, 1955), pp. 62–5; Johan Bergström-Allen, 'Carmelites and lay piety in York prior to the papal letter *Cum Nulla*' (paper delivered at the 2003 'Carmelite History and Spirituality' Symposium, York, forthcoming).

16 University of York, Borthwick Institute of Historical Research, Register of Archbishop Bowet (Reg. 18), f. 402, fos 404v and 409v.

17 Sometimes entitled *Regula vivendi (Rule of Life), Emendatio peccatoris,*

Vehiculum Vitae or *Duodecim capitula*. Jonathan Burke Severs, Albert E. Hartung and John Edwin Wells (eds), *A Manual of the Writings in Middle English, 1050–1500* (New Haven, CT, 1967), 9, p. 3064; Michael G. Sargent, 'The transmission by the English Carthusians of some late medieval spiritual writings', *Journal of Ecclesiastical History*, 27, 3 (1976), 232, n. 3.

[18] On Rolle's life and writings, see Nicholas Watson, *Richard Rolle and the Invention of Authority* (Cambridge, 1991).

[19] British Library MS Additional 37790 (Amherst Manuscript), fos 1–95; Yale University MS Beinecke 331, fos 1–136v; Oxford, Corpus Christi College MS 236, passim. The only printed edition of the translations, based solely on the Oxford manuscript, is by Ralph Harvey, *The Fire of Love & The Mending of Life or The Rule of Living*, EETS o.s. 106 (London, 1896). All references to Misyn's translation will be taken from this edition, hereafter *fyer*. On the Amherst manuscript see Marleen Cré, 'Vernacular mysticism in the Charterhouse: an analysis of British Library MS Additional 37790 in its religious and literary context' (unpublished Ph.D. thesis, Université de Fribourg, September 2001). On the relationships between the manuscripts see Margaret Laing, 'Linguistic profiles and textual criticism: the translation by Richard Misyn of Rolle's *Incendium Amoris* and *Emendatio Vitae*', in Angus McIntosh, M. L. Samuels and Margaret Laing (eds), *Middle English Dialectology: Essays on some Principles and Problems* (Aberdeen, 1989), pp. 188–223.

[20] Misyn, *fyer*, p. 1.

[21] Ibid., p. 104.

[22] Warren, *Anchorites and their Patrons*, pp. 39, 242–53. Thanks are due to Dr Eddie Jones of Exeter University for making available some of Rotha Mary Clay's unpublished notes, which helped me to locate Margaret Heslington.

[23] Not 1428, as claimed by Jonathan Hughes in *Pastors and Visionaries: Religion and Secular Life in Late Medieval Yorkshire* (Suffolk, 1988), p. 110. On the Guild of Corpus Christi, see David J. F. Crouch, *Piety, Fraternity and Power: Religious Gilds in Late Medieval Yorkshire, 1389–1547* (York, 2000).

[24] Warren, *Anchorites and their Patrons*, pp. 184, 192, 207.

[25] York, Borthwick Institute, Probate Registry, Will 3, f. 590; Raine, *Mediaeval York*, p. 108; Warren, *Anchorites and their Patrons*, pp. 244–5. Now the National Centre for Early Music, St Margaret's is sadly not well documented, but see Philippa Hoskin, 'Some late fourteenth-century gild and fabric wardens' accounts from the Church of St. Margaret's, Walmgate, York', in David M. Smith (ed.), *The Church in Medieval York: Records edited in Honour of Professor Barrie Dobson* (York, 1999), pp. 75–86. It is my belief that the small building still standing on the side of the church there could be Heslington's anchorhold, and would once have provided a squint overlooking the altar.

[26] 'Frater Ricardus Mysyn, suffragenus, ordinis Fratrum Carmelitarum' is recorded 'in primis' as the first person admitted in 1461–2: *Register of the*

Guild of Corpus Christi in the City of York, ed. R. H. Skaife, Surtees Society, 57 (London, 1872 for 1871), p. 62.

27   Fifth ordinance (Skaife, *Register of the Guild of Corpus Christi*, pp. vi and 7).

28   Skaife, *Register of the Guild of Corpus Christi*, p. xii.

29   Lawrence, *Medieval Monasticism*, pp. 250 and 255. On the support of friars by the burgher class, see Jonathan Hughes, *Pastors and Visionaries*, p. 50.

30   Felicity Riddy, ' "Women talking about the things of God": a late medieval sub-culture', in Carol M. Meale (ed.), *Women and Literature in Britain 1150–1500* (Cambridge, 2nd edn, 1993), p. 107.

31   Misyn, *fyer*, p. 1.

32   Warren, *Anchorites and their Patrons*, p. 103.

33   Such texts for female solitaries are listed by Warren, *Anchorites and their Patrons*, pp. 103, 294–8. Clay rightly stated that 'the works of Richard Rolle and Walter Hilton were much appreciated by anchoresses' (*The Hermits and Anchorites of England*, p. 177). Carmelite interest in both these Yorkshire authors is indicative of the Order's awareness of anchoritic literary movements in England. Not only did Misyn translate Rolle into English, but a confrère, Thomas Fishlake, translated Hilton's anchoritic text *The Scale of Perfection* from English into Latin at the end of the fourteenth century. For further details, see my M.Phil. thesis, pp. 20–4.

34   On the rite of enclosure, see Clay, *The Hermits and Anchorites of England*, appendix A; and Georgia Ronan Crampton (ed.), *The Shewings of Julian of Norwich*, TEAMS (Kalamazoo, MI, 1994), p. 9.

35   Misyn, *fyer*, p. 13.

36   Ibid., p. 68.

37   The last official use of 'hermit' in the Order's title is listed by Emanuele Boaga as the Constitutions of 1281: *The Lady of the Place: Mary in the History and in the Life of Carmel* (Rome, 2001), p. 24.

38   Misyn, *fyer*, p. 2.

39   Ibid., p. 1.

40   Nicholas Watson, 'The composition of Julian of Norwich's Revelation of Love', *Speculum*, 68, 3 (1993), 665. See also Nicholas Watson, 'Censorship and cultural change in late-medieval England: vernacular theology, the Oxford translation debate, and Arundel's *Constitutions* of 1409', *Speculum*, 70, 4 (1995), 822–64.

41   I elaborate on the role of Carmelites as defenders of orthodoxy throughout my thesis.

42   *The Book of Margery Kempe*, ed. Sandford Brown Meech and Hope Emily Allen, EETS o.s. 212 (Oxford, 1940; repr. 1997), pp. 169–70.

43   Misyn, *fyer*, p. 1.

44   Watson, 'Composition', p. 666; Warren, *Anchorites and their Patrons*, pp. 79–80.

45   Misyn, *fyer*, p. 1.

46   The text is edited by Adrian Staring, 'Nicolai Prioris Generalis Carmelitarum Ignea Sagitta', *Carmelus*, 9 (1962), 237–307; and translated by Bede Edwards, *The Flaming Arrow (Ignea Sagitta)* (Durham, 1985).

47 Richard Copsey, 'The *Ignea Sagitta* and its readership: a re-evaluation', *Carmelus*, 46 (1999), 166–73.

48 Richard Copsey, 'Simon Stock and the scapular vision', *Journal of Ecclesiastical History*, 50, 4 (1999), 652–83.

49 On Philip Ribot and his writings, see Andrew Jotischky, *The Carmelites and Antiquity: Mendicants and their Pasts in the Middle Ages* (Oxford, 2002), pp. 136–50.

50 Valerie Edden, 'The mantle of Elijah', p. 83.

51 Misyn, *fyer*, p. 32.

52 Ibid., p. 76.

53 Gilchrist, *Contemplation and Action*, p. 208.

54 On the significant but underrated role of the Carmelites in English scholastic life, see Bruce P. Flood, Jr., 'The Carmelite friars in medieval English universities and society, 1299–1430', *Recherches de théologie ancienne et médiévale*, 55 (1988), 154–83; William J. Courtenay, *Schools and Scholars in Fourteenth-Century England* (Princeton, NJ, 1987), p. 371.

55 Louis Saggi et al., (eds) *Saints of Carmel: A Compilation from Various Dictionaries*, trans. Gabriel Pausback (Rome, 1972), pp. 44, 136–7; Joachim Smet, *Cloistered Carmel: A Brief History of the Carmelite Nuns* (Rome, 1986), pp. 14–15. The earliest known Carmelite anchorite was the lay-brother Franco Lippi (d. 1291) as cited in Smet, *The Carmelites*, 1, p. 27.

56 Misyn, *fyer*, p. 105.

57 Dictionary of National Biography, XVII, pp. 1085–6; Norman P. Tanner, *The Church in Late Medieval Norwich 1370–1532* (Toronto, 1984), pp. 59–60; John Bale, *Scriptorum Illustrium Maioris Brytanniae quam nunc Angliam et Scotiam vocant: Catalogus*, 2 vols (Basel, 1557–9, repr. Farnborough, Hants, 1971). *Index Britanniae Scriptorum* (John Bale's Index of British and Other Writers), ed. Reginald Lane Poole and Mary Bateson (Oxford, 1902; reissued with new introduction by Caroline Brett and James P. Carley, Cambridge, 1990), 1, pp. 629–30; Richard Sharpe, *A Handlist of the Latin Writers of Great Britain and Ireland before 1540* (Turnhout, 1997), entry 1827, pp. 679–80; Warren, *Anchorites and their Patrons*, p. 211, n. 61.

58 Tanner, *The Church in Late Medieval Norwich*, p. 59.

59 British Library MS Harley 1819, f. 197; Warren, *Anchorites and their Patrons*, p. 213.

60 Clay, *The Hermits and Anchorites of England*, p. 93; P. R. McCaffrey, *The White Friars: An Outline Carmelite History, with Special Reference to the English-Speaking Provinces* (Dublin, 1926), p. 87. Bale listed Stapleton with anchorites influenced by Netter and the Order (Oxford, MS Bodley 73; *Scriptorum*, 1, p. 565).

61 The enquiry into a would-be anchorite's life and subsequent enclosure usually required episcopal approval, and was recorded in the bishop's register, for which see Francis D. S. Darwin, *The English Mediaeval Recluse* (London, 1944), p. 49. However, 'Carmelite' anchorites seem to have operated outside episcopal control, on which see Dorothy M. Owen, *Church and Society in Medieval Lincolnshire*, ed. Joan Thirsk (Welwyn Garden City,

1971), p. 123. Friars, meanwhile, would probably carry out discernment and formation themselves. Misyn's text may have formed part of this.

[62] Warren, *Anchorites and their Patrons*, p. 213.

[63] I would like to thank: Lady Margaret Hall, Oxford, for a grant which allowed me to attend the 2002 University of Wales conference in Gregynog ('Anchorites, Wombs and Tombs: Intersections of Gender and Enclosure'); The British Province of Carmelites, for their generous and impartial support; and Liz Herbert McAvoy and Mari Hughes-Edwards for encouraging me to give my first public paper there.

II

Gender and Enclosure:
Late Medieval Intersections

7

'Crepe into that blessed syde': Enclosure Imagery in Aelred of Rievaulx's *de Institutione Inclusarum*

KRISTEN McQUINN

In the late fourteenth and early fifteenth centuries, a Middle English text was in circulation which invites its reader to 'Crepe into that blessed syde where that blood and water cam forthe, and hyde the ther as a culuer in the stoon, wel likynge the dropes of his blood, til that thy lippes be maad like to a reed scarlet hood'.[1] This text is the late medieval redaction of the high-medieval anchoritic treatise *de Institutione Inclusarum*, written originally by Aelred of Rievaulx in the early 1160s. The dramatic representation of the recluse hiding inside Christ's bloody wound and revelling in his blood is absent from Aelred's original Latin guide. In the light of this later addition to the redacted version of the text, this chapter examines the significance of this primal image and of other feminized images of enclosure in the context of late-medieval anchoritic devotion.

On the one hand, this image is suggestive of drawing nourishment directly from the body and blood of Christ and of being completely swathed, immersed, in that blood. On the other hand, it is an image of safety and comfort, of total protection within the body of Christ. This visceral description shares an implicit mutuality with female anchorites in its vivid images of blood, penetration and enclosure. Piety that was centred on the Passion and wounds of Christ was particularly appropriate for female recluses, and indeed for women in general.[2] As Roberta Gilchrist states: 'the heart may be considered especially appropriate to female devotion'.[3] A female anchorite could well have been able to connect more intimately with an image that was feminized because, as Rosalynn Voaden has shown, 'the discourse of the Sacred

Heart . . . employs images drawn from biological *female* characteristics – blood, flowing, opening and enclosure'.[4] Because of their own anatomical identities, then, female anchorites would probably be able to extract the wider significance of such imagery from a text far more readily than male anchorites. This chapter will argue that the inclusion of such feminized images allows the female recluse – and anchorites in medieval England were predominantly female[5] – to relate to the Wounded Side by recalling her own feminine experience through the emphasis on the humanity of Christ and his Passion. To this end, I will show that Aelred's redactor employs many feminized images of enclosure, in addition to that of enclosure within the heart or side of Christ. Most notably, the recluse is encouraged to draw on analogies between her cell and her fleshly body – the womb in particular – and between her cell and the garden of the biblical Song of Songs, the so-called *hortus conclusus*.[6]

The discussion of the late-medieval redaction of *de Institutione Inclusarum* can usefully be prefaced by a consideration of the rise of the devotion to the Wounded Side, which was widespread throughout medieval Europe before it was eventually superseded, in the thirteenth century, by the worship of the Sacred Heart. This devotion focused on the humanity and Passion of Christ, emphasizing his wounds and the shelter to be found within them. Such devotion has a subtle basis in the Scriptures, which was expanded by the Church Fathers.[7] Several ancient and medieval theologians referred to the Song of Songs in a manner that would eventually lead to Sacred Heart worship. For example, in the sixth century, Gregory the Great used the verse 'Come, my dove in the clefts of the rocks, in the hollow places in the wall' to refer specifically to the wound in Christ's side as a refuge for the soul.[8] Other theologians also meditated on this imagery, as Santha Bhattacharji has already demonstrated in her chapter earlier in this volume, but it was Bernard of Clairvaux's *Sermons on the Song of Songs* that aided the widespread dedication to the Wounded Side, which was assimilated in the thirteenth century into the Cult of the Sacred Heart. While his sermons do not specifically mention the Sacred Heart or Wounded Side, they nonetheless state: 'The secret of his Heart is laid open through the clefts of his body; that mighty mystery of loving is laid open . . . God . . . has even led us by the open clefts into the holy place.'[9] Bernard's sermons instigated the fervent devotion of the nuns of Helfta to the wounds of Christ, as demonstrated particularly in the writings of Gertrude the Great (1256–1302), Mechtild of Hackeborn (1241–98) and Mechtild of Magdeburg (1207–82). The Cult of the Sacred Heart primarily began in Helfta with the writings of these three women, all of whom used the imagery of taking refuge and being enclosed within Christ's wounded side. Women were the principal devotees in Eucharistic and Sacred Heart piety, and this type of devotion placed much emphasis on nuptial and Passion contemplation, which was often constructed from a feminine perspective. This is in contrast to the earlier days of the Church, which

> sought to 'regender' its female converts, to instill in them a masculine reli-
> gious identification and ideal of religious practice. Women were urged to
> divest themselves of the characteristics that male authorities deemed 'fem-
> inine' (e.g., sensuality, weakness, irrationality), and to develop 'manly'
> attributes (e.g., rationality, orderliness, and moral purity).[10]

We can see exactly this masculinist approach in the Latin original of *de Institutione Inclusarum*, which focuses on the maintenance of the anchorite's chastity and the suppression of sensuality. By the time of its late-medieval redaction, however, a new emphasis, in line with female-oriented devotional responses, like that of the Wounded Side and Sacred Heart, is clearly in evidence.

From the outset of the Middle English version of *de Institutione Inclusarum*, Aelred's redactor asserts that mere *physical* enclosure is not enough for a holy way of life:

> But many ther ben that knowe not ne charge not the profit of solitary
> liuyng, supposyng that it be ynow, oonly to shutte her body bitwene too
> walles, whan not only the thoughte rennith aboute besynes of the worlde,
> but also the tunge is occupied alday.[11]

This statement acknowledges the danger of an anchorite becoming a sinner while leading a seemingly devout life. It is not the case that anchoritic enclosure protected the recluse from the temptations of the world. In fact, paradoxically, she may have been under even more strain, since her enclosure gave ample time to think about sinning, and thus to sin in her heart.[12] In order to resist these temptations, the redactor suggests that the female anchorite engage in contemplation to focus on Christ's humanity. She should meditate upon an image of Christ's Passion so that she 'may haue mynde and se hou he sette and spredde his armes a-brood to resccyue the and al mankynde to mercy'.[13] This reminder of Christ's humanity is an elementary step toward mystical union with God, which is reinforced with the image of an open-armed Christ waiting to embrace mankind. Imagining a physical embrace thus prepares the recluse for the contemplation of a higher form of enclosure within the divine.

For the redactor, the preparation for this higher form of contemplation comes in the anchoritic work of prayer, which he links to enclosure in his construction of it as a protective refuge. He writes: 'Than shalt thow renne to som pryuat prayer, as for a gret *refute* and helpe of thyn holy purpos that thou stondist inne.'[14] Enclosure within the sanctuary of prayer will bring her closer to her enclosure within the Wounded Side. In regarding prayer as a form of envelopment, the female anchorite engages in a form of affective piety that will allow her to develop her praxis of spiritual enclosure. All the meditation the female anchorite performs is 'preparatory purification',[15] which is rewarded when she begins to come to the understanding of genuine enclosure.

Although much of the enclosure imagery in the redacted *de Institutione Inclusarum* is not based solely on meditation on the Wounded Side, the guide nonetheless reinforces devotion to it in several ways which are uniquely applicable to the anchoritic life. The redactor writes that the female recluse must cling to her devotion to Christ's wounds, especially when engaging in contemplation. The redactor does give instruction in the use of contemplation and thoughts of the Passion; he also offers several different images to use when reflecting on union with the Wounded Side. He writes, for example, 'be thou ioyful in God with-in-forthe'.[16] While the directive does not indicate enclosure in Christ's wounds, its phrasing would act as a subtle reminder of such to a person who lived the life of symbolic union with the Wounded Side.

Other enclosure imagery, such as that of the garden, also reinforces the feminization of reclusive devotion. The female anchorite enclosed in her cell is an impenetrably chaste woman, and her cell is likened to the *hortus conclusus*, the enclosed garden. The redactor says the joy found within Christ 'shuld be thy garden, thyn orcharde and thy disport [comfort]'.[17] The garden is an image of seclusion, isolation and shelter, much like the anchorhold. The use of garden imagery in religious writing originated in the Song of Songs 4: 12, which reads, 'My sister, my spouse, is a garden enclosed, a fountain sealed up'. The construction of virginity was, of course, an important element in anchoritic theology. The chaste woman and the garden are also connected to the Virgin Mary, who is associated with gardens and whom the anchorite is encouraged to emulate as an exemplum of female piety and chastity.[18]

Marian devotion is congruent with devotion to the Wounded Side; the anchorite will want to imitate Mary and Mary, in turn, tends the very wound into which the anchorite desires to withdraw.

According to Susanna Greer Fein, the redaction of *de Institutione Inclusarum* 'provides spiritual insight through a womb-centered imagery of sexual arousal, pregnancy, childbirth, and maternal pathos that analogizes anchoritic cell to female body'.[19] The analogy between the anchorhold and the body of the female anchorite is central to the theology of enclosure in the Wounded Side. The redactor tells the anchorite, 'Also beholde and meruaile the with deuocyon, what lord this myght be, the whiche vouchith-saaf to ben enclosed in a maydens wombe'.[20] The enclosure of Jesus inside the womb of Mary is an important anchoritic image. Gilchrist comments that 'interior space, be it of the house or of the body, is a feminine place; for the first dwelling place of man is buried deep in the secret places of women'.[21] Aelred writes from the perspective that women are emotional and sensual, and that their response is to Christ's humanity rather than to the abstract concept of the divinity of the Godhead. In this sense, womb imagery as applied to the anchorhold provides women with access to the complex idea of enclosure, through the mutuality between the Wounded Side and their own bodies. The anchorhold is a place of spiritual nourishment, as the womb nourishes the foetus. The recluse is, as Fein has argued, herself likened to the ripening fruit within the womb.[22] She is expected to grow spiritually while she is enclosed, and the image of the cell as the womb of Christ emphasizes that expectation in a way that also brings to mind the birth of Jesus himself from the womb of the Virgin. The recluse is also urged to enter, in contemplation, the wombs of Virgin Mary and her cousin Elizabeth. The recluse must 'falle dovn to euereither feet and in the maydens wombe wurshipe thy lorde and thyn husbonde and in the wombe of the tother beholde louely thy frende'.[23] This injunction blends veneration of Mary with the womb imagery that is complicit with devotion to enclosure within the Wounded Side.

Blood also connects womb imagery to the devotion of the Wounded Side and Sacred Heart and provides a clear example of a mutuality between the Wounded Side, vagina and female enclosure: the blood which drips from the Wounded Side is, of course, an evocation of the vagina and menstrual blood. Voaden argues that 'medieval illustrations of the Sacred Heart resemble nothing so much as a vagina'.[24] She concludes that the Wounded Side 'resembles (the vagina) in function in that it allows for entrance into the body'.[25] A female anchorite would therefore 'find a flow of blood much less threatening than [her] male contemporaries; images of blood and flowing would excite quite a different resonance'.[26] Elizabeth Robertson states: 'a woman associates her vagina with Christ's wounds. The association allows her access to a distinctively feminine voice unavailable to men; the lips of her vagina, Christ's wounds and her mouth are all linked symbolically.'[27] We see a potential link then, for the recluse, between the flow of blood from Christ's wounds and the symbolic representation of the anchorhold as a spiritual womb. We see also a further link between the penetrative image of the recluse entering the wombs of Mary and Elizabeth and the image of the anchorite entering the side of Christ, the latter an overwhelmingly sexualized and feminized construction of the soul entering into a mystical union. Caroline Walker Bynum argues that 'increasing steadily from the twelfth century on, we find female erotic and sexual experience used to describe the soul's union with Christ'.[28] The feminization of Christ's wounds and blood, then, gives women a spiritual insight that is uniquely matched to the female experience.

The use of such feminized imagery in medieval theological treatises was not exclusive to the Middle English *de Institutione Inclusarum*. One of the most well-known female anchorites, and a near-contemporary to Aelred's redactor, Julian of Norwich, employs similar imagery and discussion in the Long Text of her work, *A Revelation of Love*.[29] Here, Julian employs an explicitly feminine image of Christ, which is built upon and expanded throughout her text. As Liz Herbert McAvoy has shown, Julian conflates 'feminine spiritual insight and intimations of eroticized mystical union [which] serves also to create a female baseline . . . which asserts the mystical experience as one to which women are not only particularly empathetic, but also one to which they are especially subject'.[30] In a similar manner to the redactor of *de Institutione Inclusarum*, Julian locates a portion of her spiritual insights within the feminized imagery of the Sacred Heart, at one point depicting Christ as inviting her to creep into his wounded side: 'Than with a glad chere our Lord loked into His syde and beheld, enjoyand; and with His swete lokyng He led forth the understondyng of His creture be the same wound into Hys syde withinne.'[31]

As we have seen, the injunction to 'crepe into that blessed side' reflects much that is current about contemporary female anchoritic devotion. The physical enclosure of the anchorite within her cell, as a metaphor for the Wounded Side itself, prepares her for meditation on the sanctuary that can be found within the divine wound. The garden, a metaphor for feminine chastity and piety and often linked with the Virgin Mary, blends womb imagery and devotion to enclosure within the Wounded Side, giving the anchorite an image to which she can biologically relate. Enclosure within the heart of Christ continues this biological association, with its allusions to female menstruation and sexual penetration, establishing mutuality between the Wounded Side and female enclosure. When taken together, all these images delineate a structure of feminine piety which allows the anchorite to feel as though she has truly crept into that blessed side.

Notes

1 For the Latin text of Aelred's original guide see *de Institutione Inclusarum*, in *Aelredi Rievallensis Opera Omnia: 1 Opera Ascetica*, ed. A. Hoste and C. H. Talbot (Turnhout, 1971), p. 638. A corresponding translation of this original version of *de Institutione Inclusarum* is found as 'A Rule of Life for a Recluse', trans. Mary Paul Macpherson, in *Aelred of Rievaulx: Treatises, The Pastoral Prayer*, intro. David Knowles (Kalamazoo, 1971). All quotation in this essay is from the late-medieval English redaction of Aelred's guide extant in MS Bodley 423. See *Aelred of Rievaulx's de Institutione Inclusarum: Two English Versions*, ed. John Ayto and Alexandra Barratt, EETS o.s. 287 (Oxford, 1984), here at p. 22.

2 Ann K. Warren, *Anchorites and their Patrons in Medieval England* (Berkeley, 1985), p. 20.

3 Roberta Gilchrist, *Gender and Material Culture: The Archaeology of Religious Women* (London, 1994), p. 153.

4 Rosalynn Voaden, 'All girls together: community, gender and vision at Helfta', in Diane Watt (ed.), *Medieval Women in their Communities* (Cardiff, 1997), pp. 72–91. See especially p. 74.

5 See Caroline Walker Bynum, *Jesus as Mother: Studies in the Spirituality of the High Middle Ages* (Berkeley, 1982), p. 248, and Warren, *Anchorites and their Patrons*, p. 20.

6 See Ann Clark Bartlett, *Male Authors, Female Readers: Representation and Subjectivity in Middle English Devotional Literature* (Ithaca, 1995), p. 53.

7 See John 7: 38 and Song of Songs 2:14.

8 Song of Songs 1: 13–14. See Mary Jeremy Finnegan, O.P., *The Women of Helfta: Scholars and Mystics* (Athens, GA, 1991), p. 132.

9 Excerpt taken from Bernard of Clairvaux, 'Sermon 61', in Kilian Walsh and Irene M. Edmonds (eds and trans.), *On the Song of Songs III: Bernard of Clairvaux* (Kalamazoo, 1979), pp. 144–5.

[10] Bartlett, *Male Authors, Female Readers*, p. 37.

[11] *de Institutione*, p. 1.

[12] Elizabeth Robertson, *Early English Devotional Prose and the Female Audience* (Knoxville, 1990), p. 29.

[13] *de Institutione*, p. 15.

[14] Ibid., p. 6 (my emphasis).

[15] Mary L. Dutton, 'Christ our Mother: Aelred's iconography for contemplative union', in E. Rozanne Elder (ed.), *Goad and Nail: Studies in Medieval Cistercian History*, 10 (Kalamazoo, 1985), pp. 21–45.

[16] *de Institutione*, p. 14.

[17] Ibid., p. 14.

[18] Susanna Greer Fein, 'Maternity in Aelred of Rievaulx's letter to his sister', in John Carmi Parsons and Bonnie Wheeler (eds), *Medieval Mothering* (New York, 1996), pp. 139–56. See especially p. 147.

[19] Fein, 'Maternity in Aelred of Rievaulx's letter', p. 139.

[20] *de Institutione*, p. 18.

[21] Roberta Gilchrist, *Gender and Archaeology: Contesting the Past* (London, 1999), p. 139, citing Henri de Mondeville's *Chirurgie*, of 1306–20.

[22] Fein, 'Maternity in Aelred of Rievaulx's letter', p. 144.

[23] *de Institutione*, p. 18.

[24] Voaden, 'All girls together', p. 74. See also Gilchrist, *Gender and Material Culture*, p. 154, fig. 60.

[25] Voaden, 'All girls together', p. 85.

[26] Ibid., p. 85.

[27] Elizabeth Robertson, 'The rule of the body: the feminine spirituality of the *Ancrene Wisse*', in Sheila Fisher and Janet E. Halley (eds), *Seeking the Woman in Late Medieval and Renaissance Writings: Essays in Feminist Contextual Criticism* (Knoxville, 1989), pp. 109–34.

[28] Bynum, *Jesus as Mother*, p. 138.

[29] Julian of Norwich, *The Shewings of Julian of Norwich*, ed. Georgia Ronan Crampton (Kalamazoo, 1994).

[30] Liz Herbert McAvoy, 'Julian of Norwich and a trinity of the feminine', *Mystics Quarterly*, 28 (2002), 68–77.

[31] Julian of Norwich, *Shewings*, p. 69.

8

Gladly Alone, Gladly Silent: Isolation and Exile in the Anchoritic Mystical Experience

SUSANNAH MARY CHEWNING

Enclosure, as the subject of this collection, also comprises a suitable focus for an examination of the female mystical experience during the Middle Ages and its own incorporation of notions of both isolation and exile. This is particularly true in the case of what I consider to be the generically *feminine* mysticism,[1] which we find primarily in the *Wohunge Group* of anchoritic texts.[2] As I shall demonstrate, the texts included in this group can offer an insight into how the female anchorite as mystic may well have regarded her own particular form of isolation and exile.

It is, however, important initially to differentiate between the mystic and the anchorite, terms which can sometimes be confused. As we have seen, the female anchorite is ideally a woman who has chosen the solitary life and lives in an anchorhold in relative isolation from her community, seeing chiefly only her servants and her confessor. In England, however, the image of the mystic and that of the anchorite are closely connected, primarily because of an increased familiarity with the writing of Julian of Norwich (who was herself both anchorite and mystic) and her mystical treatise, *A Revelation of Love*. Although many anchorites and hermits did experience mystical encounters on a variety of levels, nevertheless the anchoritic lifestyle does not presuppose a mystical experience or even a pursuit of it.[3] As Robert Hasenfratz has argued, the highly popular anchoritic guide known as *Ancrene Wisse* is not in itself a mystical text, although it is often seen as deriving from a premise of mysticism. Indeed, according to Hasenfratz it encourages its readers 'to approach the spiritual life not through . . . meditative exercises, but through a relentlessly allegorical and exegetical way of reading'.[4] The anchoritic community, as posited by Nicholas Watson, however, seems to have been one which lent itself well to a mystical language and spirituality which includes notions of isolation and exile, as we shall see.[5] The main focus of this chapter is the anonymous thirteenth-century treatise entitled *Þe Wohunge of Ure Lauerd*,[6] a text specifically written for an anchoritic audience, and which does describe a mystical experience, here we find the two traditions of anchoritism and mysticism clearly coinciding within the context of the relative isolation of the anchorhold. Although, as previously stated, the anchorite and the mystic are not necessarily one and the same, nor did physical isolation exist for all mystics, in this chapter I will argue that the mystic does exist, paradoxically, in a type of *figurative* exile even from within a community; alone, though not solitary, by means of her extraordinary experience of God she is separated spiritually and emotionally from those people with whom she may have physical contact. So, too, the anchorite embodies this same kind of paradox because of the relative physical and social isolation which she experiences, often within a larger urban setting.

I shall begin my study, however, not with an anchorite, but with a beguine, Mechtild of Magdeburg, whose own writing identifies this notion of solitude within the mystical experience. In her work, *The Flowing Light of the Godhead*,[7] Mechtild continually humbles herself in the face of God. Writing of the possibility of achieving perfection on seven levels, she is 'gladly scorned, gladly mocked, gladly alone, gladly silent, gladly lowly, gladly elevated, gladly ordinary' (2: 12).[8] In a sense, Mechtild's depiction of her own humility here serves to define the nature of medieval mysticism – at least as far as it can be defined – as being a specifically 'feminine' experience: the mystic gladly, cheerfully, joyfully submits herself to the power of the Divinity through mystical, transcendent union.

In the various dictionary definitions of the word *glad*, one finds that it means 'cheerful, joyous, or merry in disposition'; 'made happy or joyful, delighted or pleased with'; or 'grateful'; 'very willing'; 'expressive of, or caused by happiness and joy'; 'full of brightness and cheerfulness'. The meaning of particular interest within the context of my argument, however, is that of 'filled with, marked by, or expressive of joy or delight'.[9] It is this combination of humility and joy, *jouissance*,[10] if you will, that marks the mystic as unique in her own time and in ours. She is one who delights in and is made glad by her own abjection and humiliation – not simply her humility. She is made low by her devotion and commitment to God. And in their union she is raised up – but not *out* of her humility; rather, she is raised to a higher level of sanctity *because* of it.

In her essay, 'La Mystérique', Luce Irigaray discusses the position of the mystic/hysteric as marginalized within and transgressive of patriarchal, phallogocentric culture. She also identifies the mystic as isolated from that same culture in her desire for a union with God, as well as in the manner in which she expresses that desire. She is made low, gladly, like Mechtild, pursuing her own abjection and submitting her will to the power of God:

[I]f in the sight of the nails and the spear piercing the body of the Son I drink in a joy that no word can express, let no one conclude hastily that I take pleasure in his sufferings. But if the Word was made flesh in this way, and to this extent, it can only have been to make me [become] God in my *jouissance*, which can at last be recognized.[11]

This description of mystical *jouissance* parallels the texts of the *Wohunge Group* very closely. In *Þe Wohunge of Ure Lauerd* the speaker is meditating on the Crucifixion and, in spite of its grisly representation, she 'joys' in its violence:

> A þat
> luuelike bodi þat henges swa rewli
> swa blodi & swa kalde . A hu schal
> I nu liue for nu deies mi lef fo
> me up o þe deore rode? Henges
> dun his heaued & sendes his saw-
> le . Bote ne þinche ham nawt ȝet
> þat he is ful pinet . ne þat rewfule dea-
> de bodi nulen ha nawt friðie.
> Bringen forð longis wið þat bra-
> de scharpe spere . he þurles his side
> cleues tat hert . cumes flo-
> winde ut of þat wide winde . þe
> þlod þat bohte . þe water þat te world
> wech of sake & sunne . A swe
> te iesu þu oppnes me þin herte
> for to cnawe witerliche & in to re-
> den trewe luue lettres . for þer
> i mai openlich seo hu muchel
> þu me luuedes. (ll. 535–54)

(Ah! That lovely body, that hangs so pitifully, so bloody, and so cold. Ah!
How shall I live now? For now my love dies for me on the dear cross. He
hangs down his head and sends out his soul. But it does not yet seem to
them that he has been tortured enough, nor will they leave that pitiful dead
body in peace. They bring forth Longinus, with that broad, sharp spear. He
pierces his side, cleaves that heart. And out of that wide wound comes flowing the blood that bought, the water that washed the world of strife and sin.
Ah! Sweet Jesus, you open your heart to me, so that I may know it inwardly,
and read inside it true love-letters; for there I may see openly how much
you loved me.)[12]

All of the elements of *la mystérique* are present in this passage, in which
the speaker reaches out while Christ is pierced by the spear and reads
(literally, as a love letter) his blood and sacrifice as the embodiment of
the Word made flesh. Again, in *On Lofsong of Ure Lefdi*, the narrator,
similar, though not provably identical to that of the *Wohunge*, beseeches
Mary to intercede for her and save her: 'for ich am / þine wurðe . bi sech
for me þine seli sune . / Milce . & merci . & ore' (ll. 36–8) (for me,
beseech your blessed son for mercy, and compassion, and grace).[13] She
then explains how Christ's suffering has redeemed her by means of his
suffering:

> . . . bi al þat he seide wrohte & þolede
> in eorðe . bi þe holi sacrement of his flech &
> of his blod þat ðe preost sacreð . þuruh þe grace of
> fuluht . þuruh alle þe oðre sacramenz. (ll. 45–9)

(. . . by all that he said, did and suffered on earth by the holy sacrament of
his flesh and his blood which the priest consecrates through the grace of
baptism through all the other sacraments.)[14]

Thus, she celebrates through the sacraments that Christ's death has
brought her eternal life: she is made whole through his suffering.

As soon as the mystic begins a dialogue with God in this way, she
begins to relinquish her own subjectivity as she moves towards what
Mari Hughes-Edwards, in her own treatment of the experience, terms
'fusion', that is to say, the moment of union and transcendence.
Similarly, Julia Kristeva has argued for a similar loss (or absence) of
female subjectivity under patriarchy.[15] Kristeva writes: 'a woman cannot "be": it is something which does not even belong in the order of

being . . . [I]n "woman", I see something that cannot be represented, something that is not said.'[16] In similar manner, the mystic, who is rarely fully integrated into mainstream religious orthodoxy and whose experience cannot be clearly represented or articulated, is feminized or is, to some extent, always already feminine. Kristeva's semiotics thus prove useful to illuminate the notion of the feminine mystic in her explanation of the Real[17] and its connection to the otherness of mystical desire.

The primary access-point to the subjectivity of the mystic, however, is through what Kristeva has termed 'the abject'. Kristeva's study of abjection constitutes an examination of the place of the abject in western culture.[18] At the centre of abjection is a human self-consciousness of the decay of living bodies, as seen in waste, blood and death. Preservation of the body becomes crucial in what has been described by Judith Butler as a western cultural fear of the abject, due to its association with otherness.[19] Kristeva writes:

> If dung signifies the other side of the border, the place where I am not and which permits me to be, the corpse, the most sickening of wastes, is a border that has encroached upon everything. It is no longer I who expel, 'I' is expelled. The border has become an object . . . The corpse, seen without God and outside of science, is the utmost of abjection. It is death infecting life. Abject.[20]

Much medieval mystical writing focuses on the sensual nature of bodily function. In this context, I would concur with Nicholas Watson who recognizes here a 'constancy of suffering, this positive activity of the manufacture of joy out of pain'.[21] In many readings of these mystical works, however, attention is drawn mainly to the erotic elements and the reader is distracted from the *other* sensuality that is present in mysticism – obsession with the body, with a focus on blood, sweat, lactation and menstruation, and the glorification of these functions in the dying body of Christ. In Þe Wohunge of Ure Lauerde, for example, the speaker exclaims:

> A iesu hwa mihte mare ðo-
> len cristen oder headen. Ðen
> mon him for schendlac i ðe
> beard spitted. And tu iði wele-
> fulle wlitc. i ðat lufsome leor
> swuche schome þoledes. (ll. 391–6)

(Ah, Jesus, who could be more humiliated, Christian or heathen, than by someone spitting in his beard as an insult? And you suffered this humiliation in your beautiful face.)[22]

Thus the author of the *Wohunge* recognizes Christ's body and its beauty in abjection as a means of identifying with his loss of subjectivity. This is crucial to the mystic's expression of her own loss of identity, an identity constituted by a phallogocentric culture in much the same way that Christ's identity was constructed by the Word. Here she is 'glad' that Christ has been humiliated; soon she will take his suffering as her own, and make herself, as we have seen, 'gladly scorned, gladly mocked . . . [and] gladly lowly'.

This preoccupation with the abject, however, is not unique to the author of the *Wohunge*. Aelred of Rievaulx, for example, describes the holes in Christ's body and the bloodstained lips of the Christian who wishes to kiss his dying body. In his *Threefold Meditation*, Aelred writes:

> Hasten, linger not, eat the honeycomb with your honey, drink your wine with your milk. The blood is changed into wine to gladden you, the water into milk to nourish you. From the rock streams have flowed for you, wounds have been made in his limbs, holes in the wall of his body, in which, like a dove, you may hide, while you kiss them one by one. Your lips, stained with his blood, will become like a scarlet ribbon and your words sweet.[23]

Aelred compels his reader to joy in the celebration of the blood and violence of the Crucifixion as a means to ultimate transcendence. Thus the blood, death and humiliation of Christ become the means by which the mystic may complete her transcendent journey and ultimately achieve fusion with God.

Another element of the abject in the tradition of mysticism is the notion that, during her experience of transcendence, the mystic wishes not only to identify with the crucified Christ but, like him, to actually *become* abject. Again, this is a further place wherein the mystic can be seen as 'feminized', in that she submits to the love of God in the same way that within a traditionally heterosexual paradigm a woman would submit physically and emotionally to her lover. The process of abjection goes deeper than mere submission, however, as Kristeva has also recognized. In this context, she argues that deeply rooted in all people is the desire for a return to the *chora* – the pre-linguistic, pre-nominal realm of the maternal.[24] For Kristeva, our desire to return to the realm of the *chora* is edged with a fascination and fear of the abject, for our experience of the *chora* takes us back to a time very close to our own conception and thus to a time when we existed, but did not yet exist as a 'self'. Kristeva describes the experience of the abject as 'a time of oblivion and thunder, of veiled infinity and the moment when revelation bursts forth . . . *Jouissance*, in short'.[25] Such oblivion and thunder is also pursued by the mystic, through contemplation and a desire for a fusion with God, which will take her into a realm where her own subjectivity dissolves. She must 'joy' in the presence of a being not only greater than herself but which also obliterates the self. In mystical literature there are a number of examples of the mystic pursuing this state of self-obliteration (which very often takes place during a contemplation and metaphorical re-enactment of the Crucifixion). Here, the mystic either describes herself in negative, humble or corrupt terms, or she describes a deliberate, self-imposed negation of self, made possible through adherence to the *via negativa*.

The first type of response is to be found everywhere in mystical and devotional literature containing ascetic discourses of self-flagellation, starvation and self-imposed exile, etc.[26] Similarly, the discourse of courtly love plays its part in the construction of the abject lover. In the anonymous mystical work, *The Cloud of Unknowing*, for example, the self-defamation of the mystic is expressed in this way: 'For it is þe condicion of a parfite louer, not / only to loue þat þing þat he loueþ more þen himself; bot also in maner / for to hate himself for þat þing þat he louiþ.'[27] In another text from the *Wohunge Group, On Ureison of ure Louerde*, the speaker exclaims:

> wei . wei . þe bitternesse of mine sunnen attri
> is þe lettunge . mine sunnen beoþ wal bi tweone me &
> þe . Mine sunnen werneþ me al þis swotnesse . Mine
> sunnen habbeþ grimliche iwreþed me . & iueed me
> towart te luueliche louerd . & þat is lute wunder . for swa
> ich am wiþ hare hori fenliche ifuled . þat ich ne mai ne ne
> dear cume lufsum god in þin ehsihþe. (11. 73–9)

(Alas! Alas! The bitterness of all my poisonous sins is the barrier. My sins are a wall between me and you. My sins deny me all this sweetness. My sins have cruelly maimed me and made me your enemy, lovely Lord – and no wonder, for I am so filthily stained with their foulness that I cannot, nor do I dare, dear God, come before your eyes.)[28]

Elsewhere in this work the mystic's pursuit of the abject is represented in another way: now the speaker demands to die in her self in order to live in the presence of God:

> Ontend me
> wiþ þe blase . of þi leitinde loue . let me beo ni .
> leofman . & her to loue þe . louie þe louende louerd .
> wa þat ic am swa fremede . wiþ þe . Ah ase þu
> licomliche iwend iwend me from þe worlde . wend
> me & heorte liche . & turnme allunge to þe. (ll. 14–20)

(Kindle me with the blaze of your fiery love. Let me be your lover, and teach me to love you, living Lord. Woe is me that I am so estranged from you! But as you have turned me wholly away from the world in my body, turn me also in my heart, and turn me altogether to you.)[29]

Here the speaker wishes to be burned away by the desire of God, to be made whole through the abandonment of her body and her self, so that her identity can be made one with that of the divine Other.

For the mystic, then, her metaphorical exile is threefold. First, it is experienced in her identification with and pleasure in the fallen and dying body of Christ and, therefore, in a similar pleasure in contemplating her own death and decay. Second, she seeks to become abject and thus worthy of union with Christ, ritually humiliating herself either through actual violence to her body (starvation, flagellation) or through a textual, rhetorical self-portrait of a debased, fallen, sinful being. Third, the mystic must, if she follows the *via negativa*, destroy any awareness of her own being in order to joy in the ecstasy of divine union.

In the *Wohunge Group*, all three of these forms of abjection are identified by the speaker. She humbles herself, glories in the sensual nature of the Crucifixion and takes part in a denial of her own subjectivity in her attempt to give language to her liminal and non-linguistic experience of transcendence. The speaker of *Þe God Urieson of God Almihti* states:

> aliht min þeostri heorte .
> ȝif mi bur brithnesse . & brihtte mine soule
> þet is suti . & make hire wurðe to þine swete
> wununge. (ll. 15–18)

(lighten my shadowy heart. Give my chamber brightness, and brighten my soul, which is dirty, and make her worthy to be your sweet dwelling.)[30]

Abjection takes the mystic to God, and it is to the language of abjection that the mystic then turns to describe how the union took place. Through her abjection, then, the mystic is truly, as Mechtild puts it, 'gladly scorned, gladly mocked, gladly alone, gladly silent, gladly lowly, gladly elevated, gladly ordinary'. She takes pleasure and satisfaction in her lowliness in the presence of God and, as a result, she is completely isolated from her own culture, as a woman, as a Christian, as a writer.

This type of cultural isolation is something which has been recognized by Elaine Tuttle Hansen, in her book *Chaucer and the Fictions of Gender*.[31] Here Hansen identifies the 'woman inside' as the culturally determined woman who fills one of the limited roles that are available to her. For Hansen, the feminine ideal as she appears in medieval literature is the courtly mistress, Chaucer's Criseyde for example, who is simultaneously read as a virgin, a mistress and a whore. Each type of 'woman inside' is celebrated and accepted for her value to masculine society. The 'woman outside', however, represents those feminine characteristics which are feared by masculine society, primarily those which will not conform to masculine metaphors of power and which are not understood and, therefore, not given a voice or a subjectivity within mainstream literary tradition. For Hansen, these two types of women (inside and outside courtly romance, same and other) represent the two categories of the feminine. Ultimately, all medieval women are both inside and outside. The masculine culture of the Middle Ages, however, does not engage itself with the woman outside because she represents its fear of disempowerment, castration and death. She is the unknown, unspeakable feminine and is manifested in medieval literature as the silent woman, the prophetess, the sorceress, the monster, the wild woman; in short, she is the cultural embodiment of the abject.

In this sense, therefore, the medieval mystic is also the 'woman outside', having been de-centred and socially marginalized, whether in the cloister, the anchorhold or the town, and being therefore less threatening to masculine power. This claim is obvious, and has been made before, but what may not be so obvious is the relationship between this notion of the female anchorite as woman 'outside' and her further isolation if she is also a mystic. As we have already seen, the anchoritic mystic exists outside tradition in several ways. She is feminine in a masculine institution (the Church); she goes against, or at least exists outside, traditional theological language, rhetoric and metaphors; she lives cloistered and relatively cut off from the rest of society and its temptations *and* away from the influences of traditional religious life (that is, the male orders). Thus she is quite literally 'outside', and, although she is enclosed and kept physically inside, she embodies many of the fears and insecurities held by traditional patriarchal, masculine society. The question which remains, therefore, is whether the type of exile experienced – indeed, passionately pursued – by the mystic, is an effort to isolate (and therefore protect) herself from the world, or to protect the world from her. Was she trying to shut herself away from the world, or to shut the world away from her own private encounter with God? If we read such works as *Ancrene Wisse* and the texts associated with the *Wohunge Group*, which everywhere insist on the dangerous and destructive nature of woman, then perhaps the female anchorite (who was, in many cases, also the mystic) was trying to protect the larger male-dominated world from what she had been conditioned to perceive as her own destructive femininity, whilst simultaneously affording herself some sense of empowerment by means of her own uniqueness, both within and without that community. After all, the world still continued to pose a number of threats to enclosed women and mystics: ecclesiastical interference, sexual danger and cultural eclipse amongst them. The act of enclosure, then, for female anchorite or mystic or both, may well have served to lock the world out, to make the world go away, leaving her most certainly gladly alone in her isolation and pursuit of spiritual transcendence.

Notes

[1] It is my contention that the cultural isolation and relinquishment of self associated with the act of mystical transcendence bring about a type of feminization of the mystic who, whether biologically male or female, nevertheless speaks from the position of the female. As a result, the entire 'genre' of mystical writing can arguably be read as feminized. For a more detailed account of this process, see my essay, 'Mysticism and the anchoritic community: "a

time . . . of veiled infinity" ', in Diane Watt (ed.), *Medieval Women in their Communities* (Cardiff, 1997), pp. 116–37.

2 There are two groups associated with English mysticism in the twelfth and thirteenth centuries, the *Wohunge Group* and the *Katherine Group*. The *Katherine Group* consists of the lives of Saint Katherine, Saint Margaret and Saint Juliana, *Sawles Warde, Hali Meiðhad* and, in some depictions, *Þe Wohunge of Ure Lauerd*, although most scholars now consider *Þe Wohunge* to be part of its own separate group. The texts that make up the *Wohunge* group include *On Uriesun of Ure Louerd, On Wel Swuðe God Urieson of God Almihti, On Lofsong of Ure Louerde* (sometimes titled *A devout praier to or Savior*), *On Lofsong of Ure Lefdi, Þe Oreisun of Seinte Marie and Þe Wohunge of Ure Lauerd*. For a more extensive discussion of these manuscripts, see *Þe Wohunge of Ure Lauerd*, ed. W. M. Thompson, EETS o.s. 241 (London, 1958). All references to the *Wohunge Group* texts will be taken from this edition. Translations of the Middle English, unless otherwise indicated, will be taken from Ann Savage and Nicholas Watson (trans. and eds), *Anchoritic Spirituality: Ancrene Wisse and Associated Works* (New York, 1991). Savage and Watson also offer an extended discussion of these texts in their introduction, as does Robert Hasenfratz in the introduction to his edition of *Ancrene Wisse: Ancrene Wisse*, ed. and trans. Robert Hasenfratz, TEAMS (Kalamazoo, 2000).

3 Mystical encounters seem also to have been experienced by women who were beguines or nuns, as well as by monks and male hermits. Thus mysticism does not seem to be restricted to any one type of lifestyle or profession, nor does it presuppose enclosure or isolation, although it seems often to be engendered by solitary experiences.

4 Hasenfratz, *Ancrene Wisse*, p. 43.

5 Nicholas Watson, 'The methods and objectives of thirteenth-century anchoritic devotion', in Marion Glasscoe (ed.), *The Medieval Mystical Tradition in England*, Exeter Symposium IV (Cambridge, 1987), pp. 132–53 (p. 144).

6 The edition used here is that of Thompson, *Wohunge*, as cited in n. 2 above. Unless otherwise indicated, the translations are taken from Savage and Watson, *Anchoritic Spirituality*, also cited above.

7 The translation used here is *Mechtild von Magdeburg: The Flowing Light of the Divinity*, ed. Susan L. Clark, trans. Christiane Mesh Galvanti, Garland Library of Medieval Literature, vol. 72, series B (New York, 1991).

8 The Middle High German text reads: 'Gerne ungeeret, gerne ungevoerhtet, gerne alleine, gerne stille, gerne nider, gerne hoch, gerne gemeine', for which see Hans Neumann Münchener (ed.), 'Das fließende Licht der Gottheit. Nach der Einsiedler Handschrift in kritischem Vergleich mit der gesamten Überlieferung', in *Texte und Untersuchungen zur deutschen Literatur des Mittelalters*, 100, 101 (Munich, 1990), 2: 12. Here (book 2, line 12), Mechtild uses the word *gerne*, which is translated by Galvanti as 'glad'. The MED definition of *glad* (also *gladde*) includes 'of will, feeling, disposition, expression, mien, etc.: joyful, cheerful, pleasant'.

[9]   OED, 'glad', definition (a).

[10] For a useful definition of the term see Robert J. Belton, 'The usual English translation [of *jouissance*], "enjoyment", does not carry the sexually orgasmic connotation that the French does in addition to the idea of taking pleasure in something. In Lacanian circles, *jouissance* is distinguished from pleasure (*plaisir*) in that the latter indicates simply the search for psychic balance (homeostasis) through the release of tension, whereas the former is supposed to be a perpetual state in violation of the pleasure principle . . . [Kristeva] offers a slight development and a bit of wordplay: she uses *plaisir* for sexual pleasure and *jouissance* (or *j'ouïs sens*, "I heard meaning") as total joy due to the presence of meaning.' Robert J. Belton, 'Words of art: *Jouissance*', Okanagan University College website (29 May 2003) <*http://www.arts.ouc.bc.ca/fina/glossary/j-list.html*>

[11] Luce Irigaray, 'La Mystérique', in *Speculum of the Other Woman*, trans. Gillian C. Gill (New York, 1985), p. 200.

[12] *Wohunge*, pp. 34–5; Savage and Watson, p. 255.

[13] *Wohunge*, p. 17; Savage and Watson, p. 329.

[14] *Wohunge*, pp. 66–9; Savage and Watson, p. 330.

[15] For a more detailed explanation of the relationship between Kristeva's sense of the abject and medieval anchoritic mysticism, see my article, 'Mysticism and the anchoritic community', pp. 116–37.

[16] Julia Kristeva, 'Woman can never be defined' ('La femme, ce n'est jamais ça'), trans. Marilyn August, *Tel Quel*, 59 (1974), repr. in Elaine Marks and Isabelle de Courtivron (eds), *New French Feminisms* (New York, 1980), pp. 137–41 (p. 137).

[17] For Kristeva, it can only be the speaking subject that pursues the 'true real', and Christian mysticism has been one way in which a feminine voice can be expressed, allowing the feminine to become a speaking subject in its pursuit of the *vréel*, the immanent union of the mystic with the love of God.

[18] Julia Kristeva, *The Powers of Horror: An Essay in Abjection* (New York, 1982).

[19] See Judith Butler, *Gender Trouble: Feminism and the Subversion of Identity* (London, 1990), pp. 133–4.

[20] Kristeva, *Powers of Horror*, p. 3.

[21] Watson, 'Methods and objectives', p. 144.

[22] *Wohunge*, pp. 30–1; Savage and Watson, p. 253.

[23] Aelred of Rievaulx, 'A Rule of Life for a Recluse', trans. Mary Paul Macpherson in *Aelred of Rievaulx: Treatises: The Pastoral Prayer* (Spencer, MA, 1971), pp. 90–1.

[24] This desire to return to the *chora* is reflected in the mystic's desire for access to the maternal which forms a common motif in anchoritic literature. For an examination of this concept see Liz Herbert McAvoy, ' "Ant nes he him seolf reclus i maries wombe": Julian of Norwich, the anchorhold and redemption of the monstrous female body', in Liz Herbert McAvoy and Teresa Walters (eds), *Consuming Narratives: Gender and Monstrous Appetites in the Middle Ages and Renaissance* (Cardiff, 2002), pp. 128–43.

[25] Kristeva, *Powers of Horror*, p. 9.

[26] For book-length discussions of the self-destruction of the body as part of the self-destruction of the subject, see Rudolph Bell's *Holy Anorexia* (Chicago, 1985) and Carolyn Walker Bynum's *Holy Feast and Holy Fast: The Religious Significance of Food to Medieval Women* (Berkeley, Los Angeles and London, 1987).

[27] *The Cloud of Unknowing and Related Treatises*, ed. Phyllis Hodgson (Salzburg, 1982), p. 45.

[28] *On Ureison* in *Wohunge*, p. 1; Savage and Watson, p. 323.

[29] *On Ureison* in *Wohunge*, p. 3; Savage and Watson, p. 322.

[30] *God Urieson* in *Wohunge*, p. 5; Savage and Watson, p. 322.

[31] Elaine Tuttle Hansen, *Chaucer and the Fictions of Gender* (Berkeley, 1992).

9

Dionysius of Ryckel: Masculinity and Historical Memory

ULRIKE WIETHAUS

It is the quiet shore of contemplation that I set aside for myself, as I lay bare, under the cunning, orderly surface of civilizations, the nurturing horror that they attend to pushing aside by purifying, systematizing, and thinking.

Julia Kristeva, *Powers of Horror*[1]

Introduction: As the Rivers of a Continent . . .

Denys of Ryckel, born in either 1402 or 1403, studied in Cologne and spent the rest of his life in the Carthusian hermitage at Roermond, named Bethlehem Mariae. He left his hermitage, in ruins today, on only two occasions in almost fifty years. Denys experienced frequent ecstasies, visions and revelations, and became known as the *doctor ecstaticus* of the Carthusian Order.[2] He died in 1471, leaving behind a copious body of writing and coveted corporal relics. His studies, combining Neoplatonic and Thomistic schemata, covered mystical subjects such as contemplation, prayer and meditation. Several decades after his death, his literary output was edited and printed by the Cologne Carthusians, an intellectual group intensely occupied with disseminating mystical texts and traditions. Through these editorial efforts, Denys became so widely known and respected that the Bollandists bestowed upon him the epithet, 'Qui Dionysium legit, nihil non legit' (He who reads Dionysius, there is nothing he does not read).[3]

In subsequent centuries, his reputation suffered from the ebb and flow of scholarly and ecclesiastical interests in mysticism generally, his writings experiencing a revival at the end of the nineteenth century. Denys of Ryckel's life and work constitute a particularly poignant case-study of late-medieval religious masculinity. Enclosed in his cell for almost half a century, with the enclosure syncopated by ecstasies and long periods of reading and writing, Denys became remembered in unusually effusive and rhapsodic discourse by prominent male scholars. In comparing scholarly judgements of Denys's significance as a Carthusian author with marginalized – if not, at times, obliterated – biographical and historical evidence, the instability at the core of historical definitions of his masculinity becomes evident. In the following pages, therefore, I will bring to centre-stage surviving stories told of Denys's corporeality, both as body and as corpse, always tied to a particular place, Roermond, and set in stark contrast to the abstractness of much of his own writing and of subsequent scholarly evocations of his masculinity.

My chapter, which I see as a prolegomenon to reading Denys's oeuvre, follows Julia Kristeva's theory of the dynamics of abjection in the creation of selfhood. Indeed, the quotation from her study cited above encapsulates the gist of my claim that well-accepted assessments by male scholars have simplified the unsettling historical context and meaning of Denys's works and have distorted our knowledge of the author himself, particularly of his gender and the nature of his literary productivity. As I shall demonstrate, the key to such simplifications lies in the symbolic use of gender stereotypes by these commentators, which serves ultimately to reduce the complexities of Denys's personhood. In this context, I will argue that, in fact, his corporeality became culturally coded as his 'femininity' – something ignored by traditional scholarly assessments of him. Enclosed and neglected while he was still alive, it proceeded to yield to mutilation and the will of others after death. The writing itself, however, as materiality and intellectual productivity, constitutes his culturally marked 'masculinity'. Both of these gender dimensions coexist in uneasy and shadowy proximity to each other, as split-off parts that signify larger ideological agendas: the 'codes on which rest the sleep of individuals and the breathing spell of societies'[4] – in this case, the masculine code of heroic academic accomplishment, a fantasy of the barely embodied scholar-monk as pinnacle of medieval civilization.

The *locus classicus* for any contemporary reflection on Denys of

Ryckel is possibly Johan Huizinga's *The Waning of the Middle Ages*. Huizinga spares no drama in sketching Denys in the context of late-medieval mysticism, indulging in superlatives whilst assuring us:

> Denys le Chartreux, of Rickel, is the most complete type of religious enthusiast at the end of the Middle Ages. His mental range and many-sided energy are hardly conceivable. To mystic transports, ferocious asceticism, continual visions and revelations he unites immense activity as a theological writer. His works fill forty-five quarto volumes. All medieval divinity meets in him as the rivers of a continent flow together in an estuary.[5]

For Huizinga, Denys as masculine type evokes the forces of nature – as flowing water, as ferociousness, as immensity, with his self conceived as a veritable biotope – many-sided, inclusive, complex beyond description. All of these attributes of his masculinity, however, work only by contrast, as technicolour foreground to a muted background, that is, the background of a great number of late-medieval female mystics who are, by implication, defined as less complete, one-sided, utterly conceivable and describable in their mental range and limited energy, tamed rather than ferocious, with only intermittent visions and barely registered writing activities; they are stagnant, rather than flowing. Predictably enough, the pages following Huizinga's extravagant praise of Denys contain a dismissal of female mystics, the women relegated to the rank of nameless stock-types, such as the 'poor nun', the 'blind woman', woman insane, woman ignorant and logically absurd, and woman hypochondriac. When mentioned by name, the female mystic can be said only to be 'supersensitive' (Saint Colette) or her visions and revelations labelled as too common to be believable (Saint Bridget of Sweden, Saint Catherine of Siena).[6]

Huizinga's piling-on of superlatives to flesh out his image of Denys is astonishing and intimidating simultaneously, and one cannot but suspect some sort of wishful thinking at work. Denys is, without doubt, extraordinary, in that he both wrote theology 'like a man' and experienced ecstasies 'like a woman'; men of comparable achievement in western Christianity during the Middle Ages are, perhaps, only the mystics Richard Rolle (*c.*1300–49) and Henry Suso (*c.*1295–1366).[7] In Huizinga's imagination, however, Denys as type finds himself sandwiched between the too-feminine Suso ('sublime', he nonetheless 'verges . . . on the ridiculous'[8]), and the too-feminine Thomas à Kempis ('no theologian . . . and hardly even a true mystic'[9]), both of whom lack unadulterated idealization due to – what else? – excessive domesticity. Suso is perceived as less masculine because of his 'craving for hallowing every action of daily life',[10] and Thomas, because he 'leads us back to everyday life'.[11]

So why Huizinga's double strategy of employing both extravagance and misogyny to communicate such capaciousness of skill and sensibility? For Huizinga, Denys seems to signify some kind of *happy end* of the mystical Middle Ages: in an oceanic flow of productivity, visions and discipline, medieval religious contradictions become resolved and the story of the individuation of an age completed.[12] All rivers are finally emptied into the sea, made representable and communicable in the figure of one paradigmatic *man*, a hermit nonetheless, in that most highly esteemed and seemingly least compromised monastic order, the Carthusians, known for their incorruptible discipline and their bookishness.[13]

Reading Huizinga's eulogy of Denys's accomplishment, one could hardly imagine a more innocently worded evocation of ideal medieval religious identity, purged of the gender trouble caused by obstreperous women mystics and the unflattering violence of a misogynist clergy. It is, however, also cleansed of other ecclesiastical contexts that determined Christian masculinity in medieval Europe, such as the privileges and abuses of ecclesiastical power, the legacy of anti-Semitism and the bloodshed committed among so-called heretics and infidels. Huizinga writes into being a male embodiment of a narcissistic masculine *coincidentia oppositorum* (coincidence of opposites), absorbing the perceived incompleteness yet nonetheless generative power of female visionaries into the productivity of male theologians, now wishfully constructed as untainted by the machinations of power. If passively endured visions come to characterize the religious feminine, the voluminous performance of writing is chosen as the signifier of medieval religious masculinity: virile and fertile, the (male) flesh begets the (written) word, its fecundity smoothly circumventing the spectre of maternity and problematic sexual desire.[14] In Denys's case, such word-flesh multiplies itself through forty-five quarto volumes or 25,000 pages.[15]

This, then, is the task of a Kristevan notion of 'counter-history' which I embark upon here, allowing to surface what was washed away in Huizinga's enthusiastic panning – to trace the outlines of religious masculinity and religious context in the actual body of Denys, whether transmitted in the telling of biographical stories or, by extension, through the materiality of his writing. With the assistance of these bodily fragments, we must ask whether Denys indeed thought of

himself as a 'most complete type of religious enthusiast'. Let us begin
with his skeletal remains and genealogy.

Re-membering the body: 1572–1898

Huizinga's clear picture of the happy Carthusian hermit carries the
weight of its shadow, earlier stories imagining an embodied masculinity
associated with death, loss and violent regeneration. From text to body:
'Qui Dionysium legit, nihil non legit' has been the widely repeated
motto for the success of having turned Denys's manuscripts into print.
Reading Denys (the *man*, that is, his male body, not quite yet his books
– or are the two fused in some way?), reading *him*, is there then nothing
one ought not to read? Stories, local legends, material traces with which
to hold on to his male body while reading *him* through time, exist in
abundance, his name even having served to preserve a trace of the
existence of a Jewish community in Roermond. In the town's local
telling, Denys's name was preserved within the family of a Jewish
contemporary whom – so the story goes – Denys converted. In his
enthusiasm, the Jewish convert changed his name to Dionysius Dionysii;
the last member of his family died in Roermond on 1 December 1859.[16]

As to Denys's grave, however, we have to contend with a lacuna
between the year of his death in 1472 and the first decade of the seventeenth century. But, on 22 March 1608, the remains of Denys's corpse
were rediscovered behind the chapel of the Virgin in Roermond – or, at
least, the collective wish was that the anonymous grave-pit in the court-
yard contained his skeletal remains. Inscribed on to the perhaps 136-
year-old bones, faint markings of individuality were read as indicators
of an unconflicted identity as a celibate writer, combined with both
saintliness and – surprisingly enough – physical vulnerability.[17] It is said
that the skull still contained protruding front teeth – Denys himself
noted that he stuttered. It is said that the skeleton was long and thick-
boned – Denys remarked on his own physical strength, singling out his
'iron head and brazen stomach'.[18] The skull especially emitted a sweet
smell – a sure sign of his former saintly lifestyle. Finally, the thumb and
the index finger of the right hand still had flesh and skin attached to
them – no doubt a supernatural reminder of his extraordinary literary
productivity.[19] Further miracles at the site seem to confirm the identity
of the bones.[20] Upon discovery, however, the corpse is not left alone:
bits and pieces proceed to attach themselves to other localities and other

stories. As the result of a theft, for example, the skull travelled to Cologne sometime after 1608. It was returned to Roermond over 170 years later, in August of 1785, adding to the reputation of both the corpse and the identity which it represented. As Denys's literary fortunes rose again in the following century, his body continued to carry the burdens of fame, yielding itself to further dismemberment. In 1858, the lower jaw was sent on its way again, now given as a gift to the Grande Chartreuse, the Carthusian mother-house in Grenoble, founded in 1084 by Bruno of Cologne (c. 1030–1101).

When Denys's skeleton was discovered in 1608, bones easier to separate than the skull – in this case, the two shins and fibulae, an upper thigh-bone, all bones of the arms and a shoulder-blade – were put in a box and joined with the more recent remains of sixteenth-century Roermond hermits. The relics' physical proximity now linked up with narrative strands of the hermits' own deaths and lives. The recently dead were all martyrs, killed by Protestant militia in 1572. Was this conjoining of bones meant to comfort and to elevate the status of the newly dead by contact with a celebrated ancestor? Whatever the case, the realm of the feminine – and thus the grotesque – reasserts itself in the gruesome story of their deaths.[21] These monks were ritually slaughtered in an act of mock cannibalism, reminiscent not only of the female-associated task of cooking, but also of the imagined savagery of the peoples of the New World. In their subversion of feminine domesticity, the troops of the Prince of Orange imitated the preparation of meat for a meal: some monks were thrown into boiling water and cooked, others were impaled and roasted over a fire, yet others were killed and their internal organs cut out and offered for mock sales of meat in the public square.[22]

In search of a 'buried logic of our anguish and hatred',[23] of images of abjection, a thematic link between the martyrs' deaths and Denys himself occurs in Denys's own association with foul foodstuffs. Peeling back further layers of memories of Denys's male body, we find his servant, the lay-brother Karl von Herck, providing another exercise in abjection when talking of his master's dietary preferences. Rancid butter, butter teeming with wriggling worms, fruit and vegetables inhabited by slugs, rotten herring may elicit our disgust, but, for Denys, are responded to with a very masculine equanimity. Karl's report of Denys's rationale suggests that, for him, slugs and worms are not poisonous and are therefore good to eat, and rot is preferable to too much salt in a fish.[24] In the stories told about female mystics, drinking pus and swallowing repulsive substances such as scabs become rituals of self-humiliation and compassion;[25] when encoding masculinity, however, the story of alimentary abjection changes its meaning. Now, rationality wins out over sensuality, and eating rot turns into a form of mastery of the domestic. And the story structure repeats itself over time. Just as Denys has ritually 'mastered'[26] his own unruly body through ingesting loathsome food, roughly a hundred years later Protestant soldiers will ritually master Carthusian bodies through turning their bodies into food 'revolting' beyond measure and comparison.

At the end of the nineteenth century, a macabre family romance is spun from these frayed narrative threads of bone, rot and human meat. Publishing his oeuvre in 1898, Denys's biographer, Mougel, invokes Tertullian in pointing to the happy circumstance that turn-of-the-century Roermond now houses a seminary for Catholic priests. Bones and bodies are invoked to create a purely masculine genealogy: 'sanguis martyrum semen levitarum' (The blood of martyrs [is] the seed of priests) – martyrs are the fathers of priests, giving of their bodies to form the bodies of their sons; their blood is their semen.[27] Through his contact with vile food, with the savage violence of Protestant persecution and with death, the bookish and stuttering hermit thus becomes a man, and then a father in good time, bringing forth sons, always eclipsing the visionary m/other – and this in stories told as late as 1898.[28]

Bibliophilia:[29] The ultimate coding of our crises

So, the paradox: 'Qui Dionysium legit, nihil non legit.' By all accounts, Denys produced an extraordinarily voluminous *body of writings*. He is not the only one to have done so among the Carthusians, but he is remembered paradigmatically as the only one.[30] But what precisely *is* being remembered of the man as author? The pithy saying seems to suggest that the sheer volume of his writings – its materiality – promises abundance, completion, the pleasure of reading all there is to be read: 'nihil non legit'. And another oceanic space is here evoked. To read everything is to read the world, to make the world one's own if one submits to such refined scopophilia. Thus, one may again be fully one with the body of the mother, even the body of the father – perhaps devouring him by reading him, as the Protestants wished to eat the Carthusians' bodies in 1608.

In 1898, Mougel hailed Denys's productivity as masculine and rigorously spiritual, as rigid, anything but flaccid. A hundred years later,
however, the contemporary reader's response seems to have become
generally one of frustration, fatigue and disappointment: Denys now
merely repeats, compiles, extracts, summarizes tirelessly. Today, his
abundance is oddly judged to be of an inferior virility: his writing is 'not
a product of original intellectual force',[31] and yet it was precisely the
encyclopedic nature of Denys's writing, rather than any originality, that
so appealed to his Carthusian brethren. Beginning in 1532, the Cologne
Carthusians undertook to print all of Denys's works – this historic
choice is perhaps the main reason why he, and not his other equally productive Carthusian contemporaries, was remembered for extraordinary
literary productivity.[32] As much as the Carthusian Order might have
been celebrated as a conservation of original Christian virtue and time-
lessness of devotion ('soli Deo'), it was simultaneously dramatically
'modern' in its emphasis on learning, education and religious reflection
and instruction.[33] Significantly, however, Denys absorbed this desire for
learning, yet chose to write only in Latin. It is not clear whether he
could not or would not write in German.[34] Although he was concerned
about a simple style, an emphasis in line with the fifteenth-century
impetus of reaching out to the laity and the religiously uneducated,[35] he
still remained within the circle of Latinate religious elites. Through his
repeated choice of Latin, Denys protected his group from cultural contamination and dissolution: 'Qui Dionysium legit, nihil non legit.' The
implicit qualification here, then, is that Denys opened the world of
learning only to those who had the magic key, the password. Writing
Latin, then, is a social code for what type of masculinity? Only those
who know Latin may read everything, may know all, may be the
beloved sons of their fathers. Thus, according to Kristeva:

> On close inspection, all literature is probably a version of the apocalypse
> that seems to me rooted, no matter what its sociohistorical conditions
> might be, on the fragile border (borderline cases) where identities (sub-
> ject/object, etc.) do not exist or only barely so – doubly, fuzzy, heteroge-
> neous, animal, metamorphosed, altered, abject . . . Even literature as such
> represents the ultimate coding of our crises, of our most intimate and most
> serious apocalypses.[36]

Writing, then, is the warding off of a threat to life and limb, of the most
serious apocalypse, a circling of wagons against the attack of the Other,

who exposes the fragility of one's own identity. In the case of fifteenth-century Carthusians, the Other is experienced as an affluent urban laity, semi-educated from a traditional theological point of view and, in any case, dogmatically untrustworthy. The pen is a weapon: as cutting as a sword. At this historical moment where a choice of language was an available option, it cut, shaped and defended religious class boundaries. The enemy? Unpredictably emerging *bodies* of knowledge, walking and talking 'a certain democratization of knowledge, thereby slowly eroding the absolute authority of the clergy in the eyes of the urban semiliterate'.[37] And here we come full circle: the soldiers of the Prince of Orange who turn Carthusians into meat to eat are the latest wave of a larger group, the militant wing of rebellious laypeople who increasingly usurp religious space and privilege through speech and writ in the vernacular. Indeed, 'Martin Luther could rely on a rather well-read and critical urban readership among the urban elites as he began his quest for church reform'.[38]

Modern authorial masculinity, given ritual birth in the Protestant act of killing the Catholic fathers and cast in scholarly discourse as 'creative', 'original' and 'vernacular', would have signified a dangerous act of betrayal for Denys. Imitating the Protestant use of the vernacular as sacred language would have been as good as leaving the order. Having worked so hard to belong, Denys could not leave his homosocial home now.[39] All his Latinate writing, compiling and gathering, then, perhaps constitute an evocation and defence of the fathers against the new generation of murderous sons, who are staging the consumption of their fathers in turn. This is, perhaps, the buried logic of sacred Christian horror: polysemic, the soldiers' massacre of the hermits also plays at preparing the Eucharist.

Counterpoint: Tears and delight

The distortion of a text, according to Freud, 'is not unlike a murder. The difficulty lies not in the execution of the deed but in the doing away with the traces.'[40] Today, as we have seen, several model masculinities compete to claim Denys's identity as a fifteenth-century man, celibate, erudite, productive, contemplative. The characterizations from which we may choose range from virile to androgynous to dull and timid. None of these intensely charged constructs, however, takes much account of Denys's statements about himself. Those fragments of his own authorial subjectivity which do remain disclose contradictions and subtle forms of resistance, as I shall demonstrate; they offer us glimpses of open, rather than closed, movements of a dynamic self. The posthumous models, claiming to represent a 'true' rendering of Denys's self, thus distort the original text of the body and the original body of the text. Indeed, these scholarly interpretations have constituted some kind of murder which, lucky for us, has also been messy enough to leave behind traces of the deed.

Being a Male Child. The boy child, Denys, is poor, pugnacious and spends his time guarding sheep. Denys remembers that he frequently fought with other boys.[41] Fighting over what and why? And why does he tell just this one memory? Why this aggression? Whatever the answer may be, Denys, the child, was not a meek and gentle lamb. His family is respected but not part of an elite. The parents are 'simplices et pauperes, honesti tamen et catholici' (uneducated and poor, yet honest and orthodox).[42] Denys's career is remarkable for its (at least initial) upward trajectory. Was he ever ashamed of his parents? Did others, later on, who came from aristocratic families, look down upon Denys, pass him by in career advancement?

As a beneficiary of the fifteenth-century emphasis on childhood education, Denys manages to attend a Benedictine school in nearby Sint-Truiden. While there, he frequently visits the grave of Christina Mirabilis (d. 1224), who cared for sheep much as he did, learns about her miracles and, so we must assume, prays and communicates with her spirit at her grave. He absorbs details from the life of the stigmatic Elisabeth of Spalbek (d. 1266). His own mystical experiences begin around the time of his schooling, while experiencing separation from home and family, both culturally and geographically. Mystical experiences take the form of 'inner visits and . . . hidden consolations'.[43] Around the age of 10, intense anxieties about the salvation of his soul begin to haunt him, and he decides to resolve the anxieties by becoming a monk. He continues his studies among the Brethren of the Common Life in Zwolle, even further away from home. At the age of 18, he asks to be admitted to the Carthusian Order.[44] His new world and new family, intensely homosocial and disciplinary, at first rejects him. He is too young for the Order, and must go even further away, this time to Cologne, and study. He hates his time at the university.[45] Finally, at the age of 21, he is permitted to enter the Carthusian Order. He is home again.

Being an Old Man. The paradox: although Denys belongs to the educated elites and produces a remarkable literary oeuvre, he does not
advance to higher positions within the Order.[46] After a short stint as
procurator, a task he seems to have failed, he does nothing but write. As
noted above, he leaves his hermitage only twice in fifty years, once
(1451–2) for a six-month-long trip through Germanic countries with
Nicolas of Cusa, and a second time, fifteen years later, to assist in the
creation of a new Carthusian house in nearby Herzogenbusch (1466–9).
Weak and discouraged, he asks to be returned to Roermond. His legs
are covered with open sores and he suffers from kidney- or gall-stones.
He knows he is going to die, and prepares himself properly, wishing not
to be a burden. He stops eating.

For Mougel, the dying body, still alive, recognizes its hard shell. The
cell in which Denys lived and died is his womb and his world, bringing
together other places, gendered both masculine and feminine – the cell
as a battlefield and a school, but also as a female teacher of wisdom, a
joyful paradise, filled with the lilies of chastity and the purple roses of
love.[47] The cell is conceived as womb and less as a tomb; indeed, the cell
is the beginning and end of all masculinity. His cell, a feminine space,
remembered as a small room attached to the church, was destroyed as
late as 1852, sacrificed to a remodelling of the church.

Writing in the womb, in contrast to writing against the open urban
spaces of the Protestant bourgeoisie, Mougel imagines Denys's quill as
his weapon of choice as much as the 'dear female companion of his life'.[48]
Denys himself, however, sees his writing as a defence against carnal sin.[49]
Writing for him would be pointless without sexual arousal; the cell is the
place that evokes the temptations of sexuality (yet of what kind?).

Cutting through all contradictions, temptations, inscriptions of masculinity as violent, loyal, hierarchical, ambitious, and of femininity as a
position of abjection, Denys invents his own definition of masculinity
after all, going back to the boy child he once remembered as pugnacious, who herded sheep together with other boys, and to the adolescent
who experienced mystical bliss at the graves of local female saints.
Forgotten is the first rejection by the Order, the hard times at the university, the labours as procurator, the anxieties about the salvation of
his soul as a young adult. Pre-oedipal bliss, indeed, but the object of
desire here is not the mother. In her stead, we find a group of other
boys. In this paradise, all women should be regarded as mothers, all
adult men as fathers – so Denys has Jesus say to a boy, to *him*.[50] Denys's
own idealized masculinity exists in a fantasy world of boy children,

whom he says Jesus loves with a particular love, a homosocial world imagined to be far away from the fierceness of patriarchy and the inscriptions of sexualized gender. For Denys, a boy child has fifteen amicable characteristics: he loves other boys and he loves to socialize with other boys; boys express compassion for each other, love to play together and make each other happy. They are not unjust toward each other and do not hurt each other. They cry easily. When they fight, they quickly reconcile and do not seek revenge. They have no sexual desire. They do not lie or manipulate. They obey their parents. They fear punishment. They do not judge each other and do not feel contempt for each other. Finally, they develop their skills and talents every day. Theirs is a body of pleasure, without conflict and violence. And, instead of producing texts, they speak, laugh and cry.[51] Together.

Notes

[1] Julia Kristeva, *Powers of Horror: An Essay on Abjection* (New York, 1982), p. 210.

[2] The epithet is taken from J. Bollandus and G. Henschenius, *Acta Sanctorum . . . editio novissima*, Mart. II (Antwerp, 1668), p. 245, as quoted in Martin Beer, *Denys des Kartäusers Lehre vom desiderium naturale des Menschen nach der Gottesschau* (Munich, 1963), p. 21, n. 54. To acknowledge Latinate and Anglicized spelling, I am using both renderings, *Denys* and *Dionysius*.

[3] Quoted by Peter J. A. Nissen, 'Dionysius von Rijkel', in Peter Dinzelbacher (ed.), *Wörterbuch der Mystik* (Stuttgart, 1989), p. 117.

[4] Kristeva, *Powers of Horror*, p. 209.

[5] Johan Huizinga, *The Waning of the Middle Ages* (Garden City, NY, 1954 [1924]), p. 189.

[6] Huizinga uncritically paraphrases Jean Gerson and then employs William James's notion of a theopathic sensibility in describing female mystics and feminized male mystics, such as Suso and Alain de la Roche, in *The Waning of the Middle Ages*, pp. 193–200.

[7] On Henry Suso's use of feminized forms of mysticism, see my recent essay, 'Thieves and carnivals: gender in German Dominican literature of the fourteenth century', in Renate Blumenfeld-Kosinski, Duncan Robertson and Nancy Bradley Warren (eds), *The Vernacular Spirit: Essays on Medieval Religious Literature* (New York, 2002), pp. 209–39.

[8] Huizinga, *Waning of the Middle Ages*, p. 152.

[9] Ibid., p. 225.

[10] Ibid., p. 152.

[11] Ibid., p. 225.

[12] For a psychoanalytically oriented study of the concept of oceanic feeling,

dating back to Freud's reception of a term coined by Romain Rolland, see William B. Parsons, *The Enigma of the Oceanic Feeling. Revisioning the Psychoanalytic Theory of Mysticism* (New York and Oxford, 1999).

[13] On the reputation of the Carthusians and the internal control mechanisms used to keep their reputation intact, see the insightful essays by Heinrich Rüthing, 'Zur Geschichte der Kartäusen in der Ordensprovinz Alemannia inferior von 1320 bis 1400', and ' "Die Wächter Israels" – ein Beitrag zur Geschichte der Visitationen im Kartäuserorden', in Marijan Zadnikar with Adam Wienand (eds), *Die Kartäuser: Der Orden der schweigenden Mönche* (Cologne, 1983), pp. 139–85.

[14] For another example of this dynamic, see Jacqueline Murray's analysis of Peter Abelard's productivity after his castration in 'Mystical castration: some reflections on Peter Abelard, Hugh of Lincoln, and sexual control', in Jacqueline Murray (ed.), *Conflicted Identities and Multiple Masculinities: Men in the Medieval West* (New York and London, 1999), pp. 73–93.

[15] Raymond Macken OFM, *Denys the Carthusian: Commentator on Boethius'* De Consolatione Philosophiae (Salzburg, 1984), p. 13.

[16] D. A. Mougel, *Dionysius der Karthäuser, 1402–1471: Sein Leben, Sein Wirken* (Mühlheim a.d. Ruhr, 1898), p. 59.

[17] Mougel describes the miraculous find, which was preceded by intensive communal prayers asking for divine inspiration: ibid., pp. 82–3.

[18] Ibid., p. 18, n. 1.

[19] Ibid., p. 82.

[20] Ibid., p. 83, n. 3.

[21] Kristeva, *Powers of Horror*, pp. 156–73, describes the double-faced nature of the mother (her body as sign) in the process of becoming a self, soothing and quotidian as much as disgusting and defiling.

[22] These events are recounted in Mougel, *Dionysius*, p. 80.

[23] Kristeva, *Powers of Horror*, p. 210.

[24] Karl's story is recounted in Michael Kaufmann, *Aegidius Romanus' de Colonna, Johannes Gersons, Dionys des Kartäusers und Jakob Sadolets Pädagogische Schriften* (Freiburg im Breisgau, 1904), p. 185. The link between eating and reading was originally drawn by the Carthusian Guigo II (1140–93), discussed in Dirk Wassermann, *Dionysius der Kartäuser: Einführung in Werk und Gedankenwelt* (Salzburg, 1996), p. 31.

[25] For a critical discussion of this issue, see Julie B. Miller, 'Eroticized violence in medieval women's mystical literature: a call for a feminist critique', *Journal of Feminist Studies in Religion*, 15, 2 (1999), 25–50.

[26] Kaufmann, *Aegidius Romanus' de Colonna*, p. 185.

[27] Mougel, *Dionysius*, p. 84.

[28] In 1963, with the threat of an all-too liberal Vatican Council II under way, Dionysius was once more invoked as the heroic fighter against the threat of the same/yet another 'Protestantization'. See Beer, *Denys des Kartäusers Lehre*.

[29] On the notion of 'bibliophilie', see Wassermann, *Dionysius der Kartäuser*, p. 27. Wassermann defines the Carthusian emphasis on books and writing in the fourteenth century as part of an internal effort to reform the Order.

[30] On this, see Hubertus Maria Blum, 'Lexikale Übersicht der Kartäuser Schriftsteller', in Zadnikar with Wienand (eds), *Die Kartäuser*, pp. 345–74.

[31] Nissen, 'Dionysius von Rijkel', p. 117. Nissen quotes Wilhelm Oehl, *Deutsche Mystikerbriefe des Mittelalters* (München und Wien, 1931); writing in 1931, Oehl comments in *Mystikerbriefe* that 'as a theologian, Dionysius is rather a compiler of enormous knowledge than a creative mind' (p. 572). It should be noted, however, that this was precisely what was commonly defined as proof of great intellectual ability in the fifteenth century. See Kent Emery, Jr., 'Dionysii Cartusiensis bibliotheca et manuscripta', in *Kartäusermystik und Mystiker*, ed. James Hogg (Lewiston, 1982), pp. 119–56.

[32] See Wassermann, *Dionysius der Kartäuser*, p. 13. On printing and issues of education, see Heinrich Rüthing, 'Zur Geschichte der Kartäusen', and ' "Die Wächter Israels" ', pp. 139–85. For a cautious note on the 'democratization of knowledge', see Klaus Schreiner, 'Gebildete Analphabeten? Spätmittelalterliche Laienbrüder als Leser und Schreiber wissensvermittelnder und frömmigkeitsbildender Literatur', in Horst Brunner and Norbert Richard Wolf (eds), *Wissensliteratur im Mittelalter und in der Frühen Neuzeit: Bedingungen, Typen, Publikum, Sprache* (Wiesbaden, 1993), pp. 296–328.

[33] See Werner Williams-Krapp, 'The erosion of a monopoly: German religious literature in the fifteenth century', in Blumenfeld-Kosinski, Robertson and Warren (eds), *The Vernacular Spirit*, pp. 239–63, and Wassermann, *Dionysius der Kartäuser*, p. 4, on the demand for contemplative monastic theology.

[34] On the Carthusians and the vernacular, see Wolfram D. Sexauer, *Frühneuhochdeutsche Schriften in Kartäuserbibliotheken. Untersuchungen zur Pflege der volkssprachlichen Literatur in Kartäuserklöstern des oberdeutschen Raums bis zum Einsetzen der Reformation* (Frankfurt/Main, 1978).

[35] Williams-Krapp, 'Erosion', p. 241. The three celebrated Carthusian values were *simplicitas*, *antiquus rigor* and *solitudo* (simplicity, rigour (of first generations of Christian ascetics) and solitude); see discussion by Wassermann, *Dionysius der Kartäuser*, pp. 18–19. Ironically, Carthusian hermitages were usually built in cities, and attracted predominantly members of the urban 'bourgeoisie' – no doubt functioning as a way to bring rebellious sons back into the lap of the Church.

[36] Kristeva, *Powers of Horror*, pp. 207, 208.

[37] Williams-Krapp, 'Erosion', p. 255.

[38] Ibid., p. 255.

[39] Although ultimately homosocial, he nevertheless kept some contact with religious women; at least three of them, all from Nijmegen, are cited in Oehl, *Deutsche Mystikerbriefe des Mittelalters*, p. 588: Mechtild, a pious woman confined to her bed due to extensive ecstatic periods, Christine, a stigmatic, and Katharine, enduring mystical inedia. Regarding the sorry nature of the status of Carthusian nuns, see the essay by James Hogg, 'The Carthusian nuns: a survey of the sources of their history', in James Hogg (ed.), *Die*

Kartäuser und Ihre Welt – Kontakte und Gegenseitige Einflüsse. Analecta Cartusiana, vol. 62 (Salzburg, 1993), pp. 190–294.

[40] Sigmund Freud, *Moses and Monotheism* (New York, 1967 [1939]), p. 2.

[41] 'Ego quoque in pueritia mea, antequam coepi frequentare scholas, custodivi et pavi oves parentum meorum . . . et eram puer valde malus, pugnans frequenter in agro contra alios pueros ovium pastores' (Also in my boyhood, before I began school, I cared and feared for my parents' sheep . . . and I was a very bad young boy, frequently fighting against other shepherd boys in the field), quoted in Mougel, *Dionysius der Karthäuser*, p. 8. Elsewhere, he says that he was almost still a child when he began to go to St Trond, perhaps indicating his sense of vulnerability (p. 10). He was aware of his intellectual gifts from childhood: 'puer eram ingeniosus capacemque mentem mihi elargitus est' (I was an intellectual child and endowed with a capable mind) (p. 10). See also Beer, *Denys des Kartäusers Lehre,* p. 12.

[42] Quoted in Wassermann, *Dionysius der Kartäuser*, p. 7, n. 2.

[43] Macken, *Denys the Carthusian*, pp. 6–7. The most comprehensive, although not the earliest, biography of Denys is by Dietrich Loër von Stratum (1500–54), the Cologne editor of the first printed edition of Denys's works, *Vita beatae memoriae Dionysii Cartusiani,* in J. Bollandus and G. Henschenius, *Acta Sanctorum* (Antwerp, 1668), pp. 245–55. Mougel's rendering is painstakingly based on Loër, but embellished with nineteenth-century Catholic sentiment and politico-religious need.

[44] Wassermann, *Dionysius der Kartäuser*, p. 7.

[45] This was probably not without reason. For a study of male-on-male violence at medieval universities, see Ruth Mazo Karras, 'Separating the men from the goats: masculinity, civilization and identity formation in the medieval university', in Murray, *Conflicted Identities,* pp. 189–215.

[46] This is noted by Wassermann, *Dionysius der Kartäuser*, p. 12.

[47] Quoted in Mougel, *Dionysius der Kartäuser*, p. 56; the images are developments of themes found in Basil the Great's (d. 379) writings.

[48] Ibid., p. 77.

[49] 'Of course, these exclusively mental labours are endowed with much difficulty, exertion, and frustration, but precisely for this reason, they were extremely useful to me. They aided in reining in the senses and in combating evil inclinations, and lastly, they maintained my love for the hermitage'. Quoted in ibid., p. 2. On writing as an ascetical exercise in the Devotio Moderna movement, see Wassermann, *Dionysius der Kartäuser*, p. 43.

[50] Denys's numerous pedagogical writings on masculine identity formation deserve more analysis than given here. All statements about boys referred to in the text above are taken from his treatise, 'On the characteristics of young men'. Regarding mothers and fathers, the full quotation reads: 'Ninth, in the way of children, love all older men like fathers, but love women with a spiritual love like mothers.' Dionysius of Ryckel, 'On the characteristics of young men', in Kaufmann, *Aegidius Romanus' de Colonna,* p. 318.

[51] Ibid., p. 315.

10

'Wrapt as if to the third heaven': Gender and Contemplation in Late Medieval Anchoritic Guidance Writing

MARI HUGHES-EDWARDS

In his second letter to the Corinthians, St Paul writes:

> I know a man in Christ. Above fourteen years ago (whether in the body, I know not, or out of the body, I know not: God knoweth), such a one was caught up to the third heaven. And I know such a man (whether in the body, or out of the body) . . . was caught up into paradise and heard secret words which it is not granted to man to utter. (2 Corinthians 12: 2–4)

Paul refers, in this passage, to himself, possibly to his Damascus road conversion.[1] He concedes that to describe this event adequately is beyond him, because it is beyond the realms of mortal linguistic possibility. As much, then, as he is able to, Paul describes his experience as one which took him so far beyond the temporal world that he cannot subsequently determine whether he was literally taken up or, rather, overwhelmed by a powerful visionary force. The book of Acts tells us that, following his conversion, Paul was for three days deprived of the bodily sense of sight and that he could neither eat nor drink.[2] It is exactly this state of rapturous oblivion to the temporal world to which the late medieval anchoritic guidance writers Richard Rolle, Walter Hilton, the anonymous *Speculum Inclusorum* author and his vernacular translator urge their recluses to aspire. This chapter examines some of the ways in which these writers construct this kind of experience for the male and female anchorites for whom they write, and explores some of the implications of the contemplative practice of fusion for the perpetuation of the anchoritic ideal. There is a subtle but significant difference between the experience of contemplative rapture or fusion, which is beyond the body, beyond language and therefore beyond gender, and the description of it, which is inherently embodied and thereby gendered. This chapter proposes, then, that gender enters the contemplative equation at the point of the *communication* of contemplative experience, and not at the point of the experience itself.

The four guides under consideration here are two fourteenth-century vernacular texts, Rolle's *The Form of Living* and Hilton's *The Scale of Perfection* (Book I), both originally intended for women, the anonymous fourteenth-century Latin guide *Speculum Inclusorum*, written originally for male anchorites, and its fifteenth-century vernacular translation, the *Myrour of Recluses*, which was widened to include a female audience. Their discussion of, and directions about, contemplative experience are based on a threefold system of meditation (the lowest level of contemplative experience), vision (a higher level) and fusion (the highest, and rarest, level). Through fusion the recluse transcends the earthly world, abandoning the senses and, consequently, the flesh. These texts conceive of this highest form of contemplative experience as a fusion or union of the anchorite's spirit or soul with God. It is as rare as it is brief and is gifted by grace, rather than acquired through practice. No guidance writer can lead the recluse to it or even, in keeping with Paul's conclusions, communicate it adequately. The guides suggest that while meditation and vision *can* foster fusion, they do not of necessity culminate in it. Accomplished and experienced meditative or visionary anchorites may never achieve this highest level of contemplative experience.

Contemplative fusion has its precedent in earlier guidance writings for recluses. As with so much else, the contemplative perspectives of the later guides may be traced in embryonic form in high medieval guides, such as *de Institutione Inclusarum* and *Ancrene Wisse*. The influential binary constructed in Ann Warren's *Anchorites and their Patrons in Medieval England*, which proposes the rigid separation of anchoritic guides into a high medieval penitential model and a late medieval contemplative one, does not allow for the considerable similarities between the contemplative spiritualities of these two groups. She writes:

> In marked contrast to this early literature, the works of the second half of the fourteenth century . . . lead the anchorite toward mystical union with God . . . Anchorites in the eleventh, twelfth, and thirteenth centuries were

described as ascetics in their own literature and it was only with the flowering of mysticism in the fourteenth century that this focus changed.[3]

It is clearly the case that high medieval guides deal extensively with asceticism as a preparation for contemplation, while late medieval guides prefer to focus upon the process and rewards of that contemplation. Yet it is by no means clear that medievals understood penitence and contemplation to be as mutually exclusive as Warren constructs them. It is reductive to look only at the differences between these two groups of texts. It may well be as useful to consider the high and later medieval anchoritic guides in terms of their similarities as it is to reiterate their differences.[4] The contemplative material of the later guides is certainly far more developed than that of their high medieval counterparts, but the threefold contemplative system is clearly discernible in the earlier texts and, as this chapter will show, the notion of fusion is far from alien to the high medieval anchoritic guidance writer.

Aelred describes contemplative experience in terms of an ascent:

> quotiens orantem in quoddam ineffabile desiderum sui rapiebat, quotiens mentem tuam a terrenis subtractam ad caelestes delicias et paradisiacas amoenitates transportabat . . .

> (how often he carried you away with a certain unspeakable longing for himself while you were at prayer, how often he lifted up your mind from the things of the earth and introduced it into the delights of heaven and the joys of paradise . . .)[5]

He continues: 'quotiens aestuanti prae amore ipse se tuis uisceribus infundebat' (how often he infused himself into your inmost being when you were on fire with love). The recluse is encouraged to disregard the temporal sphere: 'Non has delicias tuas somnus interpolet, nullus exterior tumultus impediat' (Do not let these delights of yours be interrupted by sleep or disturbed by any tumult from without).[6] Aelred's construction of the recluse's meditation on the Magdalene's meeting with Jesus in the garden approaches a fusion-like transcendence of time, place, language and the body: 'Nam plura dicere lacrymae prohibent, cum uocem occludat affectus, omnesque animae corporisque sensus nimius amor absorbeat' (Tears preclude any further utterance as the voice is stifled by emotion and excess of love leaves the soul dumb, the body without feeling).[7] *Ancrene Wisse* similarly constructs the whole experience of contemplation as a height to be attained.[8] The contemplative soars upwards in flight, like one of the birds of which this guide makes so much:

> alswa schal ancre fleon wið contemplatiun. þat is wið heh þoht & wið hali bonen . . . toward heouene & . . . hire sawle fode.

(In the same way an anchoress must fly by night toward heaven with contemplation – that is, with high thoughts and holy prayers – and gather her soul-food by night.)[9]

The demands of the body have periodically to be reasserted, which of course implies, as did Aelred's guide, that in this experience they have been partially abandoned:

> þe gode ancre. ne fleo ha neauer se heh ha mot lihten oðerhwiles dun to þer eorðe of hire bodi. Eoten. drinken. slepen. wurchen. speoken. héren of . . . eorðliche þinges.

(the good anchoress, fly she ever so high, must at some times alight down on the earth of her body to eat, drink, sleep, work, speak and hear about . . . earthly things.)[10]

Ancrene Wisse describes fusion in a prescribed moment of ecstasy, which takes the mass for its stimulus:

> Efter þe measse cos hwen þe preost sacreð. þer for þeoteð al þe world. *þer beoð al ut of bodi* þer i sperclinde luue bicluppeð ower leofmon þe in to ower breostes bur is iliht of heouene.

(After the kiss of peace when the priest consecrates the host, forget all the world, *be wholly out of your body*, embrace in shining love your lover, who has alighted into the bower of your breast from heaven.)[11]

While Aelred approaches the idea of fusion tentatively, constructing it, even at its height, only in terms of an absence, or resignation, of the flesh, *Ancrene Wisse* celebrates the union of the recluse's body with Christ's. The two have become one.

The later medieval guides build upon these high medieval constructions in their equation of fusion with ravishment. The *Speculum* author describes it as a moment 'quando usus sensuum est ligatus, vel quasi in raptu, quando mens non considerat res sensibiles circumstances' (a rauisschynge, whan þe herte or þe þouȝt considereth nat þe sensible þinges standinge or beynge oboute).[12] The late medieval recluse is, as was her/his high medieval counterpart – particularly in *Ancrene Wisse*'s case – ravished by love. Rolle writes: 'þei ben contemplatif men . . . rauist in loue, for contemplacioun is a sight, and þai seth in to heuyn with har gostly eigh [spiritual eye]'.[13] Both Hilton and the *Speculum* author and his vernacular translator use St Paul's example overtly, likening such experience to being, as he was, ravished 'into the thridde hevene'.[14] The *Speculum* author, in a passage missing from *Myrour*, draws on a sermon of Aelred's to gloss this further – and this is not the only time that he looks to the high-medieval period for the corroboration of his perspective. He writes:

> narrat sanctus Alredus . . . quibus orantibus mira quedam suavitas superveniens omnes mundanas cogitaciones et carnales affectus extinxit. Moxque rapti quasi ad tercium celum cum beato Paulo et incomprehensibili luce perfusi, quadam beatifica visione Dei, licet inperfecta, vel saltem quodam excellenti ac inenarrabili gaudio perfusi, sic inebriati sunt, quod ab aliis pulsati, cum difficultate ad corporales sensus, quos reliquerant, redire valebant.

> (holy Aelred says . . . while certain people were praying a wonderful surpassing sweetness extinguished all worldly thoughts and all carnal affections. And soon, wrapt as if to the third heaven along with St Paul, infused with incomprehensible light and by a certain beatific vision of God, even though it is imperfect, they are so inebriated with an excellent and unspeakable joy that cannot be told, that they have to be struck by others and only with difficulty are they able to return to the bodily senses which they have left behind them.)[15]

Hilton similarly negotiates this through the language of force. Contemplative experience

> maketh the bodi, yif grace come myghtili, for to stire and turne heer and theer as a man that were mad or dronken and can have noo reste . . . [L]ove . . . bi grete violence and maistrie breketh doun alle lustis and likynges of alle ertheli thinges, and it woundeth the soule with the blisful swerd.[16]

The soul is wrested from the body as 'the bodi faileth and falleth doun

and mai not bere it'.[17] The subsequent fusion, however, is constructed
as a peaceful union. The recluse is

> as it were mykil ravysschid out of the bodili wittes . . . with a soft swete
> brennande love in hym, so perfightli that bi ravyscynge of this love the
> soule is ooned for the tyme . . . fastned to God, thanne God and a soule
> aren not two but bothe oon. Not in fleisch, but in oo spirit. And sotheli in
> this onynge is the mariage maad bitwixe God and the soule, which schal
> nevere be brokyn.[18]

Rolle similarly writes that the experience of the third degree of 'synguler'
love subsumes the anchorite's identity, specifically into that of Christ:
'þan þe sowl is Ihesu louynge . . . Ihesu desyrynge . . . in hym restynge'.[19]

These guidance writers, then, conceive of a contemplative state
which, at its height, transcends the flesh and, indeed, the world. At their
most daring they construct this as an absence of body, just as Aelred's
guide and *Ancrene Wisse* did, manifested in a trance-like abandonment
of the senses. They also conceive of an absence of language, for such an
experience is literally, in the *Speculum* author's words, unspeakable, and
cannot be told. Nonetheless, in order to articulate this subjugation of
the human to the divine they must use language, however inadequate,
and such language is, of course, inherently embodied and thereby subject to gendered performance. Gender, after all, resides in the flesh and
the word. This spiritual fusion, which is in essence bodiless and word-
less, is, *as an experience*, genderless. It is beyond gender, just as it is
beyond language. It becomes gendered only in the process of its communication, through the language which can never do it justice. These
writers accordingly ascribe sensory characteristics, such as touch and
sight, to the ravished soul, and it is here, of course, that the burning of
the fire of love becomes an effective tool in the communication of this
kind of fusion. Another powerful method of its communication is found
in the bridegroom and marriage metaphors, which feminize the ravished body and soul in their passive submission to the will of a superior
authority. Through this kind of gendered imagery these writers convey
powerfully the intimacy of such a consummation or fusion relationship,
and open up notions of the paradoxical empowerment that comes from
surrender. Yet the actual *experience* is a resignation of the flesh and a
transcendence, therefore, of the biological and social constructs which
derive from it. These guides show us, then, that gender intersects with
contemplative experience only at the level of the communication of that

experience to others. This is, of course, in itself highly significant, for it shows us how medievals attempted to conceive of an experience that was literally beyond them. Yet we must remember that these gendered concepts are methods of intellectual assimilation, rather than reflections of the reality of the experience. The gendering – and in particular the feminization – of the contemplative experience of rapture or fusion occurs and is significant only at a textual level. It is, by these guidance writers' own admission, evidence of limitation, of their inability to express the inexpressible.[20]

Grace Jantzen argues, in terms of the ineffability of God, in her study of *Power, Gender and Christian Mysticism*, that all mystical writers take it for granted that their depictions of him, because of the limitations of language, carry their own negation within themselves. She insists: 'they are fatally misunderstood . . . if their self-negation is not taken into account'.[21] Tarjei Park argues in an article on the role of the flesh in the writings of Water Hilton and Julian of Norwich that 'Human action, sensation and imagination are signifiers for limitation', for 'ultimately . . . contemplation has little to do with embodiment'.[22] An awareness of humanity's inadequate comprehension of this type of fusion is behind Hilton's desire to clarify the location of the fire of love. He is motivated by the ignorance of those 'symple' folk who believe that it is bodily rather than spiritual, largely because it is described to them through embodied language. He writes: 'it is neither bodili, ne it is bodili feelid. A soule mai fele it . . . whiche soule is in the bodi, but he felith it not bi no bodili witt . . . the fier of love is not bodili, for it is oonly in the goostli desire of the soule.'[23] He also concedes crucially that 'what it is I can not telle thee'; he can describe it only in terms of what it is not, because he has a language at his disposal which has no mode of expression for this type of experience. If it is beyond the body, then it is, Hilton concludes, beyond the language which is inherently rooted in that body. This was the conclusion, too, of a whole host of contemporary visionaries, such as Julian of Norwich and Margery Kempe, who bemoan the accurate linguistic recovery of the irrecoverable. Julian declares: 'I cannot ne may not shew it as hopinly ne as fully as I wolde.'[24] Margery concludes that she 'cowd neuyr telle þe grace þat sche felt, it was so heuenly, so hy abouen hyr reson & hyr bodyly wyttys . . . þat sche myth neuyr expressyn it wyth her word lych as sche felt it in hyr sowle'.[25] Richard Kieckhefer, in his evaluation of the tenor of fourteenth-century sainthood, has gathered together numerous examples of the disconsolate reactions of those gifted with such experience in their attempts to communicate it.

Perhaps the most striking is that of Catherine of Siena, whose compan-
ions sometimes tested the authenticity of her trance-like states by kick-
ing her or pricking her with needles. Catherine observes that she has
seen 'divine mysteries that no living soul can utter because memory has
no hold over them and there are no words capable of describing things
so sublime: any words that were used would be like mud compared with
gold'.[26]

There is a gap, then, which these writers acknowledge, between the
experience and the expression of it, a gap which is of necessity filled by
a language which, they concede, obscures its true meaning. This is true
not only of contemplative experience, but of the communication of
other concepts vital to anchoritic guidance writing. Anke Bernau has
recently identified a similar paradox in *Ancrene Wisse*'s construction
of virginity. Arguing for the fundamental dependence of the
virginal/anchoritic identity on language, she finds that: 'virginity prolif-
erates and generates images and metaphors that blur the outlines the
text seeks to fix'. The concept is 'not elucidated but hidden from view
by descriptions that constantly defer its meaning and fail to pinpoint its
"essence" '.[27] The same is certainly true of the later medieval constructions of contemplative rupture or fusion, which require a language for
their elucidation that inevitably contributes to their obfuscation.

Identifying anchoritism with this kind of sophisticated contemplative
state, as all these guides do, reinforces the need for a contemplative vocation at a time of great debate about the usefulness of the contemplative
life. It also reinforces the desirability of the anchoritic ideals of solitude
and social separation from the community. The anchorite who sits
enraptured within the cell conforms at the most extreme of levels to the
solitary anchoritic exemplum. The world, which causes every guidance
writer so many difficulties, is unlikely to be a problem for such a sophisticated contemplative and, conversely, s/he is unlikely to be a problem for
the world. In continually aspiring to such contemplation and engaging,
because s/he is thus inspired, in a programme of self-improvement and
devotions, the anchorite is led quite naturally away from a world which
does not hold an experience which can match this fusion rapture. These
guidance writers no longer need to maintain anchoritic ideals through
the fear which is the consequence of dire warnings of gender-specific
potential transgression. The anchoritic ideal is joyfully maintained by
aspiration. The recluse, as Susannah Chewning has argued elsewhere in
this volume in the context of the mystic (ch. 8), turns gladly, not fearfully,
away from her/himself.

At the same time, however, the fusion state is potentially hazardous, since it is difficult to interpret, regulate and control it within the bounds of the orthodoxy which is such a contemporary concern for these guidance writers. That the anchorite, whether male or female, is able to negotiate a liberation from the confines of the enclosures of cell and flesh, that this gender-neutral experience bypasses all the attendant implications of gender-specific post-lapsarian transgression, is of potential concern for these men, and in particular for the later writers, Hilton and the *Speculum* author. Anchoritic guidance writers are, after all, the representatives of a patriarchy which has fundamental responsibility for the bodies and minds of its recluses. These guides betray some uneasiness, therefore, in their negotiations of fusion. Even as they approve of it, they must concern themselves, in its re-presentation and reconstruction, with the limitation of its potential fallout. In so doing they are resigned, despite themselves, to worrying away at traditional gendered anchoritic guidance issues, such as the transgressive role of the flesh, and the female flesh in particular, in their perpetuation of the anchoritic ideal. It is this paradox which generates and motivates their texts and their enthusiastic attempts to define and redefine their position and the positions of their charges within the contemplative vocation. The ineffability and inadequacy of language does not, of course, lead a writer to speechlessness. Jantzen writes that 'to look for a way of speaking does not result in finding no such way but in finding all of them – an embarrassment of riches', none of which are ultimate, but all of which are provocative.[28] This is certainly true of these anchoritic guides, each of which attempts to reinterpret an ideal which continues to elude interpretation, and none of which can be looked to as the definitive guide to anchoritism, which alters and develops over time, is never stable, is never wholly definable, and always, like the anchorites these texts attempt to represent, remains hidden, just out of reach.

Much scholarly work which has been done, as Chewning's chapter in this volume again demonstrates, focuses on the feminization which occurs at the point of the communication of anchoritic contemplative experience and on the different topic of potential feminine empowerment which may arise through the elevation in status of a female contemplative. In conclusion, however, I want to suggest that if we perceive fusion to be gender-neutral as an experience, then we must begin to accept that it is intended to be equally empowering for men and women – and perhaps that is truly liberating. This chapter has focused on a subtle point of difference, which has been rather overlooked in scholarship's entirely justifiable eagerness to explore the gendered themes which these writers themselves construct as part of their linguistically creative attempts to express the inexpressible. Although such readings are effective at the level of the construction, or rather the reconstruction, of such experience, they do not, if the model of Paul and its development in these guides is taken into account, reflect the reality of the experience itself, and this is something of which these guidance writers are themselves all too aware.

Notes

1 Paul breaks a vow of silence when he mentions this ecstatic experience which occurred fourteen years earlier (see Corinthians 12: 2). This would place the event during the so-called silent years, when Paul was in the region of Syria and Cilicia (see Acts 9: 30; Galatians 1: 21).

2 Acts 9: 8–10.

3 Ann K. Warren, *Anchorites and their Patrons in Medieval England* (Berkeley, 1985), p. 115.

4 My recent article on anchoritic asceticism traces the development of high-medieval ascetical perspectives through to their natural conclusions in the later-medieval texts. It argues for a reading of the later guides which is firmly contextualized within high-medieval anchoritic perspectives. See Mari Hughes-Edwards, 'Hedgehog skins and hairshirts: the changing role of asceticism in the anchoritic ideal', *Mystics Quarterly*, 28, 1 (2002), 6–25.

5 All quotation from *de Institutione Inclusarum* will be taken from *Aelredi Rievallensis Opera Omnia: 1 Opera Ascetica*, ed. A. Hoste and C. H. Talbot (Turnhout, 1971). The corresponding translation of every quotation from *de Institutione Inclusarum* is taken from Mary Paul Macpherson's translation of the guide, entitled 'A Rule of Life for a Recluse', in *Aelred of Rievaulx: Treatises: The Pastoral Prayer* (Spencer, MA., 1971). For this quotation see *de Institutione*, p. 676; Macpherson, p. 96.

6 *de Institutione*, p. 673; Macpherson, p. 92.

7 *de Institutione*, p. 672; Macpherson, p. 91.

8 All quotation from *Ancrene Wisse* will be taken from the Corpus revision: *The English Text of the Ancrene Riwle: Ancrene Wisse: Edited from MS. Corpus Christi College Cambridge 402*, by J. R. R. Tolkien, EETS o.s. 249 (London, New York and Toronto, 1962). The corresponding translation of every quotation from *Ancrene Wisse* is taken from *Anchoritic Spirituality: Ancrene Wisse and Associated Works*, trans. and ed. Anne Savage and Nicholas Watson (New York and Mahwah, 1991).

9 *Ancrene Wisse*, p. 751; Savage and Watson, p. 71.

10 *Ancrene Wisse*, p. 70; Savage and Watson, p. 98.

11 *Ancrene Wisse*, p. 21 (my emphasis); Savage and Watson, p. 59.

12 All quotation from *Speculum* is taken from 'Speculum Inclusorum', ed.

P. L. Oliger, *Lateranum*, n.s. 4 (1938), 1–148, here at 83. The author of the original Latin version is referred to throughout this chapter as 'the *Speculum* author'. The corresponding Middle English translation is taken from *The Myrour of Recluses* ed. Marta Powell Harley (London, Ontario, 1995), here at pp. 16–17). The author of this later vernacular translation of the guide is referred to throughout as 'the translator'. This translation is only partial and those passages of *Speculum* quoted in the chapter which do not have a corresponding vernacular translation in *Myrour* have been translated into modern English by myself. I am grateful to Dr J. W. Binns for assistance with this translation.

[13] Richard Rolle, *The Form of Living*, in Sarah J. Ogilvie-Thompson (ed.), *Richard Rolle: Prose and Verse from MS Longleat 29 and Related Manuscripts*, EETS o.s. 293 (1988), p. 25.

[14] Walter Hilton, *The Scale of Perfection*, ed. Thomas Bestul, TEAMS (Kalamazoo, 2000), p. 50.

[15] *Speculum*, p. 129.

[16] Hilton, *Scale*, p. 29.

[17] Ibid., p. 30.

[18] Ibid., p. 7.

[19] Rolle, *Form of Living*, p. 17.

[20] It must be reiterated here that this does not refer to vision or meditation, which is, as previously asserted, distinct from this higher state, and which is certainly gendered as an experience, and not simply in the communication of it as an experience.

[21] Grace Jantzen, *Power, Gender and Christian Mysticism* (Cambridge, 1995), pp. 281–2.

[22] Tarjei Park, 'Reflecting Christ: the role of the flesh in Walter Hilton and Julian of Norwich', in Marion Glasscoe (ed.), *The Medieval Mystical Tradition in England*, Exeter Symposium V (1992), pp. 28 and 29 respectively.

[23] Hilton, *Scale*, p. 26.

[24] *The Shewings of Julian of Norwich*, ed. Georgia Ronan Crampton (Kalamazoo, 1994), p. 50.

[25] *The Book of Margery Kempe*, ed. Sandford Brown Meech and Hope Emily Allen, EETS o.s. 212 (London, New York and Toronto, 1997), p. 3.

[26] Richard Kieckhefer, *Unquiet Souls: Fourteenth Century Saints and their Religious Milieu* (Chicago and London, 1984), p. 155. Kieckhefer here cites Raymond of Capua's *The Life of Saint Catherine of Siena*, trans. George Lamb (New York, 1960), pp. 213–16.

[27] Anke Bernau, 'Virginal effects: text and identity in *Ancrene Wisse*', in S. J. E. Riches and S. Salih (eds), *Gender and Holiness: Men, Women and Saints in Late-Medieval Europe* (London and New York, 2002), p. 44.

[28] Jantzen, *Power, Gender and Christian Mysticism*, p. 284.

III

Beyond the Tomb:
The Question of Audience

11

'Efter hire euene': Lay Audiences and the Variable Asceticism of *Ancrene Wisse*

ROBERT HASENFRATZ

The late twelfth and early thirteenth centuries saw an unprecedented expansion in the possibilities for lay spirituality. The heresies that disturbed southern Europe (themselves largely lay movements) motivated the ecclesiastical hierarchy to turn much more of its attention to lay preaching, and the period saw the creation of the Dominican Order, the preaching friars. A number of third or tertiary orders arose in this period as well, allowing lay people to associate themselves with established mendicant orders under a quasi-rule, sometimes in communities. The Franciscans, Dominicans and Carmelites formed tertiary orders, with their own rules and liturgy (often based on the Little Office of Our Lady),[1] and beguine[2] and beghard communities, for lay women and men respectively, were forming in the late twelfth and early thirteenth centuries in the Low Countries. It is in this context of these emerging lay movements that *Ancrene Wisse* is best viewed.[3]

In view of its special lay audience, *Ancrene Wisse*'s view of asceticism and ascetic practices seems potentially confusing. On the one hand, *Ancrene Wisse* assumes a deeply ascetic approach to the spiritual life, one demanding a careful regulation and training of the body. Part 2, for example, imagines the body's five senses as dangerous portals that the Devil can attack and penetrate. For this reason the body must be enclosed, silenced and controlled. Part 3 goes even further by insisting that the spirit cannot fly to God until the body – naturally fat, heavy and unruly – is trained, disciplined and made light: 'Ah ancre schal . . . temie ful wel hire flesch, sone se ha i-feleð þet hit awilgeð to swiðe, mid feasten, mid wecchen, wið here, wið heard swinc, wið hearde disceplines'

(An anchoress must . . . tame her flesh very well as soon as she feels it becoming too wilful, with fasting, with keeping vigil, with haircloth, with hard work, with harsh disciplines).[4] The following sections develop further the notion of spiritual warfare, fought largely on the field of the body, culminating in part 6, where the anchoritic life itself is seen as the embodiment of pain, penance and torn bodies. Thus, in *Ancrene Wisse* the ascetic denial of the flesh appears the fundamental basis on which all spiritual progress is built.

In the climatic sections of *Ancrene Wisse*, however, the author seems to place ascetic practices firmly in the province of the outer rule, subject not only to wide variation in practice, but also rendering them far less important than the inner rule of love (part 7):

Seinte Pawel witneð þet alle uttre heardschipes, alle flesches pinsunges, ant licomliche swinkes, all is ase nawt aȝeines luue þe schireð ant brihteð þe heorte. Exercitio corporis ad modicum ualet, pietas autem ualet ad omnia. Thet is, 'licomlich bisischipe is to lute wurð, ah swote ant schir heorte is god to alle þinges'.

(Saint Paul witnesses that all outward hardships, all mortifications of the flesh and bodily labour, all are as nothing compared to love, which purifies and brightens the heart. *Exercitio corporus . . . omnia* (1 Timothy 4: 8). 'Bodily effort is worth little, but a sweet and pure heart is good for everything.')[5]

Part 8, which turns to the outer rule at length, goes on to make a case *against* several ascetic practices, from fasting on bread and water to the wearing of hair shirts, whipping and self-mutilation.

The answer to this seeming contradiction is, I believe, that the *Ancrene Wisse* author sees ascetic denial of the body *in general* as the necessary foundation of all contemplative life, but views *specific* ascetic practices as appropriate for different kinds of contemplatives, from the very advanced to beginners. As Cate Gunn argues elsewhere in this volume (ch. 12), *Ancrene Wisse* is keenly aware of the wide range of its audience, from advanced female anchorites to laywomen living in the world, and the nature of this lay audience conditions the careful approach to ascetic practice in *Ancrene Wisse*, the subject of this chapter.[6] The female anchorites for whom this guide was originally intended were themselves laywomen. Parts 4, 5 and 6 of *Ancrene Wisse*, in particular, seem to be addressed to a wider-than-anchoritic lay audience and, since they concern the understanding of sin, confession and penance, respectively, they would seem particularly appropriate for wide distribution in the years following the Fourth Lateran Council, of 1215, which codified the system of sacramental penance for lay Christians. The concern with variability in practice is present from the very beginning of *Ancrene Wisse*, and can be seen most clearly in a passage from the preface, which throws light on the kinds of audiences the author imagines:

Ah alle ne mahe nawt halden a riwle, ne ne þurue nawt, ne ne ahe nawt halden on a wise þe uttre riwle . . . For þi mot þeos changin hire misliche *efter euchanes manere ant efter hire euene*. For sum is strong, sum unstrong, ant mei ful wel beo cwite ant paie Godd mid leasse. Sum is clergesse, sum nawt, ant mot te mare wurchen ant on oðer wise seggen hire bonen. Sum is ald ant eðelich ant is þe leasse dread of. Sum is ȝung ant luuelich ant is neod betere warde. Forþi schal euch ancre habben þe uttre riwle *efter hire schriftes read*, ant hwet-se he bit ant hat hire in obedience, þe cnaweð hire manere ant wat hire strengðe. He mei þe uttre riwle changin efter wisdom as he sið, þet te inre mahe beo best ihalden.

(But all cannot keep to one rule, and need not and ought not to keep in one way the outer rule . . . Therefore the one changes in different ways, *according to each individual's character and capacity*. For one is strong, another is not strong and may be very well acquitted and pay God with less. One is learned, another not and must work more and say her prayers in another way. One is old and weak and is the less to be feared, for another is young and lovely and has need of closer watch. Therefore each anchoress shall keep the outer rule according to her confessor's counsel, and do whatever he asks and commands her in obedience.)[7]

The first thing to notice here is that the author defines the outer rule exclusively in terms of asceticism: it is the outer rule that makes one fast, hold vigils, wear harsh clothing, etc. The outer rule as described here *is* the mortification of the body. More importantly, the passage reveals a special concern for lay spirituality in its awareness of a broad range of potential readers[8] and in its desire to regulate lay practice through a confessor (one of the goals of the Fourth Lateran Council). These concerns are embodied in two important phrases that repeat in discussions of ascetic practice throughout *Ancrene Wisse*: 'efter hire euene' (according to her character or capacity) and 'efter hire schriftes leaue' (by her confessor's permission).

This chapter, therefore, will examine *Ancrene Wisse's* handling of asceticism and ascetic practices in light of its very mixed audience. The challenge facing the *Ancrene Wisse* author was how to construct a working ascesis (often based on the astoundingly stringent ideals of early desert monasticism, as identified in the first section of this volume)[9] for laypeople of differing abilities and interests. Part of the solution, I shall argue, was to separate the theory from the praxis of asceticism, both of which are discussed in turn below.

I

Basic ascetic theory[10] emerges in *Ancrene Wisse* with special clarity in part 3, although part 2, on the guarding of the five senses, lays the groundwork for this discussion, particularly in its urging that the organs of the body associated with the senses be closed and protected against infernal attack and in its vivid painting of Christ's sufferings in each sense, as a means of psychologically mortifying and closing the anchorite's body. Asceticism is seen as necessary because the fallen body is a potential ally to the Devil in his quest to defeat and enslave the spirit of the believer. However, since the body is joined to the spirit, the body cannot be conquered in such a way that it is dangerously weakened or, perhaps, even killed. Instead, the body must undergo an education, always according to the capacity of the individual.

Part 3, in general, draws its most memorable images from the natural world, allegorizing animals in the style of bestiaries (another popular form), and its symbols for the body–spirit unity are particularly colourful. The female anchorite, dominated by her body, appears as a comically heavy ostrich attempting to fly, a pig in the sty of her anchorhold and as a fat and ill-natured calf, a dog on a dungheap, etc., while she with a properly subdued body appears as a pelican, a night-bird and a swallow. The dominant image for the contemplative life is that of a bird in flight: the body tends to be a heavy weight pulling the spirit towards the earth. If it is too heavy, she cannot fly, but if it has been made lean, she can soar above the earth and earthly things. Thus the section hinges on a number of images of heavy and light, fat and lean, low and high. As it turns out, the need for caution has everything to do with the nature of the amalgamation of body and soul. Since the two are inextricably linked, slaying the body, however inclined to evil, would mean killing the soul as well:

Þah þe flesch beo ure fa, hit is us i-haten þet we halden hit up. Wa we moten don hit as hit is wel ofte wurðe, ah nawt fordon mid alle. For hu wac se hit eauer beo, þenne is hit swa i-cuplet, ant se feste i-feiet to ure deore-wurðe gast, Godes ahne furme, þet we mahten sone slean þet an wið þet oþer.

(Though the flesh is our enemy, we are commanded to uphold it. We must cause it grief as it very often deserves, but not destroy it altogether, since however weak it is it is so joined and so tightly fixed to our precious soul, God's own image, that we could easily kill the one with the other.)[11]

Ancrene Wisse restates this idea in terms of the governing image of the bird in flight by pointing out that, however high in spirit the female anchorite may soar, she must return to the 'eorðe of hire bodi' (earth of her body),[12] in order to eat, sleep and work. Thus, *Ancrene Wisse* recognizes theoretical limits to ascetic practice – no mortification of the body should proceed far enough to endanger it.

Throughout the section, the author uses two central metaphors to explain how asceticism can conquer the body: the first is leanness – that the fat, heavy body should be made as light as possible; the second is taming – that the body is a difficult and wilful animal (a wild horse or calf that must be trained). From this perspective, *Ancrene Wisse*'s ascetic theory does not see the body as irrevocably evil. In a real sense, education, and not literal 'mortification' or deadening, is the goal. Asceticism alone, then, cannot achieve the goals of the contemplative life. In fact, the subduing, lightening and training of the body emerge here as a preliminary practice. Only by first applying disciplines to the heavy body can it be made lean enough for the enclosed woman *then* to fly towards spiritual contemplation. In *Ancrene Wisse* asceticism is, as Mari Hughes-Edwards has put it elsewhere, 'a means to an end, loved not in itself but for what can be accomplished through it'.[13]

While part 4 continues the idea of spiritual combat on the field of the contested body, and part 5 offers the female anchorite an important weapon in cleansing sins of body and mind (that is, confession), part 6 is of particular interest to the ascetic theory of *Ancrene Wisse*, in that it constitutes a wide-ranging meditation on the value of ascetic pain. After treating confession (part 5) as part of the sacramental system of penance (contrition of heart, confession of mouth, penance and absolution) aimed at a broad audience, part 6 somewhat unexpectedly discuss penance, not as a step in the sacramental system, but as part of a generalized suffering. This part modulates *Ancrene Wisse*'s ascetic theory

significantly, and is particularly wily in its handling of audience. One of
its main aims is to rewire the emotions of its readers so that they feel
actual joy in pain: 'for al hare blisse is forte beon ahonget sariliche ant
scheomeliche wið Iesu on his rode' (for all their joy is to be hung,
painfully and shamefully with Jesus on his cross).[14] Although it would
seem from the opening section, which places the anchoritic audience in
the highest category of those chosen by God, pilgrims on earth, the
dead and those on the cross with Christ, in fact, the end of part 6 reveals
rather startlingly that preceding discussion of pain and mortification
has been directed to the less advanced, *not* towards the advanced:

> Al þet ich habbe i-seid of flesches pinsunge nis nawt for ow, mine leoue sus-
> tren—þe oðer-hwile þolieð mare þen ich walde—ah is for sum þet schal
> rede þis inoh-reaðe, þe grapeð hire to softe. No-ðe-les, ȝunge impen me big-
> urd wið þornes leste beastes freoten ham hwil ha beoð mearewe. ȝe beoð
> ȝunge impen i-set i Godes orchard; þornes beoð þe heardschipes þet ich
> habbe i-speken of. Ant ow is neod þet ȝe beon biset wið ham abuten, þet te
> beast of helle, hwen he snakereð toward ow for-te biten on ow, hurte him
> o þe scharpschipe ant schunche aȝein-wardes.

> (All that I have said of the mortification of the flesh is not meant for you,
> my dear sisters, who sometimes suffer more than I would like; but it is for
> anyone who handles herself too gently who reads this willingly enough.
> Nevertheless, one surrounds young saplings with thorns in case beasts
> chew them while they are tender. You are young saplings planted in God's
> orchard; thorns are the hardships I have spoken of, and you need to be sur-
> rounded by them so that the beast of hell, when he comes sneaking toward
> you to bite you, may hurt himself on the sharpness and shrink back again.)[15]

This passage posits a remarkably mixed audience for *Ancrene Wisse*: the
original female anchorites, presumably very advanced in the contemplative life, though themselves quasi-laywomen, as well as potential lay
readers at a much lower level. In this section, the author betrays some
anxiety about potential lay readers who lack supervision or who might
approach the contemplative life without the proper degree of serious-
ness or preparation.
     Something more radical, however, is afoot in part 6. The book closes
with the fascinating anecdote of a man, known to the author, who seeks
out the most extraordinary means to mortify his body[16] and who

bereð ba togederes heui brunie ant here, i-bunden hearde wið irn – middel, þeh, ant earmes – mid brade þicke bondes, swa þet tet swat þrof is passiun to þolien. Feasteð, wakeð, swinkeð, ant, Crist hit wat, meaneð him þet hit ne greueð him nawt ant bit me ofte teachen him sum-hwet wið hwet he mahte his licome deruen.

(bears a heavy coat of mail and a hair shirt, both at once, his middle, thighs and arms bound tight with iron in broad, thick bands, so that the sweat from it is an agony to bear. He fasts, keeps vigil, works, and, Christ knows, he complains that it does not hurt him at all, and often asks me to teach him something with which he can mortify [that is, 'torment' perhaps even 'harm'] his body.)[17]

The author puts this man's ascetic suffering in the realm of the saintly and the unreachable, referring even to the 'passiun' or martyrdom of sweat he endures, finally commenting that the audience can do nothing but admire this man's miraculous strength (and that of an unidentified woman who suffers 'little less'):

ah nis þer bute þoncki Godd i strengðe þet he ȝeueð ham, ant i-cnawen eadmodliche ure wacnesse. Luuie we hare god, ant swa hit is ure ahne, for as Sein Gregoire seið of swa muchel strengðe is luue, þet hit makeð oþres god wiðute swinc ure ahne.

(There is nothing to do but thank God for the strength that he gives them, and humbly to acknowledge our weakness. Let us love their good, and so make it our own, for as St Gregory says, love has such power that it makes the good of others our own, without labour.)[18]

The phrase 'without labour' hints at a quite different approach to the ascetic life. While the author holds up extreme asceticism as an admirable thing here, he seems throughout part 6 to want to modulate suffering into a vicarious practice. That is, he encourages a kind of identification with, and emotional participation in, foremost Christ's sufferings on the cross, but also the saints' sufferings in their martyrdoms.

The martyrdom of the saints becomes a symbol of the ascetic life, though nowhere does part 6 suggest that contemplatives should strive for saint like suffering and the actual tearing or destruction of the body. Everything about the body–spirit unity explored so thoroughly in part 3 argues against martyrdom as a goal for contemplatives. In fact, the opposite is true; there is a call for moderation and reason:

> euch mon wið wisdom weie hwet he mahe don, ne beo nawt se ouer swiðe i gast þet he forȝeme þe bodi, ne eft se tendre of his flesch þet hit iwurðe untohen ant makie þe gast þeowe.

(everyone should measure out with wisdom what they can do, and not be so extravagantly spiritual that they are heedless of the body, or, again, so soft on his flesh that it becomes undisciplined, and makes the spirit its servant.)[19]

The focus in part 6 thus falls far less than one might expect on the physical pain in believers' bodies than on the quasi-mystical joy of their *identifying* with the pain of Christ and the saints. The athletic sufferers at the end of part 6, both male and female, do not serve as models for advanced ascetic practice, but are indeed somewhat mysterious, saintly types, beyond the possibility or desirability of imitation. They become the objects of what Hughes-Edwards terms 'ascetical meditation', an asceticism of mind favoured particularly in the late-medieval anchoritic guides but, as she points out, also clearly present in the high-medieval guides, like *Ancrene Wisse*.[20]

II

Ancrene Wisse treats the praxis of asceticism as part of the outer rule, allowing for a maximum amount of variability and adaptability for lay contemplatives of different levels, though in general it seems that, as *Ancrene Wisse* evolved, the author attempted to restrain extreme practices in the most advanced amongst his audience and to encourage stricter, though surprisingly vague, self-denial for beginners. The most complete catalogue of ascetic practices appears in part 6, where *Ancrene Wisse* describes the mortification of the flesh thus: 'wið feasten, wið wecchen, wið disceplines, wið heard werunge, heard leohe, wið uuel, wið muchele swinkes' (with fasts, with vigils, with disciplines, with rough clothing, a rough shelter, with illness, with heavy labours),[21] though there are similar lists, particularly in parts 3 and 6, almost always beginning with fasting and vigils. The following survey of ascetic practice in *Ancrene Wisse* attempts to provide a complete list of specific techniques, discussed in the rough order of severity, beginning with the most common and least controversial practices.

Fasting. Although fasting is almost always mentioned first in any list of ascetic practices in *Ancrene Wisse*, there is little formal discussion of it, outside of how it fits into the liturgical calendar, and little mention of it in the general directions about food in part 8. In the later section, the author writes that

> ȝe ne schulen nawt eoten flesch ne seim, bute for muche secnesse oðer hwa-se is ouer-feble. Potage eoteð bliðeliche, ant wunieð ow to lutel drunch. No-ðe-les, leoue sustren, ower mete ant ower drunch haueð i-þuht me ofte leasse þen ich walde. Ne feaste ȝe na dei to bread ne to weattre, bute ȝe habben leaue.

> (You must not eat meat or fat, except in the case of great illness, or unless someone is very weak. Eat vegetable stew willingly, and accustom yourself to little drink. Nevertheless, dear sisters, your food and drink have often seemed less to me than I would want you to have. Do not fast on bread and water unless you have leave.)[22]

As is often the case in part 8, the author is at pains to curb the more extreme practices of the advanced female anchorite, and sees fasting on bread and water as just such an extreme practice, as is clear here and in a passage from part 4 on remedies against pride, where he notes that the body, which the foolish may be tempted to take pride in, can be reduced to a state of weakness with 'feasten a seoueniht to weater ant to breade, þreo niht togederes wakien' (fasting a week on water and bread, keeping vigil for three nights together).[23] Besides fasting, *Ancrene Wisse* mentions the eating of poor or substandard food as a mortification, associating it with the bitter gall that Christ was forced to drink on the cross.

On the whole, it is curious that *Ancrene Wisse* spends so little time on such an important ascetic practice as fasting. The *Vitas Patrum* contains a multitude of anecdotes about either the heroic abstinence or the disgusting food of the desert saints,[24] and in fact Aelred spends considerable space enjoining his sister to lift up the impenetrable shield of fasting, discussing the particular importance of the Lenten fast.[25] *Ancrene Wisse*'s suggested ban on fasting on bread and water would seem to exclude one of the more common penances and seems very mild.

Keeping of Vigils. Ancrene Wisse sees the keeping of vigils primarily as a way to deprive the body of sleep and thus to keep it under control, and mentions it in most of the catalogues of ascetic practices. Vigils are also associated with intercessory prayer and are discussed at some length in part 3. At first glance, it seems that vigils are an integral part of a contemplative's task of subduing her body:

þet is ancre rihte muchel for-te wakien. Ecclesiasticus: Vigilia honestatis tabefatiet carnes [Ecclesiasticus 31: 1]: "Na þing ne awealdeð wilde flesch, ne ne makeð hit tomre, þen muche wecche".

(It is proper for an anchoress to keep frequent vigils. Ecclesiasticus: *Vigilia . . . carnes* [Ecclesiasticus 31: 1]: "Nothing rules wild flesh or makes it tamer than many vigils".)[26]

The passage just cited on fasting suggests that, while it might take a week to weaken the body fully on a fast of bread and water, staying awake for three nights in a row would be just as effective.[27] The further discussion of vigils in part 3 has a marked tendency to make vigils (a specific ascetic practice) into vigilance (an interior attitude) – wakefulness and watchfulness in the face of the coming judgement. The following eight reasons to 'wake' focus on this looser metaphorical vigilance.[28]

Clothing. *Ancrene Wisse* shows a remarkable range of opinion on ascetic clothing. The most straightforward advice comes in part 8, where the point seems to be that material next to the skin should be coarse and plain: 'Nest flesch ne schal nan werien linnene claŏ bute hit beo of hearde ant of greate heorden' (Next to your skin you must not wear linen cloth unless it is harsh and coarse flax).[29] This fits into the general notion that a contemplative should not allow the flesh any sort of ease or comfort. On the other hand, various types of restrictive or prickling clothing are generally advised against. First of all, the author prohibits belts cinched tightly across the body, as well as the wearing of heavy mailshirts (which apparently induced violent sweating), disciplines practised by the ascetic man at the end of part 6:

ʒe schulen in an hetter ant i-gurd liggen, swa leoðeliche þah þet ʒe mahen honden putten þer-under. Nest lich nan ˜ne gurde hire wið na cunne gurdles, bute þurh schriftes leaue, ne beore nan irn ne here, ne iles piles felles.

(You must sleep in a garment with a belt, tied loosely enough for you to put a hand under it. Let no one belt herself with any kind of belt next to the body, except with her confessor's leave, nor wear any iron or hair, or hedgehog skins.)[30]

The issue of hair shirts is an interesting one in that, for the bulk of *Ancrene Wisse*, the wearing of coarse and prickling hair shirts is a seemingly normal practice.[31] However, in a section added to part 8 in the Corpus Revision, the author or reviser has rethought the original advice (the addition unique to Corpus appears in angle brackets):

Sum wummon inoh-reaðe wereð þe brech of here ful wel i-cnottet, þe streape-les dun to þe vet i-lacet ful feaste, <ah eauer is best þe swete ant te swote heorte – me is leouere þet ȝe þolien wel an heard word, þen an heard here>.

(A woman will sometimes wear breeches of haircloth very firmly knotted, the legs laced very tightly down to the feet. <But always a sweet and tender heart is best. I would rather that you well endure harsh words than harsh hairclothes>.)[32]

These additions show a tendency, particularly in part 8, to add more advice against purely physical mortifications, and it seems likely that the author or reviser was responding to actual practices among anchoritic women.

Heavy Labour.   Some of the lists of ascetic practices refer somewhat vaguely to hard work ('heard swinc').[33] It is difficult to understand exactly what is meant by this: it might refer to manual labour, which for the female anchorites in question consisted mainly of handiwork (see part 8), to the *opus Dei*, the work of God (that is, prayer), or perhaps, more generally, to the travail of the anchoritic life in general. Again, *Ancrene Wisse* refers to an ascetic practice without defining it in detail.

Sickness.   It may seem strange to list sickness as an ascetic practice, since illness is involuntary. However, the ascetic man at the end of part 6 prays for sickness and despairs when it does not come, and in part 6's discussion of suffering there is an extensive section devoted to sickness and medicine, spiritual versus physical, where spiritual health is to be preferred over the physical. In two colourful anecdotes drawn from Cistercian sources,[34] we see men anxious about their health comically refused spiritual medicine because they were so anxious to take care of their bodies with physical medicine. Adapting a substantial passage from Aelred's *de Institutione Inclusarum*, the *Ancrene Wisse* author suggests that, even though moderation is best:

> soð wisdom is don eauer sawle heale biuore flesches heale. Ant hwen he ne mei nawt ba somet halden, cheose ear licomes hurt þen þurh to strong fondunge sawle þrowunge.

> (true wisdom always puts the health of the soul before the body's health, and when it cannot keep both, rather chooses bodily hurt than suffering in the soul through too strong a temptation'.)[35]

This reverses somewhat *Ancrene Wisse*'s preference for caution, preserving Aelred's harder attitude, though by this stage in the discussion, as with the notion of vigils and vigilance, the sick person seeking a physical healing has become a looser type for those overly concerned with their bodies in general.

Whipping and Mutilation.   In part 8's discussion of clothing (see above), the author uses the question of hedgehog skins to address more extreme forms of mortification, namely whipping or self-flagellation, as well as the cutting of the body. The Corpus version adds two phrases (indicated in angle brackets below) not present in the earlier versions: a female anchorite should not wear hedgehog skins:

> ne beate hire þer-wið, ne wið scurge i-leadet, wið holin ne wið breres, ne biblodgi hire-seolf wið-ute schriftes leaue, <no-hwer ne binetli hire, ne ne beate biuoren, ne na keoruunge ne keorue,> ne ne neome ed eanes to luðere disceplines, <temptatiuns for-te acwenchen>.

> (let her not beat herself with them, nor with a leaded scourge, with holly or briars, nor draw blood from herself without her confessor's leave; <let her not sting herself with nettles anywhere, nor beat herself in front, nor cut herself,> nor impose on herself too many severe disciplines <to quench temptations at one time>.)[36]

It again seems very likely that, in expanding the list of potentially dangerous practices, the author was responding to the actual practices of the women under his direction. Since flagellation was administered on the bare back,[37] beating 'on the front' would represent a possibly harmful deviation from normal practice.

Though flagellation as a devotional practice seems to have been popularized by Peter Damian in the eleventh century in his monastery at Fonte Avella in Italy, it quickly spread in popularity and by the thirteenth century was practised by devout laypeople.[38] *Ancrene Wisse* elsewhere presents flagellation and the use of self-inflicted pain as an appropriate defence against temptations to lechery,[39] as part of the system of sacramental penance[40] and as a method of purification before high feast-days.[41]

Ancrene Wisse refers very briefly to self-mutilation[42] in its advice that the female anchorite should not 'cut herself' (literally the phrase reads 'let her cut no cut'). Presumably any ascetic practice that draws blood, like the severe whippings, could in theory endanger the health of the body and thus go beyond the limits set by *Ancrene Wisse*'s ascetic theory.

In conclusion, although *Ancrene Wisse* invokes the spirit of desert asceticism, its discussion of common ascetical practices like fasting, keeping vigil, manual labour, etc. is not detailed, and is prone to move from actual physical practice to an inner attitude. It seems that *Ancrene Wisse* wants contemplatives to admire, but not to imitate athletic asceticism (like that of the ascetic man and woman at the end of part 6). In his life of Marie d'Oignies, roughly contemporary with *Ancrene Wisse*, Jacques de Vitry takes a similar position on the extreme asceticism practised by Marie after her marriage and later on (heavy manual labour, sleeping on hard planks and binding her body with a rough cord, rolling in fires, cutting out bits of her flesh): 'I do not say these things to commend the excess but so that I might show her fervour. In these and in many other things wherein the privilege of grace operated, let the discreet reader pay attention that what is a privilege for a few does not make common law. Let us imitate her virtues but we cannot imitate the works of her virtues without individual privilege.'[43] Advanced female recluses, judging from the additions in part 8, however, *did* want to imitate some of the extremes, particularly with regard to clothing and disciplines (like flagellation).[44] In creating a lay asceticism for a mixed audience *Ancrene Wisse* spends a fair amount of energy in laying down basic ascetic theory but leaves most of the practices purposefully vague, generalizing others to the point of the symbolic.

Notes

[1] See the articles 'Tertiary' and 'Third order', in F. L. Cross (ed.), *The Oxford Dictionary of the Christian Church*, 2nd edn (Oxford, 1983).

[2] For a recent study, see Walter Simons, *City of Ladies: Beguine Communities in the Medieval Low Countries, 1200–1565* (Philadelphia, 2001).

[3] All quotation from *Ancrene Wisse* will be taken from the Corpus revision: *The English Text of the Ancrene Riwle: Ancrene Wisse: Edited from MS. Corpus Christi College Cambridge 402*, ed. J. R. R. Tolkien, EETS o.s. 249 (London, New York and Toronto, 1962). The corresponding translation of every quotation from *Ancrene Wisse* is taken from *Anchoritic Spirituality: Ancrene Wisse and Associated Works*, trans. and intro. Anne Savage and Nicholas Watson (New York and Mahwah, 1991).

[4] *Ancrene Wisse*, p. 92; Savage and Watson, pp. 99–100.

[5] *Ancrene Wisse*, p. 195; Savage and Watson, p. 189.

[6] Bella Millett's work, in particular, has shown the many connections between *Ancrene Wisse* and thirteenth-century sermon literature and pastoral writing intended for lay audiences (see, in particular, '*Ancrene Wisse* and the conditions of confession', *English Studies*, 80 (1999), 193–214), while Cate Gunn's essay in this collection, 'Beyond the tomb: *Ancrene Wisse* and lay piety', maps out how the adaptations and versions of this guide respond differently according to its various lay audiences.

[7] *Ancrene Wisse*, pp. 7–8 (my emphasis); Savage and Watson, pp. 48–9.

[8] Part 5, on confession, shows a very similar sense of mixed audience in its sample confession, where the penitent is to identify herself as 'an ancre, a nunne, a wif i-weddet, a meiden, a wummon þet me lefde se wel', etc. (*Ancrene Wisse*, p. 163) (an anchoress, a nun, a wedded wife, a maiden, a woman loved so well) (Savage and Watson, p. 165).

[9] *Ancrene Wisse* frequently admires and quotes the *Vitas Patrum* (see J. P. Migne, *PL Cursus Completus* ([Paris, 1885]), pp. 73–4). This is a compilation of many originally distinct texts about the ascetic saints of the Egyptian desert. Although it may seem to be a document of high monasticism, the *Vitas Patrum* was used from very early on as a collection of exempla for popular preaching and was translated into Old English, Middle English and a number of European vernaculars. See J. Welter's *L'Exemplum dans la littérature religieuse et didactique du moyen âge* (Paris, 1927), pp. 14–55. Jocelyn Wogan-Browne, *Saints' Lives and Women's Literary Culture c. 1150–1300: Virginity and its Authorizations* (Oxford, 2001), has recently examined the popularity of vernacular versions of the *Vitas Patrum* in the thirteenth century and concludes that 'they seem to have functioned as an ancillary and "informal" hagiographic genre, part-way between the *vita* and the conduct book, and to have provided models not only for professional religious, but for semi-religious and lay people . . . *Vitae patrum* tales figure in the books of lay as well as professed women in newly translated and recycled forms, and the asceticism of the desert fathers becomes associated

with female pious lives, even and especially the lives of married women'
(p. 135).

[10] The best guide to *Ancrene Wisse*'s ascetic theory is Mari Hughes-Edwards,
'Hedgehog skins and hairshirts: the changing role of asceticism in the
anchoritic ideal', *Mystics Quarterly*, 28, 1 (2002), 6–25. Hughes-Edwards
surveys anchoritic writings from the high to late Middle Ages, concluding
that 'anchoritic guides reflect a shift during the Middle Ages from an interest in asceticism as it is physically experienced, to an interest in it as a mental construct' (p. 24). Although *Ancrene Wisse* constructs an asceticism
experienced primarily through the body, it foreshadows the concerns of the
later guides.

[11] *Ancrene Wisse*, p. 73; Savage and Watson, p. 100.

[12] *Ancrene Wisse*, p. 70; Savage and Watson, p. 98.

[13] Hughes-Edwards, 'Hedgehog skins and hairshirts', 17.

[14] *Ancrene Wisse*, p. 180; Savage and Watson, p. 178.

[15] *Ancrene Wisse*, p. 193; Savage and Watson, p. 187.

[16] Aelred's *de Institutione Inclusarum*, an important source for *Ancrene Wisse*,
describes two similar figures who make war on their bodies. The first is a
monk (perhaps Aelred himself), who plunges his body into ice-cold waters
and rubs it with nettles in order to overcome lust, the second, a man who
made war on his body in adolescence with the most extreme practices and
who dies happily of an illness in old age, having achieved a fitful victory over
his evil body. See *de Institutione Inclusarum*, in *Aelredi Rievallensis Opera
Omnia: 1 Opera Ascetica*, ed. A. Hoste and C. H. Talbot (Turnhout, 1971),
pp. 652–3. A translation of this may be found in 'A Rule of Life for a
Recluse', in *Aelred of Rievaulx: Treatises: The Pastoral Prayer*, trans. Mary
Paul Macpherson and intro. David Knowles (Spencer, M.A., 1971),
pp. 66–7.

[17] *Ancrene Wisse*, pp. 194–5; Savage and Watson, p. 188.

[18] *Ancrene Wisse*, p. 195; Savage and Watson, p. 188.

[19] *Ancrene Wisse*, pp. 189–90; Savage and Watson, p. 184.

[20] Hughes-Edwards, 'Hedgehog skins and hairshirts', 22.

[21] *Ancrene Wisse*, p. 187; Savage and Watson, p. 183.

[22] *Ancrene Wisse*, p. 211; Savage and Watson, p. 199.

[23] *Ancrene Wisse*, p. 143; Savage and Watson, p. 150.

[24] See for example the story of Arsenius' delight in eating stinking palm leaves
stewed in water not changed for a year (*Vitas Patrum PL*, 73, col. 764A).

[25] *de Institutione Inclusarum*, pp. 647–8, 655–6; Macpherson, pp. 59–60, 69–70.

[26] *Ancrene Wisse*, p. 75; Savage and Watson, pp. 100–2. The translation of the
verse from Ecclesiasticus is particularly loose: a literal rendering would be
'Vigils of honesty consume the flesh'. The Douai translation is 'Watching for
riches consumeth the flesh'.

[27] The *Vitas Patrum* takes a much harsher view of vigils, with Arsenius, for
example, grudgingly closing his eyes for a few minutes after an entire night
of prayer and claiming that a good monk need sleep no more than one hour
a day. See *PL*, 73, col. 763.

[28] Significantly, the Pepys version of *Ancrene Wisse* changes the notion of vigil (remaining awake through the night) into a call for rising early, continuing the process of metaphor already seen here; see *The English Text of the Ancrene Riwle: Edited from Magdalene College, Cambridge, MS. Pepys 2498*, ed. A. Zettersten and B. Diensberg, EETS, o.s 274 (London, 1976), p. 60.

[29] *Ancrene Wisse*, p. 214; Savage and Watson, p. 202.

[30] *Ancrene Wisse*, p. 214; Savage and Watson, p. 202.

[31] See for example *Ancrene Wisse*, p. 69, where the author says that the good anchoress must be like Judith in her fasting, keeping vigils, hard labour and in wearing of hair shirts.

[32] *Ancrene Wisse*, p. 214; Savage and Watson, p. 202.

[33] *Ancrene Wisse*, p. 72.

[34] See *Ancrene Wisse, Parts Six and Seven*, trans. Geoffrey Shepherd (London, 1959), p. 44, note to p. 12, line 35.

[35] *Ancrene Wisse*, p. 189; Savage and Watson, p. 184. In Aelred, this passage justifies the extreme asceticism of a man he knows.

[36] *Ancrene Wisse*, p. 214; Savage and Watson, p. 202.

[37] See Pierre Gougaud, *Devotional and Ascetic Practices in the Middle Ages*, trans. G. C. Bateman (London, 1927), p. 192.

[38] See Jean Leclercq's article on 'Disciplina', in *Dictionnaire de Spiritualité, Ascétique et Mystique Doctrine et Histoire*, vol. 3 (Paris, 1957), cols. 1291–1302. For a recent psychoanalytic approach to medieval and post-medieval flagellation, see Patrick Vandermeersch, *La Chair de la passion: un histoire de foi, la flagellation* (Paris, 2002).

[39] In part 4's discussion of lechery, St Benedict rolls in thorns to subdue physical lust (p. 152) and, though *Ancrene Wisse* does not recommend his severity, it suggests that the contemplative should apply 'a smeort discepline' to quell lust (p. 152). See Savage and Watson, p. 156.

[40] At the very end of part 5, *Ancrene Wisse* says that a confessor may add 'disceplines' to a list of rather mild penances (p. 177). See Savage and Watson, p. 175.

[41] See *Ancrene Wisse*, p. 210; Savage and Watson, p. 199.

[42] See Claire Marshall, 'The politics of self-mutilation: forms of female devotion in the late Middle Ages', in Darryll Grantley and Nina Taunton (eds), *The Body in Late Medieval and Early Modern Culture* (Aldershot, 2000), pp. 11–21.

[43] Jacques de Vitry, *The Life of Marie D'Oignies*, trans. Margot H. King (Toronto, 1993), p. 47.

[44] In this they were not unlike a group of pious thirteenth-century widows, recently studied by Wogan-Browne, who were involved as patrons in the writing of ascetic saints' lives (St Edmund of Canterbury and St Richard of Chichester): 'Ascesis confers authority in claiming hegemonies and resources, not least among them the resources of wealthy widows. It also offers several points of identification with ascetic heroes in Edmund and Richard's lives: the penitential practices of fasting, vigils, and mortification are standardly represented as the particular hallmark and occupation of pious widows and chaste churchmen.' See *Saints' Lives*, p. 179.

12

Beyond the Tomb:
Ancrene Wisse and Lay Piety[1]

CATE GUNN

*A*ncrene *Wisse* is often studied – especially by those concerned with issues of gender – for information on female recluses: the nature of their spirituality and corporeality; the effects of misogyny and enclosure on their constructions of the self; their place within the history of female piety, and so on.[2] I want, however, to examine the development of the textual tradition of *Ancrene Wisse*, a guide for anchorites which existed in many different versions throughout the Middle Ages, and to shed light on the ways in which its textual development implies a relationship between anchoritism and lay piety. *Ancrene Wisse* was always a work in progress, and was continually adapted to the needs of a changing audience.[3] As Bella Millett has suggested: 'At an early stage it was adapted for a larger group of recluses; and it was later reworked for nuns, for male religious, for a mixed general audience including both religious and laity, and for a lay audience.'[4] Millett also suggests that: 'The key to the textual instability of *Ancrene Wisse* lies in its functionality.'[5] What we are looking at, therefore, is a work which always contained within itself different functions and the possibility of being used by different audiences. Despite Nicholas Watson's assertion that *Ancrene Wisse* and its associated works were 'clearly professional tools' and are best understood when the original anchoritic readers are taken into account,[6] I believe that it may be more interesting to consider *Ancrene Wisse* as a 'process' rather than as the 'product' of literary composition.[7]

That *Ancrene Wisse* was written in the vernacular in the first half of the thirteenth century, originally for three sisters who were following a religious life as lay anchorites rather than as nuns, invites us to read it in the context of the literature of lay piety as much (if not more than) as a traditional institutional product. The spirituality evinced by *Ancrene Wisse* – a spirituality that is incarnational and affective – although itself a product of monasticism, is also the spirituality that motivated the growth of lay piety. I use the term *lay* with a certain amount of caution; the first recording in English of the adjective *lai* is from around 1400 and includes concepts of illiteracy in Latin and of not belonging to the priesthood.[8] The term *lay* is usually used to indicate those who have not devoted their entire lives to a religious vocation – a definition which would exclude the anchorites for whom *Ancrene Wisse* was written. The female anchorites were not, however, following a traditional religious vocation; as they occupied a liminal position in society, so *Ancrene Wisse* has a transitional locus. The upsurge in lay piety in the late twelfth and early thirteenth centuries led to new religious movements, but also to a demand for religious literature directed towards a new middle-class readership; the roots of *Ancrene Wisse* are in monasticism, but it anticipates the developing lay piety and vernacular theology of the thirteenth and fourteenth centuries. By placing *Ancrene Wisse* within this context of lay piety, we can usefully compare it with other devotional and pastoral works written for a lay audience. Millett has already made some comparisons, comparing part 5 of *Ancrene Wisse* with the European tradition of confessional literature,[9] and the devotional routine as set out in part 1 with the development of Books of Hours.[10] It is also possible to argue that the directions for prayers in *Ancrene Wisse*, with their repeated Aves associated with meditations on the Virgin Mary, are looking forward to the development of the rosary: a passage in part 1 of *Ancrene Wisse*, in which the anchoresses are advised to say multiple Hail Marys and Psalms associated with the Virgin Mary,[11] can be seen as fitting in with what Anne Winston-Allen writes about the development of the rosary as a 'meditative exercise', used by laypeople as well as nuns, and as a prayer to be said during Mass for those unable to follow the Latin of the service.[12]

Ancrene Wisse, written in the vernacular, was intended to be read by the anchorites, but in its composition and language it shows traces of the rhetoric of the preaching aids, confessional manuals, penitential treatises and other *pastoralia* used by clerics. The Fourth Lateran Council of 1215, which required all adults to take communion and make confession at least once a year, stimulated the production of such *pastoralia*; parts 5 and 6 of *Ancrene Wisse* bear closest comparison to this literature. The major pastoral works directed at laypeople, however, were probably sermons; I intend to draw some preliminary comparisons between *Ancrene Wisse* and sermons of the period.

The author borrowed some of the techniques of sermon composition – in terms both of the construction and of the 'tools', such as *exempla*, which were hallmarks of the 'modern', thirteenth-century sermon. Thirteenth-century sermons are noted for their structure – they progress by the division of the theme.[13] While the author of *Ancrene Wisse* may not use this very precise and formal structure, division is very important as an organizational device and as a method of progressing his argument. Erwin Panofsky explains division and subdivision in dialectic works as the 'mental habit' of scholasticism, designed for elucidation and clarification.[14] David d'Avray argues that thirteenth-century mendicant sermons are not scholastic, but does admit that they share 'the subdividing mentality' with scholastic works of this period.[15] Something of this mental habit is apparent in *Ancrene Wisse*: the work as a whole is divided into parts and the parts themselves are sometimes divided in the manner of a sermon. The use in *Ancrene Wisse* of the term *destinctiuns*[16] for its division into eight parts is ultimately derived from the later-twelfth-century revision of the constitutions of the Premonstratensian order, which divided them into four *distinctiones* 'as much for the variety of the contents as for the convenience of the readers'.[17] *Distinctiones* as subdivisions or chapters of a larger work were used for the sake of clarity, accessibility and to make the reading more interesting. In the high Middle Ages, works began to be presented differently – with divisions, indices, chapter headings and so on – because they were being used differently; instead of being read through from beginning to end, texts were used for reference purposes.[18] *Ancrene Wisse* can thus be read as a library of texts of lay piety.

Part 2 of *Ancrene Wisse* uses the five senses as a means of dividing the theme of the custody of the heart, and part 5 starts with an explicit statement of the intention to proceed by means of division. While some parts of *Ancrene Wisse*, most notably those on Temptation and Confession, use elaborate division and subdivision, the progress of ideas in other parts is almost in the manner of a stream of consciousness, as one image or thought leads to another. Louis-Jacques Bataillon makes a distinction between two kinds of sermons, those organized by the *distinctiones* into which the theme is divided and those that use lengthy *similitudines* to form a structure. The latter, he claims, are practically never found in university sermons but are an element in the effort of preachers to reach the people and explain the Scriptures to them.[19]

Distinctiones, in the particular sense of the dividing of a word or theme, are not present in *Ancrene Wisse*,[20] but part 3 could be described as being structured by lengthy *similitudines* (how the anchoresses are like birds) and so fits in with what Bataillon sees as a deliberate tactic in lay preaching. Taking a verse from Psalm 101, 'Similis factus sum pellicano solitudinis' (I am become like to a pelican of the wilderness),[21] the author suggests the anchoresses are like pelicans in their passion and in being thin;[22] they are like birds in their nests,[23] the night-bird under the eaves[24] and the sparrow alone on the roof.[25]

In this part, on the Inner Feelings, we can see the author reaching out to his female audience through his use of images and figures: as well as likening the anchoresses to birds, he urges them to follow the examples of Judith and Esther; he illustrates his argument with *exempla* and defends it by the use of etymologies; he calls on the Scriptures, Church fathers and even the poet Horace as authorities. The presence of Judith and Esther might alert us to a particular awareness of the female audience, as in sermons, preached to nuns by a Dominican, which included the figures of the woman who killed Abimelech, Judith, who slew Holofernes, and Jael, who dispatched Sisera with a nail. V. M. O'Mara has pointed out, in a survey of sermons preached to women that 'there is clearly a pronounced emphasis on women';[26] Stephen Langton made much of the story of Esther in his *Sermo de Virginibus*, in which he presented the 'ideal of virginity as applied to female religious',[27] and Humbert of Romans used the figures of both Judith and Esther in his sermon to 'mulieres religiosas inclusas' (enclosed religious women) (a sermon in which he, significantly, also holds up Marie d'Oignies – that pioneer of the quasi-religious, or semi-regular, life for women – as an example).[28] The story of Judith as representing confession, cutting off the head of sin, Holofernes,[29] is not gender-specific, however; Odo of Cheriton and Thomas of Chobham, both educated in Paris and preachers in the early thirteenth century, state that Judith is interpreted as confession.[30] Neither is the use of Esther and Judith confined to thirteenth-century pastoral literature; they are mentioned by the eleventh-century Peter Damian[31] and by Aelred of Rievaulx.[32] Bernard mentions Judith in a list of people who triumphed over their enemies, even though she was a woman: 'Iosue, Iephte, Gedeon, Samson, Iudith quoque, quamquam femina, gloriose in diebus suis triumpharunt de hostibus' (Joshua, Jephthah, Gideon, Samson, Judith also, although a woman, triumphed gloriously in their day over their enemies).[33] Caroline Walker Bynum has argued, in an essay on 'The female body and religious practice', that 'medieval thinkers used gender imagery fluidly, not literally': it was not uncommon for female imagery and models to be used of and for men.[34] What is interesting, I believe, is not so much that descriptions of 'strong women' were used in sermons intended for women and in a handbook for anchorites, but that such women could also be used as role models for men. In this context, then, the moral and spiritual teaching of *Ancrene Wisse* should be seen as applicable to men and women, religious and secular.

Thus far, I have been referring to the text of *Ancrene Wisse* found in Cambridge, Corpus Christi College, MS 402, a text which was revised, probably by the original author, for an increased number of female anchorites. *Ancrene Wisse*, however, soon 'escaped into the outside world', to use Dobson's terminology,[35] and was adapted for an audience beyond the walls of the original anchorhold. This wider application is, I believe, a fruitful area to explore; we can see that elements of *Ancrene Wisse* could be used by devout laypeople living in the world, and its rich manuscript tradition implies its continued usefulness for many different groups and is a witness to its broad appeal. The versions found in the Gonville and Caius manuscript and the Titus manuscript, both dating from around the middle of the thirteenth century, were adapted for male readers. The editor of the Titus manuscript, Frances Mack, has pointed out 'confusion' and 'carelessness' in the use of personal pronouns, suggesting that the 'attempt made in the Titus version to address the teaching of the work to men as well as to women recluses' was 'very superficial'.[36] This could suggest that not much alteration was considered necessary to adapt the text for a male readership: the basic teaching was relevant to both female and male readers. As Roger Dahood has pointed out:

> The existence, for example of MS Titus, with its relatively superficial if unsystematic revisions for a male audience, should remind us that the English educated classes of the first half of the thirteenth century may not have perceived a gulf between male and female religious sensibilities.[37]

Some of the changes, however, are interesting. The she-wolf, 'wuluene', in part 3 becomes a wolf, but the reader is still advised to throw off the rough hide and 'makien hire smeðe & softe as is cundeliche wumones huide. oðer wepmonnes' (make it as smooth and soft as a woman's – or man's – is naturally).[38] The text found in the Gonville and Caius manuscript also 'has occasional substitutions of masculine words and forms', with 'sustren' changed to 'frend' and, in one instance, to 'breþren'.[39] This text also omits the section at the beginning of part 6 which, in the Corpus version, starts 'Al is penitence ant strong penitence þet ʒe eauer dreheð mine leoue sustren' (Everything that you have to bear, my dear sisters, is penance, and hard penance),[40] so that, according to Dobson, 'it too is adapted for reading by a man' – more accurately, it is adapted for someone who is not an 'anchoress'.[41]

A version of *Ancrene Wisse* is also found in the Vernon manuscript, which contains an extensive range of vernacular religious texts adapted for a pious lay audience as well as a religious audience. A. I. Doyle points out that there is a presumption that a collection of vernacular religious literature of this scope was made for nuns 'or other devout women' but that some items, such as 'How to hear Mass' point away from this presumption: 'some items are couched specifically for lay listeners or readers'.[42] As Spencer points out in her introduction to the Vernon version of *Ancrene Wisse*, the compilers 'evidently had knowledge of (and could get access to) an impressively wide range of the existing religious literature in the vernacular'; the section in which *Ancrene Wisse* is found contains other material which belongs 'to the genre of letters of religious counsel written by men for women religious'.[43] According to Derek Pearsall, the Vernon manuscript, although probably produced in a monastery, may have catered 'for a women's religious community, or indeed for a group of women banded together in a more irregular community, like that for which the *Ancrene Wisse* was originally written'.[44] Felicity Riddy points out that, while it is true that *Ancrene Wisse* is found in the Vernon manuscript among other works written by male clerics for women readers, 'we should not assume that women were merely passive recipients of books'.[45] The Vernon manuscript was produced between 1380 and 1400 and its contents are, on the whole, 'conservative';[46] N. F. Blake has suggested that: 'It is not impossible that the onset of the Lollard heresy may have prompted someone to prepare a collection which was free of heresy for those who were considered not to be so able to judge such things for themselves.'[47]

The version of *Ancrene Wisse* found in the Pepys manuscript, also from the second half of the fourteenth century,[48] however, was rewritten and adapted for a very different audience, an audience that was secular, both male and female and possibly less orthodox.[49] Like the Corpus version in Corpus Christi 402, the Pepys version refers to the definition of the religious life found in the epistle of St James, but here the exclusivity of the anchoritic life is rejected: it insists that 'all men and women must hold a rule within' and that the second part of the definition of the religious life, to keep oneself pure and unspotted, is to apply to all people.[50] The reader is advised to avoid wicked folk, but not the goods of the world, since none may properly live and serve God unless they have their sustenance;[51] similarly, when the choice is to be made between Mary and Martha, it is acknowledged that Mary, sitting at the feet of Christ, chose the better part, but it is argued that it is not for anyone to make that choice for themselves; rather, they should pray for grace to come to that high degree.[52] God's will should be done in the world, lest the Devil take advantage of spiritual pride. The Pepys version rejected the exclusivity of the anchoritic way of life and its spirituality, substituting for it a spirituality that could be attained by pious people in the world, and here we see *Ancrene Wisse* placed within a tradition of religious literature continuing into the fourteenth century and beyond.

The original author himself seems to have accepted the evolution and textual instability of the work and to have valued its functionality over 'textual integrity'.[53] It is surely the genius of *Ancrene Wisse* that it can survive outside the confinement of the anchorhold, and there may be much profit in studying its manifold nature, in embracing its variability. *Ancrene Wisse* was not confined to the tomb of the anchorhold: it was – and still is – a living text, re-created in every new reading and for every new audience.

Notes

1   Thanks are due to Bella Millett for reading through this paper and making useful suggestions.

2   Cf. 'Much recent literary criticism analyzes the ramifications of patriarchy, misogyny, and female corporeality in *Ancrene Wisse* Group works', Roger Dahood, 'The current state of *Ancrene Wisse* group studies', *Medieval English Studies Newsletter* 36 (1997), 6–14 (see especially p. 9).

3   *The English Text of the Ancrene Riwle: Ancrene Wisse: Edited from MS. Corpus Christi College Cambridge 402*, by J. R. R. Tolkien, EETS o.s. 249 (London, New York and Toronto, 1962), p. 25. All subsequent quotation from the Corpus revision of *Ancrene Wisse* is taken from this edition. The corresponding translation of every quotation from *Ancrene Wisse* is taken from *Anchoritic Spirituality: Ancrene Wisse and Associated Works*, trans. and intro. Anne Savage and Nicholas Watson (New York and Mahwah, 1991).

4   Bella Millett, '*Mouvance* and the medieval author: re-editing *Ancrene Wisse*', in A. J. Minnis (ed.), *Late-Medieval Religious Texts and their Transmission*

(Cambridge, 1994), pp. 9–20 (p. 14). See also E. J. Dobson, *The Origins of Ancrene Wisse* (Oxford, 1976), p. 251. Throughout this chapter I adopt the current critical practice of referring to every revision of this anchoritic guide as *Ancrene Wisse*, using the respective manuscript name to differentiate between them.

5 Millett, '*Mouvance*', p. 13.

6 Nicholas Watson, 'The methods and objectives of thirteenth-century anchoritic devotion', in Marion Glasscoe (ed.), *The Medieval Mystical Tradition in England*, Exeter Symposium IV (Woodbridge, 1987), pp. 132–53 (p. 138).

7 This is in contrast to arguments such as those associated with *New Scholarship*, which claims that 'eclectic or critical editing's concentration on a single, uniform "final intention" is a chimera, and that a textual editor would be better employed describing the "process" rather than the apparent "product" of literary composition'. D. C. Greetham, *Textual Scholarship: An Introduction* (New York, 1994), p. 9.

8 See Cate Gunn, '*Ancrene Wisse*: A modern lay person's guide to a medieval religious text', *Magistra*, 8 (2002), 1–25 (especially 14–17).

9 'An investigation of the development of this theme (i.e. of conditions of confession) may help to place *Ancrene Wisse* in the context of the broader European tradition of confessional literature'. See Millett, '*Ancrene Wisse* and the conditions of confession', *English Studies*, 80 (1999), 193–215 (193).

10 '[*Ancrene Wisse*] might provide not just an instance, but a paradigm of how the supplementary devotions of monastic practice evolved into the fully-developed late-medieval "breviary for the use of the laity".' See Millett, '*Ancrene Wisse* and the Book of Hours', in Denis Renevey and Christiania Whitehead (eds), *Writing Religious Women: Female Spiritual and Textual Practices in Late Medieval England* (Cardiff, 2000), p. 32.

11 The Five Joys of Mary are in *Ancrene Wisse* at pp. 23–4, and in Savage and Watson at pp. 61–2.

12 Anne Winston-Allen, *Stories of the Rose: The Making of the Rosary in the Middle Ages* (Philadelphia, 1997), p. 4.

13 This is a structure defined by the *artes predicandi*, which 'define the structure of the sermon, namely the theme, the protheme or antitheme, prayer, divisions confirmed by authorities, and conclusion', for which see Mary E. O'Carroll, *A Thirteenth-Century Preacher's Handbook: Studies in MS Laud Misc. 511* (Toronto, 1997), pp. 22, 23.

14 Erwin Panofsky, *Gothic Architecture and Scholasticism* (Cleveland, 1957), pp. 30–1, 36.

15 D. L. d'Avray, *The Preaching of the Friars: Sermons diffused from Paris before 1300* (Oxford, 1985), pp. 176–7.

16 *Ancrene Wisse*, p. 11.

17 See Pl. F. Lefèvre and W. M. Grauwen (eds), *Les Statuts de Prémontré au Milieu du XIIe siècle*, Bibliotheca Analectorum, Praemonstratensium Fasc. 12 (Averbode, 1978), p. 1. The translation is my own. Dobson first identified this link in *Origins*, p. 84.

[18] Paul Saenger, *Space Between Words: The Origins of Silent Reading* (Stanford, 1997), p. 259 *passim*.

[19] Louis-Jacques Bataillon, '*Similitudines* et *exempla* dans les sermons du XIIIᵉ siècle', in Katherine Walsh and Diana Wood (eds), *The Bible in the Medieval World: Essays in Memory of Beryl Smalley*, Ecclesiastical History Society (Oxford, 1985), pp. 191–205.

[20] 'A biblical *distinctio* distinguishes (hence the name) the various figurative meanings of a word in the Bible, supplying for each meaning a text of Scripture in which the word is used with that meaning.' Richard H. Rouse and Mary A. Rouse, ' "*Statim invenire*", schools, preachers, and new attitudes to the page', in Robert Benson and Giles Constable with Carol D. Lanham (eds), *Renaissance and Renewal in the Twelfth Century* (Toronto, 1991), pp. 201–25 (p. 213). These two meanings of the term *distinctio* can cause confusion.

[21] *Ancrene Wisse*, p. 63; Savage and Watson, p. 93.

[22] *Ancrene Wisse*, p. 67; Savage and Watson, p. 96.

[23] *Ancrene Wisse*, pp. 70–1; Savage and Watson, p. 98.

[24] *Ancrene Wisse*, p. 74; Savage and Watson, p. 101.

[25] *Ancrene Wisse*, p. 75; Savage and Watson, p. 101.

[26] The quotation continues: 'particularly virginal women, with biblical women being seen as role-models (Rebecca, Esther, the virgin of the Song of Songs, and the Virgin Mary), anti-role-models (Lot's wife, and the sinful Jerusalem), and poor role-models turned to good (Mary Magdalene with the ointment)'. V. M. O'Mara, 'Preaching to nuns in late medieval England', in Carolyn Muessig (ed.), *Medieval Monastic Preaching* (Leiden, 1998), pp. 93–119 (see especially p. 114).

[27] Phyllis B. Roberts, 'Stephen Langton's *Sermo de Virginibus*', in Julius Kirshner and Suzanne F. Wemple (eds), *Women of the Medieval World: Essays in Honor of John H. Mundy* (Oxford, 1985), pp. 103–18 (see especially p. 104).

[28] Humbert of Romans, 'Ad mulieres religiosas inclusas quascumque', in Carla Casagrande (ed.), *Prediche alle donne del secolo XIII: Testi di Umberto da Romans, Gilberto da Tournai, Stefano de Borbone* (Milan, 1978), pp. 57–60.

[29] *Ancrene Wisse*, p. 72.

[30] Millett quotes the *Summa de Penitentia* of Odo of Cheriton: 'Sed Iudit, que interpretuatur confessio . . .' from MS Cambridge University Library, Peterhouse 109, f. 237r. See the notes to her forthcoming edition of *Ancrene Wisse* for EETS, *Ancrene Wisse* vol. 1, EETS o.s. 325 (Oxford: Oxford University Press, 2005). We also find 'Iudith interpretatur confessio . . .' in Thomas of Chobham's *Summa de Commendatione Virtutum et Extirpatione Vitiorum*, ed. F. Morenzoni, CCCM vol. 82B (Turnhout, 1997), pp. 14–15. H. L. Spencer has compared Odo to the author of *Ancrene Wisse*. See her *English Preaching in the Late Middle Ages* (Oxford, 1993), p. 82.

[31] Peter Damian, *de perfectione monachorum* (in a section on the praise of tears) in *PL*, 145, col. 308B.

[32] Aelred saw in Judith the figure of Ecclesia, who destroyed the Devil when

she decapitated Holofernes, sermon 45 in '*Sermones*', *Opera Omnia*, ed.
G. Raciti CCCM 2A (Turnhout, 1989), p. 358.

33 Bernard of Clairvaux, *Sermones super Cantica Canticorum*, sermon 13 in
Opera, vol. 1, eds J. Leclercq, C. H. Talbot and H. M. Rochais (Rome,
1957), p. 71.

34 Caroline Walker Bynum, *Fragmentation and Redemption: Essays on Gender
and the Human Body in Medieval Religion* (New York, 1992),
p. 218.

35 Dobson, *Origins*, p. 293; Dobson also writes of 'contamination' of the text.

36 See Introduction to *The English Text of the Ancrene Riwle: Edited from
Cotton MS. Titus Dxviii*, ed. Frances Mack, EETS o.s. 252 (London, 1963
(for 1962)), pp. xiv-xv. Millett believes that at some point the version in
Titus was adapted back for a female audience, since there are feminine pronouns in *Titus* which do not appear in the other manuscripts.

37 Dahood, 'The current state of *Ancrene Wisse* group studies', p. 9.

38 Titus, p. 32. The translation is my own. This is, presumably, just a quick and
careless adaptation of the text for a male reader, but one would like to think
that the ascription of smoothness and softness to a man's skin was a deliberate strike for gender equality. See 'ant hwat ʒif eni ancre iesu cristes spu-se
is forschupped to wuluene . . . & mid softe seihtnes makien hire smeðe &
softe ase is cundeliche wommo-ne hude', *The English Text of the Ancrene
Riwle: Edited from Cotton MS. Nero A.xiv*, ed. Mabel Day, EETS o.s. 225
(London, 1952), p. 53.

39 Dobson covers this in *Origins*, p. 296. For comparison see *Ancrene Wisse*,
Corpus, p. 182; at this point, the Titus version of *Ancrene Wisse* has the word
'childre', p. 129.

40 *Ancrene Wisse*, p. 177; Savage and Watson, p. 176.

41 See Dobson, *Origins*, p. 296. At first reading, it appears that Dobson suggests that men are not equipped to lead lives of harsh penitence, but, as
Millett points out, the Gonville and Caius revision of *Ancrene Wisse* loses
most of the specifically *anchoritic* bits – it also lacks part 1, much of parts 2
and 3 and part 8 and modifies its intended audience, substituting *religiuse* for
ancre [*n*] at pp. 31 and 54.

42 Introduction to *The Vernon Manuscript: A Facsimile of Bodleian Library,
Oxford, MS. Eng. Poet. a. 1*, ed. A. I. Doyle (Cambridge, 1987), p. 14.

43 H. L. Spencer, Introduction to *The English Text of the Ancrene Riwle: The
'Vernon' Text, edited from Oxford, Bodleian Library MS Eng. poet. a. 1*, ed.
Arne Zettersten and Bernhard Diensberg, EETS o.s. 310 (Oxford, 2000), pp.
xii, xiii. See also S. S. Hussey, 'Implications of choice and arrangements of
texts in part 4', in Derek Pearsall (ed.), *Studies in the Vernon Manuscript*,
(Cambridge, 1990), pp. 61–74.

44 Derek Pearsall, Introduction to *Studies in the Vernon Manuscript*, p. x.

45 Felicity Riddy, ' "Women talking about the things of God": a late medieval
sub-culture', in Carol Meale (ed.), *Women and Literature in Britain,
1150–1500* (Cambridge, 1993), p. 107.

46 Spencer, Introduction to EETS Vernon edition of *Ancrene Wisse*, p. xiii.

47 N. F. Blake, 'Vernon Manuscript: contents and organisation' in *Studies in the Vernon Manuscript*, pp. 58–9. Spencer adds 'or, at least, for those whom Church authorities considered to be unable to judge for themselves', Introduction to *Vernon*, p. xiv.

48 *The English Text of the Ancrene Riwle: Edited from Magdalene College, Cambridge, MS. Pepys 2498*, ed. A. Zettersten and B. Diensberg, EETS o.s. 274 (London, 1976).

49 Colledge argues that this revision was by a Lollard, but this view is now open to dispute; Eric [Edmund] Colledge, '*The Recluse:* a Lollard interpolated version of the *Ancrene Riwle*', *Review of English Studies*, 15 (1939), 1–15 and 129–45.

50 Pepys, pp. 2, 4.

51 Pepys, p. 4.

52 Pepys, p. 28.

53 Millett, '*Mouvance*', p. 15.

13

The Anchoritic Elements of
Holkham Misc. 41

CATHERINE INNES-PARKER

Bodleian Library MS Holkham Misc. 41 is a fascinating manuscript which adds to our understanding of the tradition of *Ancrene Wisse* and its legacy to future generations of women readers and authors.[1] A small book, easily held in the hand, this manuscript was clearly intended for private devotion. Dating from the mid-fifteenth century, it is a lovely manuscript, with 'initials in red, pink, green and blue on gold grounds, each with a partial border of leaf design on pages 1, 6, and 99',[2] suggesting that it was commissioned (either for personal use or as a gift) by someone with the means to afford more than the basic utilitarian manuscripts that contain many of the anchoritic texts of, for example, the Katherine Group. It contains only two texts, *The feitis* (sometimes read as *festis*) *and the passion of oure lord Ihesu Crist* (found only in this manuscript), and a rendition of the third Middle English version of Flete's *De Remediis*, here identified as *Consolacio anime*. A brief lyric ('Syke and sorowe depely') is appended to the first of these.

Both texts are addressed to women, and both reflect a background in the anchoritic literature of the early thirteenth century, as well as a thorough grounding in the devotional literature of the fourteenth century, such as *A Talkyng of the Love of God*, *The Doctrine of the Hert*, *The Prickyng of Love* and the works of Rolle and Hilton, many of which were addressed, at least in the first instance, to women. Like *The Chastising of God's Children* (also addressed to a female audience), Flete's treatise opens with the metaphor of God as a mother who chastises her children, which is drawn from *Ancrene Wisse*. However it is the first text, *The feitis and the passion*, which offers the most interesting evidence of the legacy of *Ancrene Wisse* and its sister texts. The text is unedited, with the exception of excerpts included by Alexandra Barratt in her anthology of women's writing in Middle English, and, with the notable exceptions of the work of Alexandra Barratt and William Pollard, very little critical attention has been paid to this text.[3]

Yet, *The feitis* has a great deal to tell us about how the women to whom *Ancrene Wisse* and its sister texts were addressed might have read these male-authored guides to their spiritual lives. If Pollard is correct in his speculation that this particular copy was made by a religious for a wealthy patron,[4] the manuscript may also reveal much about lay piety in the fifteenth century.[5] *The feitis* was written by a professional religious woman for an enclosed woman reader. The text itself consists of a Prologue, a General Confession (which the author calls 'the sweping awey the filthe of oure sinnes in a corner',[6] a series of fifty-three prayers and an Epilogue.[7] The manuscript is designed to be easily read, and each prayer is clearly identified with the Paternoster and Ave at the beginning, in red. This enables the reading pattern that is suggested in the epilogue, where the reader is instructed not to read all the prayers every day, but to 'seye summe on oon day. & summe on a nothir day. as ye haue leyser and tyme'.[8] However, the author expresses the wish that her reader will, in time, come to pray these prayers without the text, for inward prayer brings more comfort and union with God than prayer 'by the book'.[9]

The prayer cycle is, at first glance, fairly conventional, moving through Christ's life, Passion and death, and applying each of these to the spiritual life of the reader. Yet the text is original and bold, carefully constructed to create units of prayer that represent the progression of contemplative union with Christ. Meditation on the events of Christ's life prepares the reader for meditation on the Passion, which excites the reader's compassion and contrition, preparing her heart to melt into the burning love of Christ, which will merge her heart and Christ's wounded heart in love and union.

The author is clearly well-educated and familiar with the major devotional literature of her day: as Colledge and Chadwick point out, 'she is well-versed in Scripture, able in pastoral theology, [and] interested in the techniques and the theory of prayer'.[10] She appears to do her own translations of the Gospels, and uses Latin quotations with ease.[11] This deep familiarity with the Gospels enables her careful selection of stories and events from Christ's life to be included in the prayer cycle. Pollard suggests that the text is the product of an enclosed order, probably

Bridgettine, and proposes Joanna North, abbess of Syon from 1421–33, as a possible author.[12] The author's bold voice and her wide reading certainly suggest a woman with an education such as might have been provided at Syon, and her authoritative authorial stance would be consistent with an abbess of such an institution.

The text contains consistent, if subtle, references to the author and the act of writing. The authorial voice is clearly heard in the prologue and epilogue, where phrases such as 'I have written', 'I have set . . . in this writing' and the bold 'and to them so I answer' occur in every paragraph. The author boldly claims that she has written more than she has found in the Passion of the Gospels, claiming as her authority the Gospel writers themselves, who attest that there were more stories than they had written down.[13] Both prologue and epilogue include a conventional humility topos, but it is consistently undermined by the authoritative tone and by the demands that the author makes of her reader.

The authorial voice is heard not only in the prologue and epilogue, where it is to be expected, but also throughout the prayers. The didactic tone of the epilogue is reflected in the prayer that God will grant wit and wisdom to all who preach and teach his word, a group from which the author clearly does not exclude herself.[14] The author herself is evidently in a position of authority, and refers to the 'burdens of charge' that fall to her as a form of *imitatio Christi*, comparable to the bearing of Christ's cross in penance and contemplation.[15] She is deeply familiar with the contemplative life and presents herself as one who guides others in that life. She includes herself (and her reader) in the ranks of those who, like Mary, have chosen the solitary life, speaking of her writing, thinking and speaking as Christ's work.[16]

A deep identification of author and reader sounds throughout the text, as the authorial voice merges with the voice of the reader in prayer. The author views even private prayer as a communal experience, encouraging her reader to take both herself and her fellow Christians with her as she prays. The goal of prayer, however, is clearly the contemplative union of the soul with its heavenly spouse, a union that the author herself has experienced, and that she expects her reader to achieve through the teachings of her text.

Such union is rooted in the enclosed life of the anchoritic tradition, and there is a stress on the solitary life throughout the prayer cycle. For example, there are specific prayers for leaders of the Church[17] and solitaries – specifying anchorites, hermits and recluses[18] – but not for any other religious or laypersons. Christ's fasting in the wilderness is the model for the solitary life,[19] and both author and reader have joined the ranks of solitaries who have forsaken the world for Christ's sake.[20] The text also draws upon language and imagery familiar from anchoritic works. The hardships and poverty of Christ's life are allied with penance, as an example of the penance which the author and reader live out in their lives, asserting in the tradition of *Ancrene Wisse* that 'Penaunce with preiere and contricion is weye & ledere to gete us grace of yow. & foryeunesse of oure sinnes'.[21] Penance is also allied with contemplation in the bearing of the cross, particularly in the author's authority over others. The anchoritic tone of the imagery continues in the imagery of the female body applied to the enclosed body and heart, but without the vitriolic fear and mistrust of the female body often found in anchoritic texts. For example, the image of the enclosed body as a building in which Christ dwells is altered to excise the body and focus on the soul, which is likened to a house, which must be swept clean before it is fit for the indwelling of Christ,[22] and to the temple, which must be cleansed so that Christ can rest fully in her in mutual indwelling.[23] Significantly, it is the soul, not the body, which is the focus of both cleansing and union.

Similarly, *The feitis* also draws on *Ancrene Wisse*'s comparison of the enclosed female body and the heart, which it, in turn, compares to Christ's enclosure in the tomb and in Mary's womb.[24] But, again, the focus is on the heart, not the body, as the reader prays that Christ will take her heart from all earthly things and bury and enclose it in him, as his body was buried in the sepulchre.[25] The Virgin's womb is an image for the heart and soul of the reader, who prays that she might feel Christ stir in her by his divine grace, as Mary felt him stir when he took flesh and blood in her womb.[26] Elsewhere, the author draws on the imagery of pregnancy and its intimate indwelling to represent the fastening of her heart to Christ, appealing to Mary's love in bearing him between her 'preciouse sides' for forty weeks, and her tender care in nursing him with sweet milk after his birth.[27]

The Virgin Mary is consistently presented as a model of love and union with Christ throughout the early prayers, dealing with Christ's birth and youth, and the Passion section, where her grief and joy alternate, inspiring the reader to tears and joyful dalliance with Christ. Yet, it is not her virginal purity which is stressed, but her love, grief and joy, which open her to union with Christ. Indeed, the image of the virginal body is striking by its absence in this text. This is paralleled by the total lack of reference to sexual sin, even in the stories of the woman taken in adultery and of Mary Magdalene. Indeed, the prayer dealing with the woman taken in adultery is aimed at those who attack the Holy Church and her members, like the Pharisees who accuse the woman, and it is their sin which is foregrounded. The woman's sin is mentioned only once, and then only to identify her as the nameless 'woman who was taken in adultery'. Unlike the Pharisees, she is condemned neither by Christ nor by the reader.[28]

By providing positive female role-models, the text subtly undermines the emphasis on sin and temptation which characterizes many of its sources, even as it uses self-examination and repentance to evoke an emotional and meditative response to Christ's suffering. This is true in spite of the fact that, with the exception of the Virgin Mary, all of the women who are introduced here are sinners or marginalized in some way. Yet, all are models of the soul which, alienated through sin, is yet called and welcomed by Christ when she approaches him in faith and love.

The section of prayers dealing with Christ's public ministry is framed with the stories of the Samaritan woman and the Canaanite woman (women who are marginalized both morally and ethnically). The Samaritan woman is a model of those who are enlightened by Christ and united with him, and her story draws on the symbolism of water as an image of ecstatic union, found in previous prayers. The Canaanite woman is an example of those who persevere in prayer, even when Christ makes himself strange and seems to refuse to answer. Perseverance with faith, in the face of one's own unworthiness and Christ's estrangement, is rewarded with the bread of life, part of the recurring imagery of feeding and nourishment to express the soul's union with God. Both the Canaanite woman and the Samaritan woman illustrate that, with meekness and faith, unworthiness or sin is not a barrier to union with Christ.

The central role-model is, not surprisingly, Mary Magdalene, who is introduced in a series of prayers which focus on contrition, tears, tribulation, forgiveness and love. In keeping with the text's overall expurgation of the sinfulness of the female body, the extent of Mary Magdalene's sin is identified not by sexual sin, but by the demons that Christ cast out from her. Indeed, it is significant that Mary Magdalene is conflated with Mary of Bethany, but *not* with the woman taken in adultery. The demons figure the temptation and tribulation of the reader, and are patterned on Christ's own temptation in the wilderness – temptations which are overcome, even as Mary is delivered from her demons.

Mary Magdalene's primary role, however, is as a model of contrition, devotion and love, imaged in her weeping at Christ's feet, an action which the reader emulates in her soul. The reader recalls that Christ 'excused' Mary Magdalene three times – once to the Pharisee, when she wept at Christ's feet, once to Martha, for choosing the better part, and once to Judas, for anointing Christ's feet with precious ointment. Here, Mary's two acts of devotion and contrition at Christ's feet frame her identification with Mary of Bethany as the exemplar of the contemplative and solitary life. The reader seeks to emulate Mary's loving familiarity with Christ, identifying herself with the contemplative and solitary life which Mary exemplifies, rather than with her sin.

The emphasis on contemplation and union with Christ is also reflected in the author's treatment of sin and temptation. Significantly, as in the story of Mary Magdalene, passages in the prayer cycle which deal with temptation and tribulation alternate with passages on union, love-longing and compassion. This mirrors the very real alternation between mystical union and alienation that is typical of contemplative experience in the mystical tradition of the fourteenth century.[29] The author's stance on sin is both demanding and benign, and her call for perfection is qualified (a stance which, incidentally, fits well with the second text in the manuscript). For example, in spite of her insistence on self-examination and acknowledgement of sin, the author stresses that what is important is the will and desire for virtue, which will be accepted as if it were the deed.[30] Although she stresses humility and includes a long passage on the dangers of pride, she undercuts this by asserting that her reader is to *consider* herself sinful, although she is not so sinful as she has been portrayed.[31]

Both the passages on sin and temptation and the positive female role-models presented to the reader encourage her not to wallow in her sense of her own sin, but, rather, to recognize her sinfulness, repent and do penance, and *move on* to the devotion that will unite her with Christ. This is reinforced by the Passion section, the final and most contemplative section of the text. As Pollard has pointed out, this section utilizes many of the typical images of contemplative writing in a dramatic climax, which raises the reader to an ecstatic union with Christ through prayer and meditation. For example, the imprint of Christ's face in Veronica's veil is referred to as a love token given by Christ, and the reader's union with Christ is evoked, as Christ's fastening to the cross with nails and cords is imaged as the knitting of a love knot which cannot be unknit. This prayer implies that union with Christ is possible only through the cross, continuing the focus on the contemplative life as *imitatio Christi*. The reader's compassion with Christ is evoked in powerful images: for example, as his clothes are stripped away, then so too is his flesh, glued to his clothing with his blood. As the cross falls and is replaced, causing Christ's sides to burst and bleed, the contemplation of Christ's agony causes the reader to cry out, 'O myn herte whi ne cleuist on tweyne [split in two] for pite of thin lord. þat alle thises cruel turmentis hadde. O. treuli I may seie þat my herte is more hard than is the hard ston. for stones lord at youre deth to bursten. and cleuedin on tweine.'[32] She prays for Christ to soften her heart, to send her a 'sparkle' of the Holy Spirit, and to anoint her heart with the 'licour' of his love. This introduces a series of prayers which develop the union between the reader's heart and Christ's, as Christ's heart is cloven by Longinus' spear, and the water and blood which pour from the wound open the spiritual eyes of the reader, so that her heart may be buried with Christ and inflamed with Christ's presence, as was the Virgin Mary's. The Passion section culminates in the penultimate prayer, addressed to Christ's heart, as the reader prays for her heart to be wounded and ravished in Christ's love.[33]

The feitis and the passion suggests that we need to re-examine the way in which the male-authored texts that are its sources might have been read by the women to whom they were addressed. It is true that this text picks up on the emphasis on sin and temptation and the need for a recognition of one's own unworthiness that characterize its sources. But this emphasis is tempered with a stress on Christ's acceptance of the unworthy and the importance of desire, faith and perseverance – and, indeed, the insistence that the desire for virtue is more important than its pure performance. As well, what this text does *not* retain from its sources is significant. In particular, the stress on sexual sin and the dangers of the female body are notable for their absence.

This text illustrates that at least one woman reader of the male-authored tradition did not simply internalize the fear and mistrust of women's sexuality present in these texts, but, rather, focused on the ways in which texts like *Ancrene Wisse* and *Þe Wohunge of Ure Lauerd* used the imagery of the female body to portray woman's unique capacity for union with Christ in a specifically feminine way. The ambiguity of *Ancrene Wisse*'s treatment of the female body is entirely absent in this text, as women's capacity for tears and devotion, compassion and love, is transformed into a path which leads from the recognition of sin to contrition and contemplation on the remedy for sin, and union in love with the one whose death embodies that remedy. In the process, the author creates a bond with her reader, binding them together as women with shared experiences, shared weaknesses, shared needs, shared strengths and shared devotions, weaving a sense of community in reclusion and offering a unique glimpse into how women religious in the fifteenth century perceived themselves and each other.

Notes

1   My study of Holkham Misc. 41 was made possible by generous funding from the Social Sciences and Humanities Research Council of Canada.

2   Quoted from an unpublished catalogue description of the Holkham manuscripts, supplied by Peter Kidd of the Bodleian Library.

3   Excerpts from the manuscript are edited in Alexandra Barratt (ed.), *Women's Writing in Middle English* (London, 1992). In addition to Barratt's anthology, see Alexandra Barratt, '*Stabat matres dolorosae*: women as readers and writers of Passion prayers, meditations, and visions', in A. A. MacDonald et al. (eds), *The Broken Body: Passion Devotion in Late-Medieval Culture* (Groningen, 1998), pp. 55–72; Edmund Colledge and Noel Chadwick, '*Remedies Against Temptations*: the third English version of William Flete', *Archivo italiano per la storia della pietà*, 5 (1968), 199–240; William F. Pollard, 'Bodleian MS Holkham Misc. 41: a fifteenth-century Bridgettine manuscript and prayer cycle', *Birgittiana*, 3 (1997), 43–53; William F. Pollard, 'Mystical elements in a fifteenth-century prayer sequence: "The festis and the passion of oure lord Ihesu Crist" ', in Marion Glasscoe (ed.), *The Medieval Mystical Tradition in England*, Exeter Symposium IV (Exeter, 1987), pp. 47–61; and Josephine Koster Tarvers, ' "Thys ys my mystrys boke": English women as readers and writers in late medieval England', in Charlotte Cook Morse, Penelope Reed Doob and Marjorie Curry Woods (eds), *The Uses of Manuscripts in Literary Studies: Essays in Memory of Judson Boyce Allen*, Studies in Medieval Culture, 31 (Kalamazoo: 1992), pp. 305–27. I am most grateful to Jo Koster for starting my love affair with this manuscript by giving me her (unedited) transcription of this text to study.

4   Pollard, 'Bodleian MS Holkham Misc. 41', p. 43.

5   It is possible, for example, that this manuscript was copied for a reader like Joan Holand or Joanna Newmarche, widows who retired into religious seclusion after their husbands' deaths. Joan Holand owned MS BL Harley 5036, and gave MS BL Cotton Vitellius F. vii, containing an Anglo-Norman version of *Ancrene Wisse*, to Eleanor Cobham. She also owned MS Takamiya 8, containing, among other things, Love's *Mirror*, which she gave to Alice Belacyse. Joanna Newmarche owned MS BL Harley 2254, containing Hilton's *Mixed Life* and *The Prickyng of Love*. For these and other

examples of such devout widows, see Carol M. Meale, ' "oft siþis with grete deuotion I þought what I miȝt do pleysyng to god": the early ownership and readership of Love's *Mirror*, with special reference to its female audience', in Shoichi Oguro, Richard Beadle and Michael G. Sargent (eds), *Nicholas Love at Waseda: Proceedings of the International Conference 20–22 July, 1995* (London, 1997), pp. 19–46; See also the following by Mary C. Erler, 'Exchange of books between nuns and laywomen: three surviving examples', in Richard Beadle and A. J. Piper (eds), *New Science Out of Old Books: Studies in Manuscripts and Early Printed Books in Honour of A. I. Doyle* (Aldershot, 1995), pp. 360–73; 'English vowed women at the end of the Middle Ages', *Mediaeval Studies*, 57 (1995), 155–203; 'Three fifteenth-century vowesses', in Caroline M. Barron and Anne F. Sutton (eds), *Medieval London Widows, 1300–1500* (Rio Grande, 1994), pp. 165–84; 'Syon's "special benefactors and friends"; some vowed women', *Birgittiana*, 2 (1996), 209–22; and Margaret Wade Labarge, 'Three medieval widows and a second career', in Michael M. Sheehand (ed.), *Ageing and the Aged in Medieval Europe: Selected Papers from the Annual Conference of the Centre for Medieval Studies, University of Toronto, Held 25–26 February and 11–12 November 1983*, Papers in Medieval Studies, 11 (Toronto: 1990), pp. 159–72.

6 *Feitis*, p. 12. All page references are to the manuscript, based on my own transcription.

7 Unfortunately, a section is missing between pp. 64 and 65, where the text skips from Jesus washing the disciples' feet at the Last Supper to the bearing of the cross. The missing section would cover the Last Supper, betrayal and arrest, scourging and trial. A considerable portion of the Passion section is thus, alas, lost.

8 *Feitis*, p. 34.

9 In both the prologue and the epilogue, the author outlines her plan of beginning each prayer with a paternoster, which the author identifies as 'the most principal preire of alle other preieris', followed by a thanksgiving for an event in Christ's life and a petition. As Barratt has pointed out, in using the Lord's Prayer as a pattern or paradigm for all Christian prayer, 'she makes the highest and most daring claim for her writing – that in a sense Christ himself is the author' (Barratt, *Women's Writing*, p. 205). As the author states, 'oure lord that made that priere makith alle oþer preieris for be his grace it is doon' (p. 2). Nevertheless, Barratt's suggestion that at the same time the author minimizes her own role is, I think, inconsistent with the self-assurance expressed throughout the rest of the text.

10 Colledge and Chadwick, '*Remedies Against Temptations*', 211.

11 Ibid., 11. Jo Koster concurs, suggesting that 'the author either knows the Bible in English or knows the Vulgate and is comfortable with translating it' (personal communication).

12 Pollard, 'Bodleian MS Holkham Misc. 41', 45; see also Barratt, *Women's Writing*, p. 205, and Colledge and Chadwick, '*Remedies Against Temptations*', 218.

13 *Feitis*, p. 91.

[14] Ibid., p. 23.

[15] Ibid., p. 65.

[16] Ibid., p. 41.

[17] Ibid., p. 15.

[18] Ibid., p. 27.

[19] Ibid., pp. 26–7.

[20] Ibid., p. 41.

[21] Ibid., p. 29. Here the author of *Ancrene Wisse* quotes Bernard as saying that dishonour and torment, or shame and pain, are two sides of the ladder which leads to heaven. See *The English Text of the Ancrene Riwle: Ancrene Wisse: Edited from MS. Corpus Christi College Cambridge 402*, by J. R. R. Tolkien, EETS o.s. 249 (London, New York and Toronto, 1962), p. 181. For a translation of this reference see *Anchoritic Spirituality*: Ancrene Wisse *and Associated Works*, trans. and intro. Anne Savage and Nicholas Watson (New York and Mahwah, 1991), p. 178. All subsequent references to *Ancrene Wisse* and translations are from these two editions.

[22] *Feitis*, pp. 4–5.

[23] Ibid., p. 62.

[24] *Ancrene Wisse*, pp. 192–3; Savage and Watson, pp. 186–7.

[25] *Feitis*, p. 79.

[26] Ibid., p. 11.

[27] Ibid., p. 25.

[28] It is noteworthy that this story implies that, with the exception of Christ, all of the male models in this text are either negative or applied generally to the Church as a whole, rather than to the individual soul. The female models, on the other hand, are applied to the reader in intimate detail.

[29] This alternating progression from sin or temptation through contrition or penance to devotion and union is also reflected in the models provided by Christ himself. His baptism is a model for the cleansing of the reader's baptism, his fasting and temptation in the desert bring comfort and strength to the solitary who is tempted as he was, his poverty is paralleled to the reader's lifestyle of penance, which is the way to grace and forgiveness and, with prayer and contrition, is grounded in Christ. Finally, Christ's holy living governs the reader's living, so that she is immersed in Christ's love.

[30] *Feitis*, p. 5. This passage occurs in the context of the general confession, which includes the first allusion to the Canaanite woman, discussed above.

[31] Ibid., p. 92.

[32] Ibid., pp. 69–70.

[33] See Pollard, 'Mystical elements in a fifteenth-century prayer sequence'.

14

'Closyd in an hows of ston': Discourses of Anchoritism and *The Book of Margery Kempe*

It was with the voice of abject disappointment that the early commentator Herbert Thurston greeted the rediscovery of the unique manuscript of *The Book of Margery Kempe* in 1934, a manuscript which had been missing since the *Book* was written in 1436.[1] Responding to Margery Kempe's newly uncovered excesses and eccentricities, Thurston wrote: 'If she had really been an ancress [*sic*], living secluded in her cell, these peculiarities would not have mattered. But she insisted on going everywhere, following, as she believed, the special call of God.'[2] Damning Margery with this faint praise, Thurston's attitude to Margery's high profile and noisy persona, her weeping, her bodily contortions, her uncompromising rebuke of priests and her frequent resistance to direction was, of course, paradigmatic of a perennial, transhistorical and transcultural antipathy towards the unchecked female voice and unruly body which, taking its cue from classical and biblical tradition, is evidenced everywhere within medieval literature generally, and in *The Book of Margery Kempe* in particular.[3] Indeed, Thurston's words uncannily echo those of the Canterbury monk over six hundred years previously who, similarly incensed by Margery's transgressive body and voice, tells her in no uncertain terms: 'I wold þow wer closyd in an hows of ston þat þer schuld no man speke wyth þe.'[4] Thurston's response, therefore, merely rearticulates the same cultural given, clearly enunciated by this monk, that the best woman is not only the silent one, but the one whose problematic body is housed up within walls of stone, be they domestic, institutional, ideological or anchoritic.

Thurston's hopes for the manuscript had probably been conditioned by the speculation of another early commentator, Edmund Gardner, who, writing in 1910 in his introduction to an edition of the few surviving fragments of Margery's *Book*, hazarded the opinion:

> The revelations show that she was (or had been) a woman of some wealth and social position, who had abandoned the world to become an anchoress, following the life prescribed in that gem of early English devotional literature the *Ancrene Riwle*. It is clearly only a fragment of her complete book (whatever that may have been); but it is enough to show that she was a worthy precursor of that other great woman mystic of East Anglia: Julian of Norwich.[5]

All Gardner had to go on here was the only witness to Margery Kempe extant at that time, namely, a radically redacted text, first put into print by Wynkyn de Worde in 1501, reprinted by Henry Pepwell in 1521 and edited by Gardner in 1910. What is significant here, however, is that the 1521 Pepwell version sees fit to designate its author, Margery Kempe, as 'deuoute ancres of Lynne', and it is this redacted text and its reconstruction as anchoritic writing that will comprise the main focus of this chapter.[6]

The unique copy of this redacted text consists of a quarto pamphlet, of seven pages only, and what is most remarkable about its content is that the insistent bodily presence of the original *Book*'s female protagonist and the ungoverned and noisy manifestations of her piety seem to have been all but eradicated. What we are left with is a comparatively unremarkable and disembodied voice, which is entirely overshadowed in the text by that of Christ, whose pronouncements make up most of the content – in fact, thirteen out of the nineteen extracts which comprise the compilation. Similarly, the narrative voice and that of Margery Kempe, the visionary woman, have been wholly separated from one another, leaving the mystic herself to take up a position at the shady margins of the text, serving apparently as nothing more than a narrative trope.

Following the discovery of the original book in its entirety, analysis of this redacted version understandably fell into considerable neglect.[7] Much insight, however, can be gained into the longer, complete version – and particularly the purpose and direction of the discourses of anchoritism contained within it – by re-examining the seemingly anodyne text of the redaction. This chapter, therefore, will reassess the redacted text as witness and argue for its betrayal of a firm desire on the part of the anonymous redactor to exercise some control over Margery Kempe's hitherto ungovernable voice and body by enclosing them both securely within the stone walls of his own violently edited version of her original text. Later, this figurative enclosure will become entirely literalized by the transformation of Margery Kempe into devout anchoress in the 1521 Pepwell edition.

Until very recently *The Book of Margery Kempe* has not been considered at all in terms of anchoritic writing, in spite of the wealth of anchoritic discourses and images of enclosure contained within it. Beyond Margery's famous visit to Julian of Norwich in her anchorhold,[8] commentators have tended to ignore the range of other anchorites and anchoritic practices which permeate the text. However, an essay by Denis Renevey has recently served to open up this aspect of the *Book* to scrutiny. Here, Renevey argues for the bodily performances of Margery Kempe to be read in terms of an individualistic expression of those daily ritualistic performances normally undertaken by a female anchorite in the anchorhold.[9] As Renevey points out, much of Margery Kempe's behaviour throughout the *Book* adheres to – indeed, hyperbolizes – the type of religious performances expected of the devoted female anchorite, as documented in works of anchoritic guidance, such as *Ancrene Wisse*. The enclosed location, along with the ritualistic bodily and vocal activities required of its solitary inhabitant, are all rendered spiritually significant in the context of the anchorite's privileged relationship with God. So, Margery Kempe's complex and compulsive bodily expressions of spiritual piety are transformed into an equally significant hermeneutic in order to relay to her audience a mystical understanding which would otherwise remain inexpressible.[10] However, whereas the anchorite is expected to perform her spirituality away from the eyes of the world, with God as sole witness, Margery Kempe – as Thurston took such pains to point out – insists on disseminating her own mystical perceptions by means of a highly visible and vociferous public performance of them. The primary difference between the two, of course, is attributable in part to the different meanings associated with the spaces within which each adherent to this mode of spiritual expression – that is to say, anchorite and ambiguous 'holy woman' – was operating.[11]

As I have argued elsewhere, the rich and complex metaphoricity of the anchorhold provided a multiplicity of interconnected discourses which could serve to transform a discursively sinful female body into salvific entity: images of the womb, for example, transform both anchoress-as-womb and anchorhold-as-tomb from death-invoking space into life-giving liminality.[12] Whereas, however, the female anchorite's engagement with these discourses and their inscription upon her body offered her a level of spiritual empowerment because of the seclusion in which she engaged with them, Margery Kempe's own bodily inscriptions appear to have been perpetually misread and misunderstood because of their being ciphered through male-dominated and more worldly public spaces. Hence, whereas anchoritic guidance texts such as *Ancrene Wisse* tend to actively encourage a state of rapture, as Hughes-Edwards cogently argues elsewhere in this volume (ch. 10), Margery Kempe's own manifestations of ecstasy fail to elicit such affirming responses from her particular audience:

> Summe seyd it was a wikkyd spirit vexed hir; sum seyd it was a sekenes; sum seyd sche had dronkyn to mech wyn; sum bannyd [cursed] hir; sum wished sche had ben in þe hauyn [harbour]; sum wolde sche had ben in þe se in a bottumles boyt [boat].[13]

It is therefore significant that, as well as drawing upon the example of other female mystical precursors for her authority – Bridget of Sweden and Julian of Norwich amongst them – Margery Kempe demonstrates an awareness throughout her text of the type of endorsement which an adherence to anchoritic discourse and practices could bring about. For example, she appears to have been fully conversant with and very much influenced by the local anchoritic community;[14] indeed, one of the first instructions which she receives from Christ following the onset of her mystical experiences is to seek out a local anchorite for advice: 'I byd þe gon to þe ankyr at þe Frer Prechowrys, & schew hym my preuyteys & my cownselys which I schewe to þe, *and werk aftyr hys cownsel, for my spyrit xal speke in hym to þe*'.[15] Similarly, a little later in the text Margery will document a visit undertaken to Julian of Norwich prior to embarking on pilgrimage in 1314, professing the main reason for the visit as being: 'þe ankres was expert in swech thyngys [that is, mystical visions] & good cownsel cowd ʒeuen'.[16] During the early days of her conversion, too, the person who seems to exercise most influence over Margery is her anchorite confessor, a recluse who is clearly himself subject to dramatic visionary experiences and who enjoys the gift of prophecy.[17] In fact, her close relationship with this man, whom she describes as 'þe most special & synguler comforte þat euyr I had in erde',[18] along with her intimate friendship with the renowned Carmelite friar, Alan of Lynn, demonstrates the close connection between mysticism, Carmelite spirituality and anchoritism, which Bergström-Allen has already identified in his essay (ch. 6). Indeed, Julian of Norwich, the unnamed anchorite and the highly respected Alan of Lynn remain amongst the few who provide unreserved support for Margery's highly public performances of piety, perhaps because her behaviour echoed, parodied and performed many of those practices with which they were themselves already familiar within their own spiritual milieux.

Another of Margery's anchoritic contacts was one Thomas Brakleye, a Benedictine monk who lived as an anchorite attached to the Chapel in the Fields in Norwich, whom Margery tells us she visited soon after returning from her Jerusalem pilgrimage in 1415.[19] Brakleye, Margery is at pains to tell us, 'bar a name of gret perfeccyon & befortyme had louyd þis creatur ryth meche'.[20] However, local gossip about a child which Margery is supposed to have conceived and borne whilst in Jerusalem seems to have turned him against her and he utterly refuses to believe her protestations to the contrary. As a result, he insists that she return to him for further admonishments and guidance and categorically forbids her to adopt the traditional white clothing of the bride of Christ: ' "God forbade it," for sche xulde þan make al þe world to wondyr on hir.'[21] For this anchorite, at least, there remains a firm line between the behaviour and clothing appropriate for a woman within the anchorhold and that available to her on the outside. Indeed, his fear that she will create a travesty of the spiritual significance of both anchoritic practices and white garment by parading it in public and disrupting its metaphorical codes recalls the words of both Herbert Thurston and the Canterbury monk with which I began this chapter. In proscribing the high-profile expression of a traditionally secluded and intensely private spirituality, this antipathetic anchorite seeks to reclaim Margery for re-enclosure within the walls of those patriarchal ideologies which would insist upon the performance of a woman's private and personal devotional activities away from the eyes of the world. Nor is the irony of this lost on Margery. Resisting his admonishment and his instructions, Margery decides to consult God about this anchorite's authority and – predictably – God assures her that she should not 'be gouerneyd be hym [the anchorite]', upon which 'þerwyth sche toke hir leue at þat tyme'.[22] Within three days, Margery obtains the money to purchase the desired white clothing, the wearing of which will forever afterwards associate her – albeit obliquely – not only with her Carmelite champions but also with the authority of traditional anchoritic piety.

It is, of course, such anchoritic piety which is brought to fruition, not by Margery herself, but by the anonymous redactor of her *Book* and, in a sense, the redacted treatise comprises prophetic fulfilment of the desires of both the Canterbury monk and the anchorite, Thomas Brakleye. Indeed, in many ways, the construction of the redacted text can be read as a deliberate attempt to enclose Margery's body and silence her voice after her death in order to bring her fully under control, in line with those well-established and highly revered private practices of anchoritic piety already alluded to.

One of the few commentators to have examined the redacted treatise in detail is Sue Ellen Holbrook, who has demonstrated the extent to which Margery's voice is recessive in this text.[23] On Holbrook's calculation, sixty per cent of the narrative is concerned with the words of Christ, twenty-two per cent with the unspecified narrative voice, and a mere eighteen per cent is taken up by the words of Margery herself.[24] The redaction itself comprises a series of nineteen brief extracts, taken wholly out of context from a selection of interchanges between Margery and Christ. They do not adhere to the chronology of the original in any way, nor are they reproduced verbatim. Sometimes there is a merging of sentences from various dialogues within the original text to create a new and composite extract, whereas others are truncated and their emphases altered. The overall effect is the production of a type of instructional handbook for devotion, with Margery's subjective voice almost entirely expunged.[25]

As Holbrook has demonstrated, it is highly unlikely that the printer, Wynkyn de Worde, was himself responsible for the dissection and reassembling of the *Book*;[26] indeed, there is evidence to suggest that the extracts were put together fairly soon after the *Book*'s completion in 1436.[27] As Holbrook also suggests, the appearance of a veiled critique of the Bishop's Lynn priesthood, found in the very last extract of the redaction, makes it likely that the redactor was personally acquainted with Margery during her lifetime and fully conversant with the treatment meted out to her by a progression of antipathetic clerics in her home town and elsewhere. Holbrook also hazards that the man who most obviously fits the profile in this capacity is Robert Spryngolde, Margery's parish priest and the man who took over as her principal confessor following the death of her favourite anchorite. Moreover, contemporary court records reveal that Spryngolde was still alive after the production of the book in 1436;[28] indeed, Margery's original text ends with the account of a reconciled quarrel between herself and Spryngolde, due to a final major act of disobedience on her part.[29] Spryngolde, therefore, would have been privy to all Margery's concerns about the abuses she was receiving at the hands of local ecclesiastics.

He had also demonstrated on a number of occasions that he was entirely capable of offering sharp interventions in her life in an evident desire to bring her into line with more acceptable modes of behaviour. Indeed, from Margery's own account in the original text, Spryngolde appears to have shared many of the highly orthodox viewpoints which are subsequently promoted in the redaction. On one occasion, for example, when Margery has been refused entry to church, he tells her bluntly: 'Þer is no mor aȝen ȝow but þe mone & vij sterrys. Anethe is þer any man þat heldith wyth ȝow but I alone.'[30] Spryngolde's words here evidence a tension between his knowledge of and affection for Margery and his ecclesiastic duty to bring into line her noisy, performing body within the boundaries of the orthodox. Indeed, elsewhere in the *Book* we learn from Christ what Spryngolde's most insistent advice to Margery is:

> Maistyr Robert, þi gostly fadyr . . . biddith þe þu xuldist *sittyn stille* [you should sit still] & ȝeuyn thyn hert to *meditacyon* & *thynkyn* swech *holy thowtys* as god wyl puttyn in þi mende. And I haue oftyntymys bodyn þe so myself, & ȝet þu wilt not don þeraftyr but wyth meche grutchyng [complaining].[31]

Of course, Spryngolde is doomed to failure in his attempts to silence and control Margery during her lifetime, since she sometimes fails to adhere to even Christ's instructions without wholehearted 'grutchyng', and even as an old woman Margery proves herself wholly capable of contravening Spryngolde's orders. Perhaps, then, it is worth speculating (as, indeed does Holbrook) that upon Margery's death Spryngolde took it upon himself to enclose her safely within his own highly truncated version of her self-revelatory text. In so doing, he could produce a version which systematically seeks to eradicate her troublesome body and voice and to reconstruct both woman and text as orthodox embodiments of anchoritic piety, with just the type of lay audience in mind identified by Cate Gunn in her study of *Ancrene Wisse* (ch. 12). Such an undertaking would not only constitute a personal tribute to a holy woman, for whom he evidently had much respect and no small measure of affection, but it would also ensure that Margery's reputation be rehabilitated in death, with the removal from her text of her troublesome public persona and its replacement by the ecclesiastically approved anchoritic voice.

The redaction itself opens with one of Margery's more histrionic pronouncements: 'She desyred many tymes that her hede myght be smyten of with an axe vpon a blocke for the loue of our lorde Ihesu.'[32] Most commentators have read this opening as the compiler's attempt to establish from the outset the discourse of revilement as a primary one in the text he is constructing.[33] Although a perfectly valid reading, which coincides conveniently with my argument for the reformulation of the *Book* as an anchoritic text, it seems to me that the primary purpose of placing this passage here is to establish an ascetic rather than a performative Margery Kempe as its focus. Although asceticism involves a certain degree of performativity, of course, as Robert Hasenfratz also intimates in his own treatment of *Ancrene Wisse* (Ch. 11), nevertheless its performance tends to be in a more private, personal arena than the highly public one in which the performances of Margery Kempe normally take place, and comprises an intrinsic part of traditional anchoritic discourse. In this instance, therefore, Margery's desire for decapitation is presented as symptomatic of a deeply personal aspiration to be martyred for the love of God, entirely in keeping with orthodox hagiographical discourse. Being privy to Margery's own text, however, we are fully aware that, in its original context, this passage documents not the orthodox desire for martyrdom by decapitation but the feeling of abject *terror* it invokes when she thinks about it. What she is actually confessing to is her own need to find the *least painful* means of death possible – something she refers to in the original as 'þe most soft deth'[34] – so that she can begin to contemplate a possible martyrdom without the concomitant fear. In the original account, too, Margery's performing body takes up its usual position at centre-stage: she desires, for example, to be 'bowndyn . . . hed & . . . fet to a stokke',[35] whereas in the redacted version this body is subject to dismemberment and silencing. Such bodily fragmentation is continued by the later inclusion of the famous meat-in-a-pot passage, uttered by Christ in gratitude at Margery's love for her fellow Christians and heathens alike: 'I thanke the . . . þat thou woldest be hacked as smalle as flesshe to the potte for theyr loue, soo þat I wolde by thy deth saue them all fro dampnacyon yf it pleased me.'[36] Again, inclusion of this passage seems to be in order to establish the selflessness of Margery's willingness for martyrdom.

Nevertheless, read in conjunction with the earlier passage it becomes the site of slippage, which casts up for scrutiny an authorial desire for female dismemberment in order to control her most threatening parts. The subtext is therefore clear: to be rendered an orthodox holy woman and admitted into the realm of the sacred, Margery must be dismembered and carefully reconstructed, according to the agenda dictated by the same masculine ideology displayed by the redactor of her text as was evidenced in the pronouncements of Thomas Brakleye. The key to the success of this mechanism of control, however, is that the woman herself must appear to be entirely complicit with this reconstructed self, thus approving her own transformation into the epitome of the invisible anchoritic female.

As a truly passive receptacle into which the Holy Sprit pours his grace, however, the female subject must also be rendered silent.[37] As a result, the conversations between holy woman and Christ filter through, not aurally but 'in her mynde', 'in [her] soule', 'in scylence', and in 'thynkynge'.[38] Indeed, so silenced does she seem to be that all those orifices which the *Ancrene Wisse* author famously entreats his anchoresses to seal up – the eyes, the ears, the mouth – are effectively cut off from the avenues of conventional communication, rendering Margery altogether more compliant to the male imaginary, which has attempted this reconstruction of her according to its own precepts. Moreover, the sealing of this silent tomb is subsequently confirmed by Christ, who is himself transformed from the gently feminized lover of the original text ('most semly, most bewtyuows, & most amiable . . . clad in a mantyl of purpyl sylke'[39]), into the primary representative of proscriptive patriarchy, telling the holy woman: 'yf þu saydeste euery day a thousande pater noster thou shoulde not please me so well as thou dost whan þu art in scylence & suffrest me to speke in thy soule.'[40]

For most commentators who have worked on this redacted text, Margery's disappearance is, therefore, complete. However, as I have intimated, on closer examination this redaction, by its very nature, is the site of subtle fissuring. Indeed, it fails in its attempt to resist the hermeneutic of Margery's turbulent body and its re-emergence through the crackle-glazed veneer of this text's unstable construction. Moreover, such an instability brings it further into line with mainstream anchoritic texts, such as *Ancrene Wisse* or *Þe Wohunge of Ure Lauerde*, in which, as Chewning also notes, can be detected the same tensions between the proscriptive male imaginary and the potentially transcendent bodily excess of the female subject contained within these texts. The result is that the redaction as a whole becomes a site of major slippage, which allows the excess of Margery's own irresistible body to start seeping back through the cracks of the literary walls within which the redactor has attempted to contain it. This is made eminently apparent by the efforts of the redactor to cement over these cracks in his expedient alignment of Christ with his own stance on appropriate female behaviour. Thus, he has Christ tell the holy woman at the start of the treatise: 'I haue often tolde þe doughter, that thynkynge, wepynge, & hye contemplacyon is þe best lyf in erthe, & thou shalt haue more meryte in heuen for one yere thynkynge in thy mynde than for an hondred yere of prayeng wyth thy mouth.'[41] Such a prioritizing of silence here, however, would appear to be at odds with later allusions in this text to Margery's 'grete mournynge', her 'grete wepyng' and her 'sorowynge' at not being able to kiss a leper on the road who has reminded her of the suffering Christ.[42] Perhaps most discordant in this context is the inclusion towards the end of the text of Margery's much commented-on desire to be 'layde naked vpon an hurdel . . . al men to wonder on me & to cast fylth & dyrt on me: & be drawen fro town to towne euery day my lyfe tyme'.[43] Although ostensibly adhering to the redaction's attempt at a discourse of revilement, there is nevertheless a strong sense of displacement created by the inclusion of these highly excessive examples of Margery's ascetic fantasies, particularly this one, which renders her both naked and spectacular in a quest to achieve universal salvation. The sheer physicality of the extract simply does not sit comfortably within a text which appears to be insistent upon its self-effacing subject and her silent, disembodied voice. Elsewhere, too, the text's anodyne narrator will suggest: 'That day she suffred noo trybulacyon for oure lordes sake she was not mery ne gladde',[44] an extract which, while purporting to represent a sober and self-sacrificial subject, nevertheless lets slip a more boisterous figure whose excess lies in a dependency upon noisy bodily suffering for her pleasure *and* – crucially – for her sense of authority. Quite simply, Margery Kempe in her original treatise speaks her body and her body – so she would have us believe – speaks the Holy Spirit with whose wisdom her voice is saturated, and her redactor fails in his task to eradicate it from his reconstructed narrative. For Margery, body, voice and W/word are, in fact, inseparable. What we are left with in the redacted text, therefore, is a narrative full of tensions and ambiguities, fissures and points of slippage. As a result, the ostensible progress of the narrative, which is to present Margery as a wholly orthodox, silent and invisible paragon of female holiness, becomes entirely destabilized, leading to the exuberant and excessive body of the original Margery Kempe seeping back through the textual fault-lines of this cut-and-paste edition of her writing.

Thus, like those apparently proscriptive discourses within traditional anchoritic texts which the redactor seems so keen to construct, indeed, like the *Book* itself, a reading of this redaction 'against the grain' exposes its insistent discourses of enclosure – and their interaction with contemporary gender politics – as ultimately *counter*-hegemonic. Quite simply, they fail to contain the text's uncontainable female subject because of the exceptional *bodiliness* of her mystical insights and aspirations. As a result, Margery's words, however de- and recontextualized they may be in this concerted attempt to control them, utterly refuse to relinquish the authority of female body and voice as primary hermeneutic and as alternative means of directly accessing God.

Notes

[1] *The Book of Margery Kempe*, ed. Sandford Brown Meech and Hope Emily Allen, EETS o.s. 212 (London, New York and Toronto, 1997). Hereafter *Book*.

[2] Herbert Thurston, Review, *Tablet* (October 24 1936), 570.

[3] This is something I examine in the last two chapters of my monograph, *Authority and the Female Body in the Writings of Julian of Norwich and Margery Kempe* (Cambridge, 2004).

[4] *Book*, p. 27.

[5] Edmund Gardner, *The Cell of Self-Knowledge* (London, 1910), pp. xx–i.

[6] The redaction appears in Cambridge University Library MS Sel. 5, 27, and the edition referred to in this chapter appears as 'Printed extracts from *The Book of Margery Kempe*', in *Book*, pp. 353–7. Hereafter Reaction.

[7] The few contemporary critics who do engage with this text are George R. Keiser, 'The mystics and the early English printers: the economics of devotionalism', in Marion Glasscoe (ed.), *The Medieval Mystical Tradition in England: Papers Read at Dartington Hall, July 1987*, Exeter Symposium IV (Cambridge, 1987), pp. 9–26; Sue-Ellen Holbrook, 'Margery Kempe and Wynkyn de Worde', in ibid., pp. 27–46; Karma Lochrie, *Margery Kempe and Translations of the Flesh* (Philadelphia, 1991), pp. 203–26. See also Rosalynn Voaden, *God's Words, Women's Voices: The Discernment of Spirits in the Writing of Late-Medieval Women Visionaries* (Woodbridge, 1999), pp. 147–54.

[8] *Book*, pp. 42–3.

[9] Denis Renevey, 'Margery's performing body: the translation of late medieval discursive religious practices', in Denis Renevey and Christiania Whitehead (eds), *Writing Religious Women: Female Spiritual and Textual*

Practices in Late Medieval England (Cardiff, 2000), pp. 197–216.

[10] On the significance of Margery's bodily gesturing see my essay, ' "wonderfully turning & wrestyng hir body": agonies, ecstasies, and gendered performances in *The Book of Margery Kempe*', in Liz Herbert McAvoy (ed. and trans.), *The Book of Margery Kempe: An Abridged Translation* (Cambridge, 2003), pp. 106–26.

[11] For a detailed examination of the metaphorical and allegorical significance of space in the Middle Ages see Christiania Whitehead, *Castles of the Mind: A Study of Medieval Architectural Allegory* (Cardiff, 2003). See in particular pp. 91–2 for a discussion of anchoritic metaphoricity.

[12] Liz Herbert McAvoy, ' "Ant neos he himself reclus i maries wombe?"': Julian of Norwich, the anchorhold and redemption of the monstrous female body', in Liz Herbert McAvoy and Teresa Walters (eds), *Consuming Narratives: Gender and Monstrous Appetite in the Middle Ages and the Renaissance* (Cardiff, 2001), pp. 128–43.

[13] *Book*, p. 69.

[14] Again, on the distribution of anchorites in medieval England see Ann K. Warren, *Anchorites and their Patrons in Medieval England* (Berkeley and Los Angeles, 1985), pp. 292–3. Warren records a total of thirty-nine anchorites in Norfolk during the fifteenth century, of whom eighteen were female, twenty were male, with one 'indeterminate'. See also Norman Tanner, *The Church in Late Medieval Norwich* (Toronto, 1984), pp. 58–66.

[15] *Book*, p. 17 (my emphasis). Voaden argues that this instruction and its fulfilment serves to construct Margery as orthodox within the doctrine of *discretio spirituum* in *God's Words*, p. 124.

[16] *Book*, p. 42.

[17] Ibid., p. 279, n. 43/35. Both Jean Gerson and Alfonso de Jaen considered that it was appropriate for the spiritual directors of mystics to be subject to the same transcendental experience themselves. For Alfonso see *Epistola solitarii ad reges*, in *Alfonso of Jaen: His Life and Works with Critical Editions of the Epistola solitarii, the Informaciones and the Epistola serui Christi*, ed. A. Jönsson (Lund, 1989), pp. 115–71 (1: 15; Appendix fol. 247v: 1–5). For Gerson, see *Jean Gerson, Oeuvres Complètes*, 10 vols, ed. P. Glorieux (Paris, 1960–73), vol. 9, p. 179.

[18] *Book*, p. 168.

[19] Brakleye was evidently an important figure in the local community, something evidenced by his will of 1417, the executors of which were powerful national figures with links to the Duke of Bedford, that ardent anti-Lollard campaigner who was to give Margery so much difficulty on her travels in the north of England also in 1417. On Brakleye see *Book*, pp. 307–8, n. 103/1*sq.*

[20] Ibid., p. 103.

[21] Ibid., p. 103. On the significance of the virginal white garb to Margery's reconstruction of virginity, see Sarah Salih, *Versions of Virginity in Late Medieval England* (Cambridge, 2001), pp. 218–24.

[22] *Book*, p. 103.

[23] Holbrook, 'Margery Kempe and Wynkyn de Worde'.

24 Ibid., p. 353.

25 This is something discussed by Lochrie in *Translations*, pp. 220–3.

26 Holbrook, 'Margery Kempe and Wynkyn de Worde'. On Wynkyn de Worde as an unlikely compiler, see p. 38.

27 Ibid., p. 38.

28 See the entry, dated 30 April 1436, regarding Spryngolde in the Norwich Institution Book X, reproduced in *Book*, p. 368.

29 *Book*, p. 247. On the often problematic relationship between holy women and their confessors see Janet Dillon, 'Holy women and their confessors or confessors and their holy women?' in Rosalynn Voaden (ed.), *Prophets Abroad: The Reception of Continental Holy Women in Late Medieval England* (Cambridge, 1996), pp. 115–40.

30 *Book*, p. 155.

31 Ibid., p. 218 (my emphasis).

32 Redaction, p. 353.

33 See, for example, Holbrook, 'Margery Kempe and Wynkyn de Worde', p. 30.

34 *Book*, p. 30.

35 Ibid., p. 30.

36 Redaction, p. 356.

37 See Holbrook, 'Margery Kempe and Wynkyn de Worde', p. 31. Here she asserts the success of the redaction in its promotion of the need for women to commune with Christ in silence.

38 Redaction, p. 353.

39 *Book*, p. 8.

40 Redaction, p. 353.

41 Ibid., p. 354.

42 Ibid., p. 355.

43 Ibid., p. 356.

44 Ibid., p. 357.

Select Bibliography

Manuscript Sources

Kew, Public Record Office
E 135/6/48
E 326/6819
E 326/10567
E 326/10568
E 326/11356
Bodleian Library MS Holkham Misc. 41
British Library MS Additional 37790 (Amherst Manuscript)
British Library MS Harley 1819
Durham Cathedral Library MS B. IV. 34
Oxford, Bodleian Library MS Bodley 73
Oxford, Bodleian Library Topography Lincs. d. 1
Oxford, Corpus Christi College MS 236
University of York, Borthwick Institute of Historical Research, Probate Registry, Will 3
University of York, Borthwick Institute of Historical Research, Register of Archbishop Bowet (Reg. 18)
Yale University MS Beinecke 331

Primary Sources

Aelred of Rievaulx, 'A Rule of Life for a Recluse', in Mary Paul Macpherson (trans.), *Treatises: The Pastoral Prayer* (Spencer, M. A.: Cistercian Publications, 1971).

——, *de Institutione Inclusarum*, in *Aelredi Rievallensis Opera Omnia: 1 Opera Ascetica*, ed. A. Hoste and C. H. Talbot (Turnhout: Brepols, 1971), pp. 635–82.

——, *de Institutione Inclusarum: Two English Versions*, ed. John Ayto and Alexandra Barratt, EETS o.s. 287 (London: Oxford University Press, 1984).

——, '*Sermones*', in *Opera Omnia*, ed. G. Raciti CCCM 2A (Turnhout: Brepols, 1989).

Aldhelmi Malmesbiriensis Prosa de Virginitate, ed. Scott Gwara, Corpus Christianorum series Latina CXXIV A (Turnhout: Brepols, 2001).

Ambrose, *Commentarius in Cantica Canticorum*, in *PL*, 15 (Paris, 1841–64), cols 1851–1961.

Anchoritic Spirituality: Ancrene Wisse and Associated Works, trans. and ed. Anne Savage and Nicholas Watson (New York: Paulist Press, 1991).

Ancrene Wisse, Parts Six and Seven, trans. Geoffrey Shepherd (London: Nelson, 1959).

Ancrene Wisse, ed. Robert Hasenfratz, TEAMS (Kalamazoo: Medieval Institute Publications, 2000).

Anselm, *Prayers and Meditations*, trans. Benedicta Ward (Harmondsworth: Penguin Classics, 1973).

Barratt, Alexandra (ed.), *Women's Writing in Middle English* (London: Oxford University Press, 1992).

Bartelink, J. M. (ed.), *Vite dei Santi*, vol. 1 (Milan: Fondazione Lorenzo Valla, 1974).

Beer, Martin, *Denys des Kartäusers Lehre vom desiderium naturale des Menschen nach der Gottesschau* (Munich: Max Hueber Verlag, 1963).

'A Benedictine of Stanbrook' (trans.), *The Monk of Farne*, with Introduction and Notes by [David] Hugh Farmer (Baltimore: Helicon, 1961).

Bernard of Clairvaux, *Sermones super Cantica Canticorum* in *Opera*, vol. 1, ed. J. Leclercq, C. H. Talbot and H. M. Rochais (Rome: Editiones Cisterciences, 1957).

Birgitta of Sweden, 'Epistola solitarii ad reges', in A. Jönsson (ed.), *Alfonso of Jaen: His Life and Works with Critical Editions of the Epistola solitarii, the Informaciones and the Epistola serui Christi* (Lund: Lund University Press: 1989).

Casagrande, Carla, *Prediche alle donne del secolo XIII: Testi di Umberto da Romans, Gilberto da Tournai, Stefano de Borbone* (Milan: Bompiani, 1978).

Chalmers, Joseph, 'Appendix two: the Rule of Saint Albert', in *Mary the Contemplative* (Rome: Edizioni Carmelitane, 2001), pp. 89–93.

Chambers, R., M. Forster and R. Flower (eds), *The Exeter Book of Old English Poetry* (London: P. Lund, 1933).

Cicero, *On Friendship and the Dream of Scipio*, ed. and trans. J. G. F. Powell (Warminster: Aris and Phillips, 1990).

The Cloud of Unknowing, ed. Phyllis Hodgson, EETS o.s. 213 (London, New York and Toronto: Oxford University Press, 1944, repr. 1973).

The Cloud of Unknowing and Related Treatises, ed. Phyllis Hodgson (Salzburg: Institut für Anglistik un Amerikanistik Universität, 1982).

Colgrave, Bertram (ed.), *Felix's Life of Saint Guthlac* (Cambridge: Cambridge University Press, 1956; repr. with English translation, 1985).

Colledge, Edmund, and Noel Chadwick, '*Remedies Against Temptations*: the third English version of William Flete', *Archivo italiano per la storia della pietà*, 5 (1968), 199–240.

Colledge, Eric [Edmund], '*The Recluse*: a Lollard interpolated version of the *Ancrene Riwle*', *Review of English Studies*, 15 (1939), 1–15 and 129–45.

Copsey, Richard, *Early Carmelite Documents* (private printing).

Crawford, Jane, '*Guthlac*: an edition of the Old English prose life together with the poems in the *Exeter Book*' (unpublished D.Phil. thesis, University of Oxford, 1967).

Cross, F. L. (ed.), *The Oxford Dictionary of the Christian Church*, 2nd edn (Oxford: Oxford University Press, 1983).

Damian, Peter, *de perfectione monachorum, PL*, 145, cols 291–328.

Edwards, Bede, *The Rule of Saint Albert*, Vinea Carmeli, 1 (Faversham: Carmelite Press, 1973).

The English Text of the Ancrene Riwle: Edited from Cotton MS. Nero A xiv, ed. Mabel Day, EETS o.s. 225 (London: Oxford University Press, 1952).

The English Text of the Ancrene Riwle: Ancrene Wisse: Edited from MS. Corpus Christi College Cambridge 402, ed. J. R. R. Tolkien, EETS o.s. 249 (London, New York and Toronto: Oxford University Press, 1962).

The English Text of the Ancrene Riwle: Edited from Cotton MS. Titus Dxviii, ed. Frances Mack, EETS o.s. 252 (London: Oxford University Press, 1963 for 1962).

The English Text of the Ancrene Riwle: Edited from Magdalene College, Cambridge, MS. Pepys 2498, ed. A. Zettersten and Bernhard Diensberg, Introduction by H. L. Spencer, EETS o.s. 274 (London: Oxford University Press, 1976).

The English Text of the Ancrene Riwle: The 'Vernon' Text, edited from Oxford, Bodleian Library MS Eng. poet. a. 1, ed. Arne Zettersten and

Bernhard Diensberg, Introduction by H. L. Spencer, EETS o.s. 310 (Oxford: Oxford University Press, 2000).

The Exeter Book, Part I: Poems I–VIII, ed. and trans. Israel Gollancz, EETS o.s. 104 (London: K. Paul, Trench, Trübner and Co., Limited, 1895).

The Exeter Book, Part II, ed. W. S. Mackie, EETS o.s. 194 (London: Oxford University Press, 1934).

Farmer, Hugh [David] (ed.), 'The meditations of the Monk of Farne', in *Studia Anselmiana* 41 (1957), 141–245.

Farrell, R. T. (ed.), *Daniel and Azarias*, Methuen's Old English Library (London: Methuen 1974).

Fundacio abbathie de Kyrkestall, in E. Kitson Clark (ed. and trans.), *Miscellanea*, Publications of the Thoresby Society, 4 (Leeds: Thoresby Society, 1893), pp. 173–208.

Gardner, Edmund, *The Cell of Self-Knowledge* (London: Chatto and Windus, 1910).

Gerson, Jean, *Oeuvres Complètes*, 10 vols, ed. P. Glorieux (Paris: Desclée, 1960–73), vol. 9.

Gertrud the Great of Helfta, *Legatus Divinae Pietatis*, in *Revelationes Gertrudianae ac Mechtildianae*, ed. Monks of Solesmes (Paris: Henri Oudin, 1875), vol. 1.

Goscelin of Saint-Bertin, 'The *Liber confortatorius* of Goscelin of Saint Bertin', ed. C. H. Talbot, *Analecta monastica, series 3, Studia anselmiana*, fasc. 37 (Rome: Herder, 1955), pp. 1–117.

——, *Writing the Wilton Women: Goscelin's Legend of Edith* and *Liber Confortatorius*, ed. Stephanie Hollis, Medieval Women: Texts and Contexts, 9 (Turnhout: Brepols, 2004)

Gregg, R. C. (trans.), *Athanasius's Life of Antony* (New York: Paulist Press, 1980).

Gregoire le Grand, *Expositio super Cantica Canticorum, PL*, 79, cols 471–548.

——, *Dialogues*, vol. 2, ed. A. de Vogüé, Sources Chrétiennes, 251 (Paris: Cerf, 1979).

Hilton, Walter, *The Scale of Perfection*, ed. Thomas H. Bestul, TEAMS (Kalamazoo, MI: Medieval Institute Press, 2000).

Hugh of Kirkstall, *Narratio de fundatione Fontanis monasterii*, in John Richard Walbran (ed.), *Memorials of the Abbey of St Mary of Fountains*, 1 Surtees Society, 42 (Durham: Andrews and Co., 1862), pp. 1–129.

Hugo, Victor, *Notre Dame de Paris*, trans. Alban Krailsheimer (Oxford and New York: Oxford University Press, 1993).

Jerome, *Letter 22, To Eustochium*, *PL*, 22, cols 394–425.

——, *Vita S. Pauli Primi Eremitae*, *PL*, 23, cols 17–30.

——, *The Letters of St Jerome*, ed. and trans. Charles Christopher Mierow (London: Paulist Press, 1963), vol. 1, pp. 134–79.

——, *The Life of Paul the First Hermit*, trans. Carolinne White, *Early Christian Lives* (London: Penguin, 1998), pp. 75–84.

Julian of Norwich, *The Shewings of Julian of Norwich*, ed. Georgia Ronan Crampton, TEAMS (Kalamazoo, MI: Medieval Institute Publications, 1994).

Kaufmann, Michael, *Aegidius Romanus de Colonna, Johannes Gersons, Dionys des Kartäusers und Jakob Sadolets Pädagogische Schriften* (Freiburg im Breisgau: Herdersche Verlagsbuchhandlung, 1904).

Kempe, Margery, *The Book of Margery Kempe*, ed. S. B. Meech and H. E. Allen, EETS o.s. 212 (London, New York and Toronto: Oxford University Press, 1997).

The Knowing of Woman's Kind in Childing, ed. A. Barratt, Medieval Women: Texts and Contexts, 4 (Turnhout: Brepols, 2001).

Lefèvre, Pl. F., and W. M. Grauwen (eds), *Les Statuts de Prémontré au Milieu du XIIe siècle*, Bibliotheca Analectorum, Praemonstratensium Fasc. 12 (Averbode: Praemonstratensia, 1978).

McAvoy, Liz Herbert (ed. and trans.), *The Book of Margery Kempe: An Abridged Translation* (Cambridge: D. S. Brewer, 2003).

Mechthild von Magdeburg, 'Das fließende Licht der Gottheit. Nach der Einsiedler Handschrift in kritischem Vergleich mit der gesamten Überlieferung', in Hans Neumann Münchener (ed.), *Texte und Untersuchungen zur deutschen Literatur des Mittelalters*, 100, 101 (Munich: Artemis, 1990; repr. 1993).

——, *The Flowing Light of the Divinity*, ed. Susan L. Clark, trans. Christiane Mesh Galvanti, Garland Library of Medieval Literature, vol. 72, series B (New York: Garland, 1991).

Memorials of the Abbey of St Mary of Fountains, 61 vols (London, 1892–1963).

Misyn, Richard, *The Fire of Love & The Mending of Life or The Rule of Living*, ed. Ralph Harvey, EETS o.s. 106 (London: Kegan Paul, 1896).

Mosca, Vincenzo, *Alberto Patriarca di Gerusalemme: Tempo, Vita, Opera* (Rome: Edizioni Carmelitane, 1996).

Münchener, Hans Neumann (ed.), *Texte und Untersuchungen zur deutschen Literatur des Mittelalters*, 100, 101 (Munich: Artemis, 1990, repr. 1993).

The Myrour of Recluses, ed. Marta Powell Harley (London, Ontario: Farleigh Dickinson University Press, 1995).

Nicholas the Frenchman, *The Flaming Arrow (Ignea Sagitta)*, ed. Bede Edwards (Durham: Teresian Press, 1985).

Oehl, Wilhelm, *Deutsche Mystikerbriefe des Mittelalters* (Munich and Vienna: Albert Langen und Georg Müller Verlag, 1931).

Ogilvie-Thompson, Sarah J. (ed.), *Richard Rolle: Prose and Verse from MS Longleat 29 and Related Manuscripts*, EETS o.s. 293 (Oxford: Oxford University Press, 1988).

Origen, *Commentary on the Song of Songs*, in *PG*, 13 (Paris, 1862), cols 37–216.

——, *The Song of Songs*, trans. R. P. Lawson, Ancient Christian Writers, 26 (London: Newman, 1957).

Ovid, *Metamorphoses*, trans. Frank Justus Miller (London and Cambridge, MA: Heinemann, 1958).

Pahta, Päivi (ed.), *Medieval Embryology in the Vernacular: The Case of De Spermate* (Helsinki: Société Néophilologique, 1998).

Patrologia Graeca, ed. J.-P. Migne (Paris, 1887).

Patrologia Latina, ed. J.-P. Migne (Paris, 1841–64).

Paul of Naples, *The Life of Mary of Egypt*, in Hugh Magennis (ed.), *The Old English Life of Saint Mary of Egypt* (Exeter: Exeter University Press, 2002), pp. 140–209.

Proper of the Liturgy of the Hours of the Order of the Brothers of the Blessed Virgin Mary of Mount Carmel and of the Order of Discalced Carmelites (Rome: Institutum Carmelitanum, 1993).

Raymond of Capua, *The Life of Saint Catherine of Siena*, trans. George Lamb (New York: P. J. Kenedy, 1960).

Register of the Guild of Corpus Christi in the City of York, Surtees Society, 57, ed. R. H. Skaife (London: Mitchell and Hughes, 1872 for 1871).

S. Anselmi Cantuariensis archiepiscopi Opera Omnia, ed. F. S. Schmitt, vol. 3 (Edinburgh: Thomas Nelson and Sons, 1946), pp. 3–91.

Sévère, Sulpice, *Vie de Saint Martin*, ed. J. Fontaine, Sources Chrétiennes, 133, vol. 1 (Paris: Cerf, 1967).

Severs, Jonathan Burke, Albert E. Hartung and John Edwin Wells (eds), *A Manual of the Writings in Middle English, 1050–1500* (New Haven, CT: Archon Books, 1967).

Speculum Inclusorum, ed. P. L. Oliger, *Lateranum*, n.s. 4 (1938), 1–148.

Staring, Adrian, 'Nicolai Prioris Generalis Carmelitarum Ignea Sagitta', *Carmelus*, 9 (1962), 237–307.

Stratum, Dietrich Loër von (ed.), *Vita beatae memoriae Dionysii Cartusiani*, in J. Bollandus and G. Henschenius, *Acta Sanctorum* (Antwerp, 1668) pp. 245–55. Martii, t. II (Antwerp, 1668).

Thomas of Chobham, *Summa de Commendatione Virtutum et Extirpatione Vitiorum*, ed. F. Morenzoni, CCCM, vol. 82B (Turnhout: Brepols, 1997).

The Vercelli Book, ed. Celia Sisam, Early English Manuscripts in Facsimile, 19 (Copenhagen: Rosenkilde and Bagger, 1976).

The Vercelli Homilies and Related Texts, ed. D. G. Scragg, EETS o.s. 300 (Oxford: Oxford University Press, 1992).

The Vernon Manuscript: A Facsimile of Bodleian Library, Oxford, MS. Eng. Poet. a. 1, ed. A. I. Doyle (Cambridge: D. S. Brewer, 1987).

Vitry, Jacques de, *The Life of Marie D'Oignies by Jacques de Vitry*, trans. Margot H. King (Toronto: Peregrina, 1993).

Waddell, Chrysogonus (ed.), *Narrative and Legislative Texts from Early Cîteaux* (Brecht: Cîteaux Commentarii Cistercienses, 1999).

White, Carolinne (trans.), *Early Christian Lives* (London: Penguin, 1998).

Þe Wohunge of Ure Lauerd, ed. W. Meredith Thompson, EETS o.s. 241 (London: Oxford University Press, 1958).

Secondary Sources

Althusser, Louis, 'Ideology and ideological state apparatuses', as reproduced in *Literary Theory: An Anthology*, ed. Julie Rivkin and Michael Ryan (Oxford: Blackwell, 1998; various reprints), pp. 294–304.

Auberger, Jean-Baptiste, *L'Unanimité Cistercienne primitive: mythe ou réalité?* (Achel, Belgium: Cîteaux Commentarii Cistercienses, 1986).

Bale, John, *Scriptorium Illustrium Maioris Brytanniae quam nunc Angliam et Scotiam vocant: Catalogus*, 2 vols (Basel, 1557–9; repr. Farnborough, Hants: Gregg International Publishers Limited, 1971).

——, *Index Britanniae Scriptorum (John Bale's Index of British and Other Writers)*, ed. Reginald Lane Poole and Mary Bateson (Oxford, 1902; reissued with new introduction by Caroline Brett and James P. Carley, Cambridge: Boydell and Brewer, 1990).

Barratt, Alexandra, 'Anchoritic aspects of *Ancrene Wisse*', *Medium Aevum*, 40 (1980), 33–56.

——, ' "In the lowest part of our need": Julian and medieval gynecological writing', in Sandra McEntire (ed.), *Julian of Norwich: A Book of Essays* (New York and London: Garland, 1998), pp. 240–56.

——, '*Stabat matres dolorosae*: women as readers and writers of Passion prayers, meditations, and visions', in A. A. MacDonald et al. (eds), *The Broken Body: Passion Devotion in Late-Medieval Culture* (Groningen: Egbert Forsten, 1998), pp. 55–72.

Bartlett, Anne Clark, *Male Authors, Female Readers: Representation and Subjectivity in Middle English Devotional Literature* (Ithaca: Cornell University Press, 1995).

Bataillon, Louis-Jacques, 'Similitudines et exempla dans les sermons du XIIIᵉ siècle', in Katherine Walsh and Diana Wood (eds), *The Bible in the Medieval World: Essays in Memory of Beryl Smalley*, Ecclesiastical History Society (Oxford: Blackwell, 1985), pp. 191–215.

Bell, Rudolph M., *Holy Anorexia* (Chicago: University of Chicago Press, 1987).

Bennett, Judith, *Sisters and Workers in the Middle Ages* (Chicago: University of Chicago Press, 1989).

Bergström-Allen, Johan, ' "Heremitam et Ordinis Carmelitarum": a study of the vernacular theological literature produced by medieval English Whitefriars, particularly Richard Misyn, O. Carm.' (unpublished M.Phil. thesis, University of Oxford, 2002).

——, 'Looking behind to see ahead: finding a future from the early Carmelites', *Assumpta*, 46, 4 (2003), 13–27.

——, 'Carmelites and lay piety in York prior to the papal letter *Cum Nulla*' (York: Saint Albert's Press, forthcoming).

Berman, Constance H., 'Were there twelfth-century Cistercian nuns?', *Church History*, 68 (1999), 824–64.

——, *The Cistercian Evolution: The Invention of a Religious Order in Twelfth-Century Europe* (Philadelphia: University of Pennsylvania Press, 2000).

Bernau, Anke, 'Virginal effects: text and identity in *Ancrene Wisse*', in S. J. E. Riches and S. Salih (eds), *Gender and Holiness: Men, Women and Saints in Late-Medieval Europe*, (London and New York: Routledge, 2002), pp. 36–48.

Blake, N. F., 'Vernon Manuscript: contents and organisation', in Derek Persall (ed.), *Studies in the Vernon Manuscript* (Cambridge: D. S. Brewer, 1990), pp. 45–59.

Blum, Hubertus Maria, 'Lexikale Übersicht der Kartäuser Schriftsteller', in Marijan Zadnikar and Adam Wienand (eds), *Die Kartäuser: Der Orden der schweigenden Mönche* (Cologne: Wienand Verlag, 1983), pp. 345–74.

Boaga, Emanuele, *The Lady of the Place: Mary in the History and in the Life of Carmel* (Rome: Edizioni Carmelitane, 2001).

Bourdieu, Pierre, *The Logic of Practice*, trans. Richard Nice (Cambridge: Polity; Stanford: Stanford University Press, 1990).

Brown, Peter, 'The rise and function of the holy man in late Antiquity', repr. in Peter Brawn (ed.), *Society and the Holy in Late Antiquity* (London: Faber and Faber, 1982), pp. 103–52.

——, *The Body and Society: Men, Women and Sexual Renunciation in Early Christianity* (London: Methuen, 1990).

Butler, Judith, *Gender Trouble: Feminism and the Subversion of Identity* (London: Routledge, 1990).

——, *Bodies that Matter: On the Discursive Limits of 'Sex'* (New York and London: Routledge, 1993).

Bynum, Caroline Walker, *Jesus as Mother: Studies in the Spirituality of the High Middle Ages* (Berkeley: University of California Press, 1982).

——, *Holy Feast and Holy Fast: The Religious Significance of Food to Medieval Women* (Berkeley: University of California Press, 1987).

——, *Fragmentation and Redemption: Essays on Gender and the Human Body in Medieval Religion* (New York: Zone Books, 1992).

Cadden, Joan, *The Meanings of Sex Difference in the Middle Ages: Medicine, Science and Culture* (Cambridge: Cambridge University Press, 1993).

Casey, Michael, 'Bernard and the crisis at Morimond: did the Order exist in 1124?', *Cistercian Studies Quarterly*, 38 (2003), 119–75.

Chartier, M.-C., 'Reclus', in *Dictionnaire de Spiritualité*, 13, pp. 221–3.

Chewning, Susannah Mary, 'Mysticism and the anchoritic community: "a time . . . of veiled infinity" ', in Diane Watt (ed.) *Medieval Women in their Communities* (Cardiff: University of Wales Press, 1997), pp. 116–37.

——, 'The paradox of virginity within the anchoritic tradition: the masculine gaze and the feminine body in the *Wohunge Group*', in Angela Weisl and Cindy Carlson (eds), *Constructions of Widowhood and Virginity in the Middle Ages* (New York: Palgrave, 1999), pp. 112–34.

Clark, J. P. H., 'A defence of the Carmelite Order by John Hornby, O. Carm., A.D. 1374', *Carmelus*, 32 (1985), 73–98.

Clay, Rotha Mary, *The Hermits and Anchorites of England* (London: Methuen, 1914; repr. Detroit: Singing Tree Press, 1968).

Coon, Lynda L., *Sacred Fictions: Holy Women and Hagiography in Late Antiquity* (Philadelphia: University of Pennsylvania Press, 1997).

Copsey, Richard, *Carmel in Britain 3: The Hermits from Mount Carmel* (Faversham, Kent: Saint Albert's Press, 2004).

——, 'Establishment, identity and papal approval: the Carmelite Order's creation of its legendary History', *Carmelus*, 47 (Rome: Instituto Carmelitano, 2000), pp. 41–53.

——, 'The *Ignea Sagitta* and its readership: a re-evaluation', *Carmelus*, 46 (1999), 166–73.

——, 'Simon Stock and the scapular vision', *Journal of Ecclesiastical History*, 50, 4 (1999), 652–83.

Courtenay, William J., *Schools and Scholars in Fourteenth-Century England* (Princeton, NJ: Princeton University Press, 1987).

Cré, Marleen, 'Vernacular mysticism in the Charterhouse: an analysis of British Library MS Additional 37790 in its religious and literary context' (unpublished Ph.D. thesis, Université de Fribourg, 2001).

Crouch, David J. F., *Piety, Fraternity and Power: Religious Gilds in Late Medieval Yorkshire, 1389–1547* (York: York Medieval Press, 2000).

d'Avray, D. L., *The Preaching of the Friars: Sermons diffused from Paris before 1300* (Oxford: Oxford University Press, 1985).

Dahood, Roger, '*Ancrene Wisse*, the Katherine Group, and the *Wohunge* Group', in A. S. G. Edwards (ed.), *Middle English Prose: A Critical Guide to Major Authors and Genres* (New Brunswick, NJ: Rutgers University Press, 1986), pp. 1–34.

——, 'The current state of *Ancrene Wisse* group studies', *Medieval English Studies Newsletter*, 36 (1997), 6–14.

Darwin, Francis D. S., *The English Mediaeval Recluse* (London: Society for Promoting Christian Knowledge, 1944).

Deanesly, Margaret, *A History of the Medieval Church 590–1500* (London: Routledge, 1969).

Degler-Spengler, Brigitte, 'The incorporation of Cistercian nuns into the Order in the twelfth and thirteenth centuries', in John A. Nichols and Lillian Thomas Shank (eds), *Hidden Springs: Cistercian Monastic Women* (Kalamazoo: Cistercian Publications, 1995), pp. 85–134.

Dobson, Barrie, 'Mendicant ideal and practice in late medieval York', in P. V. Addyman and V. E. Black (eds), *Archaeological Papers from York Presented to M. W. Barley* (York: York Archaeological Trust, 1984), pp. 109–22.

——, 'The city of York', in Boris Ford (ed.), *Cambridge Cultural History: Volume II, Medieval Britain* (Cambridge: Cambridge University Press, 1992), pp. 201–13.

Dobson, E. J., *The Origins of* Ancrene Wisse (Oxford: Clarendon, 1976).

Doyère, Pierre, 'Érémitisme en Occident', in *Dictionnaire de Spiritualité*, 4, i (Paris: Beauchesne, 1969) pp. 953–82.

——, 'Ermites', in *Dictionnaire de Droit Catholique*, 5, 412–29.

Dutton, M. L., 'Christ our Mother: Aelred's iconography for contemplative union', in E. Rozanne Elder (ed.), *Goad and Nail: Studies in Medieval Cistercian History*, 10 (Kalamazoo: Cistercian Publications, 1985), pp. 21–45.

Edden, Valerie, 'The mantle of Elijah: Carmelite spirituality in England in the fourteenth century', in Marion Glasscoe (ed.), *The Medieval*

Mystical Tradition, England, Ireland and Wales, Exeter Symposium VI (Cambridge: D. S. Brewer, 1999), pp. 67–83.

Egan, Keith J., 'The establishment and early development of the Carmelite Order in England' (unpublished Ph.D. thesis, Cambridge University, 1965).

——, 'The spirituality of the Carmelites', in Jill Raitt (ed.), *Christian Spirituality: High Middle Ages and Reformation* (London: Routledge, 1987), pp. 50–62.

Elkins, S., *Holy Women of Twelfth-Century England* (Chapel Hill, NC: University of North Carolina Press, 1988).

Emery, Jr., Kent, 'Dionysii Cartusiensis bibliotheca et manuscripta', in *Kartäusermystik und Mystiker, Analecta Cartusiana*, vol. 55, ed. James Hogg (Salzburg: Institut für Anglistik und Amerikanistik, Universtät Salzburg; Lewiston, NY: Edwin Mellen Press, 1982), pp. 119–56.

Erler, Mary C., 'Three fifteenth-century vowesses', in Caroline M. Barron and Anne F. Sutton (eds), *Medieval London Widows, 1300–1500* (Rio Grande, OH: Hambledon Press, 1994), pp. 165–84.

——, 'English vowed women at the end of the Middle Ages', *Mediaeval Studies*, 57 (1995), 155–203.

——, 'Exchange of books between nuns and laywomen: three surviving examples', in Richard Beadle and A. J. Piper (eds), *New Science Out of Old Books: Studies in Manuscripts and Early Printed Books in Honour of A. I. Doyle* (Aldershot: Scolar Press, 1995), pp. 360–73.

——, 'Syon's "special benefactors and friends": some vowed women', *Birgittiana*, 2 (1996), 209–22.

Fein, S. G., 'Maternity in Aelred of Rievaulx's letter to his sister', in John Carmi Parsons and Bonnie Wheeler (eds), *Medieval Mothering* (New York: Garland, 1996), pp. 139–56.

Finnegan, M. J., *The Women of Helfta: Scholars and Mystics* (Athens, GA: University of Georgia Press, 1991).

Fitzgerald-Lombard, Patrick (ed.), *Carmel in Britain*, 2 vols (Rome: Institutum Carmelitanum, 1992).

Flood, Jr., Bruce P., 'The Carmelite friars in medieval English universities and society, 1299–1430', *Recherches de théologie ancienne et médiévale*, 55 (1988), 154–83.

Freeman, Elizabeth, *Narratives of a New Order: Cistercian Historical Writing in England, 1150–1220*, Medieval Church Studies, 2 (Turnhout: Brepols, 2002).

Freud, Sigmund, *Moses and Monotheism* (New York: Vintage Books, 1967; orig. pub. 1939).

Gajano, Sofia Boesch, 'Monastero, città, campagna: il culto di S. Chelidonia a Subiaco tra XII e XVI secolo', in Sofia Boesch Gajano and Lucia Sebastiani (eds), *Culto dei santi: Istitutioni e classi sociali in età preindustriale* (L'Aquila: Japadre, 1984), pp. 227–60.

——, and Lucia Sebastiani (eds), *Chelidonia: Storia di un culto* (Rome: Viella, 1997).

Georgianna, L., *The Solitary Self: Individuality in the* Ancrene Wisse (Cambridge, MA: Harvard University Press, 1981).

Gilchrist, Roberta, *Gender and Material Culture: The Archaeology of Religious Women* (New York: Routledge, 1994).

——, *Contemplation and Action: The Other Monasticism* (London and New York: Leicester University Press, 1995).

——, *Gender and Archaeology: Contesting the Past* (London and New York: Routledge, 1999).

Gillespie, Vincent, 'Cura Pastoralis in Deserto', in Michael Sargent (ed.), *De Cella in Seculum: Religious and Secular Life and Devotion in Late Medieval England* (Cambridge: D. S. Brewer, 1989), pp. 161–81.

Goldberg, P. J. P., *Woman is a Worthy Wight: Women in English Society 1200–1500* (Stroud: Alan Sutton Publishing, 1992).

Goodenough, Ewin R., *The Church in the Roman Empire* (New York: Cooper Square, 1970).

Gougaud, Pierre, *Devotional and Ascetic Practices in the Middle Ages*, trans. G. C. Bateman (London: Burns, Oates and Co., 1927).

Graves, Coburn V., 'English Cistercian nuns in Lincolnshire', *Speculum*, 54 (1979), 492–9.

Grayson, J., *Structure and Imagery in* Ancrene Wisse (Hanover, NH: University Press of New England, 1974).

Greenfield, S. B., 'The Christian saint as hero', in S. B. Greenfield and D. G. Calder (eds), *A New Critical History of Old English Literature* (New York and London: New York University Press, 1986)

Greetham, D. C., *Textual Scholarship: An Introduction* (New York: Garland, 1994).

Gunn, Cate, '*Ancrene Wisse*: A modern lay person's guide to a medieval religious text', *Magistra*, 8 (2002), 1–25.

Hallier, A., *The Monastic Theology of Aelred of Rievaulx: An Experiential Theology*, trans. Columban Heaney (Shannon, Ireland: Irish University Press, 1969).

Hansen, Elaine Tuttle, *Chaucer and the Fictions of Gender* (Berkeley: University of California Press, 1992).

Heimmel, J. P., '*God is our Mother': Julian of Norwich and the Medieval*

Image of Christian Feminine Divinity', Elizabethan and Renaissance Studies 92, 5 (Salzburg: Institut für Englische Sprache und Literatur, Universität Salzburg, 1982).

Hogg, James, 'The Carthusian nuns: a survey of the sources of their history', in James Hogg (ed.), *Die Kartäuser und Ihre Welt – Kontakte und Gegenseitige Einflüsse: Analecta Cartusiana*, vol. 62 (Salzburg: Institut für Anglistik und Amerikanistik, Universtät Salzburg; Lewiston, NY: Edwin Mellen Press, 1993), pp. 190–294.

Holbrook, Sue-Ellen, 'Margery Kempe and Wynkyn de Worde', in Marion Glasscoe (ed.), *The Medieval Mystical Tradition in England: Papers Read at Dartington Hall, July 1987*, Exeter Symposium IV (Cambridge: D. S. Brewer, 1987), pp. 27–46.

Hollis, Stephanie, *Anglo-Saxon Women and the Church: Sharing a Common Fate* (Woodbridge: Boydell, 1992).

Hoskin, Philippa, 'Some late fourteenth-century gild and fabric wardens' accounts from the Church of St. Margaret's, Walmgate, York', in David M. Smith (ed.), *The Church in Medieval York: Records Edited in Honour of Professor Barrie Dobson* (York: University of York, Borthwick Institute of Historical Research, 1999), pp. 75–86.

Howard-Johnston, James, and Paul Antony Hayward (eds), *The Cult of Saints in Late Antiquity and the Early Middle Ages: Essays on the Contribution of Peter Brown* (Oxford: Oxford University Press, 2002).

Howell, Martha C., *Women, Production and Patriarchy in Late-Medieval Cities* (Chicago: University of Chicago Press, 1986).

Hubert, Jean, 'Les recluseries urbaines au Moyen Âge', in *L'Eremitismo in Occidente nei secoli xi e xii*, (Milan: Vita e Pensiero, 1965), pp. 485–7.

Hughes, Jonathan, *Pastors and Visionaries: Religion and Secular Life in Late Medieval Yorkshire* (Woodbridge: Boydell, 1988).

Hughes-Edwards, Mari, 'Hedgehog skins and hairshirts: the changing role of asceticism in the anchoritic ideal', *Mystics Quarterly*, 28, 1 (2002), 6–25.

Huizinga, Johan, *The Waning of the Middle Ages* (Garden City, NY: Doubleday, 1954; orig. pub. 1924).

Hussey, S. S., 'Implications of choice and arrangements of texts in part 4', in Derek Pearsall (ed.), *Studies in the Vernon Manuscript* (Cambridge: D. S. Brewer, 1990), pp. 61–74.

Innes-Parker, Catherine, 'Fragmentation and reconstruction: images of the female body in *Ancrene Wisse* and the *Katherine Group*', *Comitatus*, 26 (1995), 27–52.

Irigaray, Luce, 'La Mystèrique', in *Speculum of the Other Woman*, trans. Gillian C. Gill (Ithaca, NY: Cornell University Press, 1985), pp. 191–202.

Jantzen, Grace, *Julian of Norwich* (London: SPCK, 1987).

——, *Power, Gender and Christian Mysticism* (Cambridge: Cambridge University Press, 1995), pp. 281–2.

Jedin, Hubert, *Handbuch der Kirchengeschichte*, 7 vols (Freiburg: Herder, 1962–79).

Jotischky, Andrew, *The Carmelites and Antiquity: Mendicants and their Pasts in the Middle Ages* (Oxford: Oxford University Press, 2002).

Karras, Ruth Mazo, 'Separating the men from the goats: masculinity, civilization and identity formation in the medieval university', in Jacqueline Murray (ed.), *Conflicted Identities and Multiple Masculinities: Men in the Medieval West* (New York and London: Garland Publishing, 1999), pp. 189–215.

Keiser, George R., 'The mystics and the early English printers: the economics of devotionalism', in Marion Glasscoe (ed.), *The Medieval Mystical Tradition in England: Papers Read at Dartington Hall, July 1987*, Exeter Symposium IV (Cambridge: D. S. Brewer, 1987), pp. 9–26.

Kieckhefer, Richard, *Unquiet Souls: Fourteenth Century Saints and their Religious Milieu* (Chicago and London: University of Chicago Press, 1984).

Kingsley, Charles, *The Hermits* (London: Macmillan, 1890).

Kristeva, Julia, 'Women can never be defined' ('La femme, ce n'est jamais ça'), trans. Marilyn August, *Tel Quel*, 59 (1974) repr. in Elaine Marks and Isabelle de Courtivron (eds), *New French Feminisms* (New York, London, Toronto, Sydney and Tokyo: Harvester, 1981), pp. 137–41.

——, *Powers of Horror: An Essay on Abjection* (New York: Columbia University Press, 1982).

Labarge, Margaret Wade, 'Three medieval widows and a second career', in Michael M. Sheehand (ed.), *Ageing and the Aged in Medieval Europe: Selected Papers from the Annual Conference of the Centre for Medieval Studies, University of Toronto, Held 25–26 February and 11–12 November 1983*, Papers in Medieval Studies, 11 (Toronto: Pontifical Institute of Medieval Studies, 1990), pp. 159–72.

——, *Women in Medieval Life* (London: Penguin, 2001).

Lacan, Jacques, *Écrits: A Selection*, trans. Alan Sheridan (New York: Norton, 1977).

Laing, Margaret, 'Linguistic profiles and textual criticism: the translation by Richard Misyn of Rolle's *Incendium Amoris* and *Emendatio Vitae*', in Angus McIntosh, M. L. Samuels and Margaret Laing (eds), *Middle English Dialectology: Essays on Some Principles and Problems* (Aberdeen: Aberdeen University Press, 1989), pp. 188–223.

Laqueur, Thomas, *Making Sex: Body and Gender from the Greeks to Freud* (Cambridge, MA and London: Harvard University Press, 1990).

Lawrence, C. H., *The Friars: The Impact of the Early Mendicant Movement on Western Society* (London: Longman, 1994).

——, *Medieval Monasticism: Forms of Religious Life in Western Europe in the Middle Ages* (London: Longman, 3rd edn, 2001).

Leclercq, Jean, 'Disciplina', in *Dictionnaire de Spiritualité, Ascétique et Mystique Doctrine et Histoire*, vol. 3 (Paris: G. Beauchesne, 1957), cols 1291–302.

——, ' "Eremus" et "Eremita": pour l'histoire du vocabulaire de la vie solitaire', *Collectanea Ordinis Cistercensium Reformatorum*, 48 (1963), 8–30.

Lees, Claire, and Gillian R. Overling, *Double Agents: Women and Clerical Culture in Anglo-Saxon England* (Philadelphia: University of Pennsylvania Press, 2001).

Lekai, Louis J., *The Cistercians: Ideals and Reality* (Kent, OH: Kent State University Press, 1977).

Leyser, Henrietta, *Medieval Women: A Social History of Women in England 450–1500* (London: Weidenfield and Nicolson, 2002).

Lochrie, Karma, *Margery Kempe and Translations of the Flesh* (Philadelphia: University of Pennsylvania Press, 1991).

McAvoy, Liz Herbert, ' "Ant nes he him seolf reclus i maries wombe?": Julian of Norwich, the anchorhold and redemption of the monstrous female body', in Liz Herbert McAvoy and Teresa Walters (eds), *Consuming Narratives: Gender and Monstrous Appetite in the Middle Ages and the Renaissance* (Cardiff: University of Wales Press, 2002), pp. 128–43.

——, 'Julian of Norwich and a trinity of the feminine', *Mystics Quarterly*, 28, 2 (2002), 68–77.

——, *Authority and the Female Body in the Writings of Julian of Norwich and Margery Kempe* (Cambridge: D. S. Brewer, 2004).

McCaffrey, P. R., *The White Friars: An Outline Carmelite History, with Special Reference to the English-Speaking Provinces* (Dublin: M. H. Gill and Son, 1926).

McGinn, Bernard, 'The role of the Carmelites in the history of Western mysticism', in Kevin Culligan and Regis Jordan (eds), *Carmel and Contemplation: Transforming Human Consciousness* (Washington DC: ICS Publications, 2000), pp. 25–50.

McGreal, Wilfrid, *At the Fountain of Elijah: The Carmelite Tradition* (London: Longman and Todd, 1999).

Macken, OFM, Raymond, *Denys the Carthusian: Commentator on Boethius'* De Consolatione Philosophiae (Salzburg: Institut für Anglistik und Amerikanistik, Universität Salzburg, 1984).

Maclean, Ian, *The Renaissance Notion of Women: A Study in the Fortunes of Scholasticism and Medical Science in European Intellectual Life* (Cambridge: Cambridge University Press, 1980).

Marshall, Claire, 'The politics of self-mutilation: forms of female devotion in the late Middle Ages', in Darryll Grantley and Nina Taunton (eds), *The Body in Late Medieval and Early Modern Culture* (Aldershot: Ashgate, 2000), pp. 11–21.

Meale, Carol M., ' "oft siþis with grete deuotion I þought what I miȝt do pleysyng to god": the early ownership and readership of Love's *Mirror*, with special reference to its female audience', in Shoichi Oguro, Richard Beadle and Michael G. Sargent (eds), *Nicholas Love at Waseda: Proceedings of the International Conference 20–22 July, 1995* (Cambridge: D. S. Brewer, 1997), pp. 19–46.

Miller, Julie B., 'Eroticized violence in medieval women's mystical literature: a call for a feminist critique', *Journal of Feminist Studies in Religion*, 15, 2 (1999), 25–50.

Millett, Bella, '*Mouvance* and the medieval author: re-editing *Ancrene Wisse*', in A. J. Minnis (ed.), *Late-Medieval Religious Texts and their Transmission* (Cambridge: D. S. Brewer, 1994), pp. 9–20.

——, *Ancrene Wisse, The Katherine Group, and the Wooing Group*, Annotated Bibliographies of Old and Middle English Literature, vol. 2 (Cambridge: D. S. Brewer, 1996).

——, '*Ancrene Wisse* and the conditions of confession', *English Studies*, 80 (1999), 193–215.

——, '*Ancrene Wisse* and the Book of Hours', in Denis Renevey and Christiania Whitehead (eds), *Writing Religious Women: Female Spiritual and Textual Practices in Late Medieval England* (Cardiff: University of Wales Press, 2000), pp. 21–40.

Moi, Toril, *Sexual/Textual Politics: Feminist Literary Theory* (London: Methuen, 1985).

Mougel, D. A., *Dionysius der Karthäuser, 1402–1471: Sein Leben, Sein Wirken* (Mühlheim a.d. Ruhr: Verlag von M. Hegner, 1898).

Murray, Jacqueline (ed.), *Conflicted Identities and Multiple Masculinities: Men in the Medieval West* (New York and London: Garland Publishing, 1999).

Nichols, John A., 'Cistercian nuns in twelfth and thirteenth century England', in John A. Nichols and Lillian Thomas Shank (eds), *Hidden Springs:*

Cistercian Monastic Women (Kalamazoo: Cistercian Publications, 1995), pp. 49–61.

Nissen, Peter J. A., 'Dionysius von Rijkel', in Peter Dinzelbacher (ed.), *Wörterbuch der Mystik* (Stuttgart: Alfred Kröner Verlag, 1989).

Nuth, Joan M., *God's Lovers in an Age of Anxiety: The Medieval English Mystics* (London: Darton, Longman and Todd, 2001).

O'Carroll, Mary E., *A Thirteenth-Century Preacher's Handbook: Studies in MS Laud Misc. 511* (Toronto: Pontifical Institute of Medieval Studies, 1997).

O'Mara, V. M., 'Preaching to nuns in late medieval England', in Carolyn Muessig (ed.), *Medieval Monastic Preaching* (Leiden: Brill, 1998), pp. 93–119.

Owen, Dorothy M., *Church and Society in Medieval Lincolnshire*, ed. Joan Thirsk (Welwyn Garden City: Broadwater Press, 1971).

Panofsky, Erwin, *Gothic Architecture and Scholasticism* (Cleveland: World Publishing, 1957).

Park, Tarjei, 'Reflecting Christ: the role of the flesh in Walter Hilton and Julian of Norwich', in Marion Glasscoe (ed.), *The Medieval Mystical Tradition in England*, Exeter Symposium V (Cambridge: D. S. Brewer, 1992), pp. 17–37.

Parsons, William B., *The Enigma of the Oceanic Feeling. Revisioning the Psychoanalytic Theory of Mysticism* (New York and Oxford: Oxford University Press, 1999).

Patten, B. M., *The Embryology of the Pig* (Philadelphia: Blakiston Co., 1948).

Pearsall, Derek (ed.), *Studies in the Vernon Manuscript* (Cambridge: D. S. Brewer, 1990).

Phillips, Kim L., *Medieval Maidens: Young Women and Gender in England 1270–1540* (Manchester: Manchester University Press, 2003).

Pittenger, Norman, *The Life of Saint Paul* (London: Norman Watts Ltd., 1970).

Pollard, William F., 'Bodleian MS Holkham Misc. 41: a fifteenth-century Bridgettine manuscript and prayer cycle', *Birgittiana*, 3 (1997), 43–53.

——, 'Mystical elements in a fifteenth-century prayer sequence: "The festis and the passion of oure lord Ihesu Crist" ', in Marion Glasscoe (ed.), *The Medieval Mystical Tradition in England*, Exeter Symposium IV (Cambridge: D. S. Brewer, 1987), pp. 47–61.

Raine, Angelo, *Mediaeval York: A Topographical Survey based on Original Sources* (London: John Murray, 1955).

Rasmussen, Linda, 'Order, order! Determining order in medieval English nunneries', in Linda Rasmussen, Valerie Spear and Dianne Tillotson (eds), *Our Medieval Heritage: Essays in Honour of John Tillotson for his 60th Birthday* (Cardiff: Merton Priory Press, 2002), pp. 30–49.

——, Valerie Spear and Dianne Tillotson (eds), *Our Medieval Heritage: Essays in Honour of John Tillotson for his 60th Birthday* (Cardiff: Merton Priory Press, 2002).

Riddy, Felicity, ' "Women talking about the things of God": a late medieval sub-culture', in Carole Meale (ed.), *Women and Literature in Britain, 1150–1500* (Cambridge: Cambridge University Press, 1993), pp. 104–27.

Roberts, Jane, (ed.), *The Guthlac Poems of the Exeter Book* (Oxford: Clarendon, 1979).

——, 'The Old English prose translation of Felix's *Vita Sancti Guthlaci*', in P. E. Szarmach (ed.), *Studies in Earlier Old English Prose* (Albany, NY: State University of New York Press, 1986).

Roberts, Phyllis B., 'Stephen Langton's *Sermo de Virginibus*', in Julius Kirshner and Suzanne F. Wemple (eds), *Women of the Medieval World: Essays in Honour of John H. Mundy* (Oxford: Blackwell, 1985), pp. 103–18.

Robertson, Elizabeth, 'The rule of the body: the feminine spirituality of the *Ancrene Wisse*', in Sheila Fisher and Janet H. Halley (eds), *Seeking the Woman in Late Medieval and Renaissance Writings* (Knoxville: University of Tennessee Press, 1989), pp. 109–34. Reprinted in Julia Bolton Holloway, Constance S. Wright and Joan Bechtold (eds), *Equally in God's Image: Women in the Middle Ages* (New York: Peter Lang, 1990), pp. 109–34.

——, 'An anchorhold of her own: female anchoritic literature in thirteenth-century England', in *Equally in God's Image: Women in the Middle Ages*, ed. Julia Bolton Holloway, Constance S. Wright and Joan Bechtold (New York: Peter Lang, 1990), pp. 170–83.

——, 'Medieval medical views of women and female spirituality in *Ancrene Wisse* and Julian of Norwich's *Showings*', in Linda Lomperis and Sarah Stanbury (eds), *Feminist Approaches to the Body in Medieval Literature* (Philadelphia: University of Pennsylvania Press, 1993), pp. 142–67.

Rossum, Irene van, '*Adest meliori parte*: a portrait of monastic friendship in exile in Goscelin's *Liber confortatorius*' (unpublished D.Phil dissertation, University of York, 1999).

Rouse, Richard H., and Mary A. Rouse, ' "*Statim invenire*", schools, preachers, and new attitudes to the page', in Robert Benson and Giles Constable with Carol D. Lanham (eds), *Renaissance and Renewal in the*

Twelfth Century (Toronto: University of Toronto Press, 1991), pp. 191–220.

Roy, G., '"Sharpen your mind with the whetstone of books": the female recluse as reader in Goscelin's *Liber Confortatorius*, Aelred of Rievaulx's *de Institutione Inclusarum* and the *Ancrene Wisse*', in Lesley Smith and Jane H. M. Taylor (eds), *Women, the Book and the Godly* (Cambridge: D. S. Brewer, 1995), pp. 113–22.

Rubin, M., *Corpus Christi: The Eucharist in Late Medieval Culture* (Cambridge: Cambridge University Press, 1991).

Rüthing, Heinrich, 'Zur Geschichte der Kartäusen in der Ordensprovinz Alemannia inferior von 1320 bis 1400', and '"Die Wächter Israels" – ein Beitrag zur Geschichte der Visitationen im Kartäuserorden', in Marijan Zadnikar with Adam Wienand (eds), *Die Kartäuser: Der Orden der schweigenden Mönche* (Cologne: Wienand Verlag, 1983), pp. 139–85.

Saenger, Paul, *Space Between Words: The Origins of Silent Reading* (Stanford: Stanford University Press, 1997).

Saggi, Louis, et al. (eds), *Saints of Carmel: A Compilation from Various Dictionaries*, trans. Gabriel Pausback (Rome: Carmelite Institute, 1972).

Salih, Sarah, *Versions of Virginity in Late Medieval England* (Cambridge: D. S. Brewer, 2001).

Sargent, Michael G., 'The transmission by the English Carthusians of some late medieval spiritual writings', *Journal of Ecclesiastical History*, 27, 3 (1976), 225–40.

Schreiner, Klaus, 'Gebildete Analphabeten? Spätmittelalterliche Laienbrüder als Leser und Schreiber wissensvermittelnder und frömmigkeitsbildender Literatur', in Horst Brunner and Norbert Richard Wolf (eds), *Wissensliteratur im Mittelalter und in der Frühen Neuzeit: Bedingungen, Typen, Publikum, Sprache* (Wiesbaden: Dr Ludwig Reichert Verlag, 1993), pp. 296–328.

Severs, Jonathan Burke, Albert E. Hartung and John Edwin Wells (eds), *A Manual of the Writings in Middle English, 1050–1500* (New Haven, CT: Archon Books, 1967), 9.

Sexauer, Wolfram D., *Frühneuhochdeutsche Schriften in Kartäuserbibliotheken. Untersuchungen zur Pflege der volkssprachlichen Literatur in Kartäuserklöstern des oberdeutschen Raums bis zum Einsetzen der Reformation* (Frankfurt/Main: Peter Lang, 1978).

Sharpe, Richard, *Handlist of the Latin Writers of Great Britain and Ireland before 1540* (Turnhout: Brepols, 1997).

Simons, Walter, *City of Ladies: Begune Communities in the Medieval Low Countries, 1200–1565* (Philadelphia: University of Pennsylvania Press, 2001).

Smet, Joachim, *The Carmelites: A History of the Brothers of Our Lady of Mount Carmel*, 4 vols (Rome: Institutum Carmelitanum, rev. edn 1976–88).

——, *Cloistered Carmel: A Brief History of the Carmelite Nuns* (Rome: Institutum Carmelitanum, 1986).

Southern, R. W., *The Making of the Middle Ages* (New Haven: Yale University Press, 1953).

Spencer, H. L., *English Preaching in the Late Middle Ages* (Oxford: Clarendon, 1993).

Staring, Adrian, *Medieval Carmelite Heritage* (Rome: Institutum Carmelitanum, 1989).

Stevenson, Jane, 'The holy sinner: the life of Mary of Egypt', in Erich Poppe and Bianca Ross (eds), *The Legend of Mary of Egypt in Medieval Insular Hagiography*, (Blackrock, Co. Dublin: Four Courts, 1996), pp. 19–50.

Swanson, R. N., *Religion and Devotion in Europe 1215–1515* (Cambridge: Cambridge University Press, 1995).

Szarmach, P. E. (ed.), *Studies in Earlier Old English Prose* (Albany, NY: State University of New York Press, 1986).

Tanner, Norman P., *The Church in Late Medieval Norwich 1370–1532* (Toronto: Pontifical Institute of Medieval Studies, 1984).

Tarvers, Josephine Koster, ' "Thys ys my mystrys boke": English women as readers and writers in late medieval England', in Charlotte Cook Morse, Penelope Reed Doob and Marjorie Curry Woods (eds), *The Uses of Manuscripts in Literary Studies: Essays in Memory of Judson Boyce Allen*, Studies in Medieval Culture, 31 (Kalamazoo: Medieval Institute Publications, 1992), pp. 305–27.

Thurston, Herbert, 'Review', *Tablet* (October 24 1936).

Tyler, Elizabeth, 'The collocation of words for treasure in Old English verse' (unpublished D. Phil. thesis, University of Oxford, 1994).

Vandermeersch, Patrick, *La Chair de la passion: un histoire de foi, la flagellation* (Paris: Cerf, 2002).

Voaden, R., 'All girls together: community, gender and vision at Helfta', in Diane Watt (ed.), *Medieval Women in their Communities* (Cardiff: University of Wales Press, 1997), pp. 72–91.

Waaijman, Kees, *The Mystical Space of Carmel: A Commentary on the Carmelite Rule*, trans. John Vriend (Leuven: Peeters, 1999).

Ward, Benedicta, *Harlots of the Desert: A Study of Repentance in Early Monastic Sources* (Kalamazoo: Medieval Institute Press, 1987).

Warren, Ann K., *Anchorites and their Patrons in Medieval England* (Berkeley: University of California Press, 1985).

Wassermann, Dirk, *Dionysius der Kartäuser: Einführung in Werk und Gedankenwelt* (Salzburg: Institut für Anglistik und Amerikanistik, Universität Salzburg, 1996).

Watson, Nicholas, 'The methods and objectives of thirteenth-century anchoritic devotion', in Marion Glasscoe (ed.), *The Medieval Mystical Tradition in England*, Exeter Symposium IV (Woodbridge: D. S. Brewer, 1987), pp. 132–53.

——, *Richard Rolle and the Invention of Authority* (Cambridge: Cambridge University Press, 1991).

——, 'The composition of Julian of Norwich's Revelation of Love', *Speculum*, 68, 3 (1993), 637–83.

——, 'Censorship and cultural change in late-medieval England: vernacular theology, the Oxford Translation Debate, and Arundel's *Constitutions* of 1409', *Speculum*, 70, 4 (1995), 822–64.

Welter, J., *L'Exemplum dans la littérature religieuse et didactique du moyen âge* (Paris: Occitania, 1927).

White, Carolinne (trans.), *Early Christian Lives* (London: Penguin, 1998).

Wiethaus, Ulrike, 'Thieves and carnivals: gender in German Dominican literature of the fourteenth century', in Renate Blumenfeld-Kosinski, Duncan Robertson and Nancy Bradley Warren (eds), *The Vernacular Spirit: Essays on Medieval Religious Literature* (New York: Palgrave, 2002), pp. 209–39.

Williams, Charles Allyn, 'Oriental affinities of the legend of the Hairy Anchorite', Part I, *University of Illinois Studies in Language and Literature*, 10 (1925), 1–56; Part II, *University of Illinois Studies in Language and Literature*, 11 (1926), 57–139.

Williams, David H., *The Cistercians in the Early Middle Ages* (Leominster: Gracewing, 1998).

Williams-Krapp, Werner, 'The erosion of a monopoly: German religious literature in the fifteenth century', in Renate Blumenfeld-Kosinski, Duncan Robertson and Nancy Bradley Warren (eds), *The Vernacular Spirit: Essays on Medieval Religious Literature* (New York: Palgrave, 2002), pp. 239–63.

Wilmart, A., 'Ève et Goscelin (I)', *Revue Bénédictine*, 46 (1934), 414–38; 'Ève et Goscelin (II)', *Revue Bénédictine*, 50 (1938), 42–83.

Winston-Allen, Anne, *Stories of the Rose: The Making of the Rosary in the Middle Ages* (University Park, PA: Pennsylvania State University Press, 1997).

Wogan-Browne, Jocelyn, *Saints' Lives and Women's Literary Culture c.1150–1300: Virginity and its Authorizations* (Oxford: Oxford University Press, 2001).

——, R. Voaden, ' "Inner" and "outer": conceptualizing the body in *Ancrene Wisse* and Aelred's *de Institutione Inclusarum*, in Gregory Kratzmann and James Simpson (eds), *Medieval English Religious and Ethical Literature: Essays in Honour of G. H. Russell*, (Cambridge: Boydell and Brewer, 1986), pp. 192–208.

——, 'Chaste bodies: frames and experiences', in Sarah Kay and Miri Rubin (eds), *Framing Medieval Bodies* (Manchester: Manchester University Press, 1994), pp. 24–42.

——, A. Diamond, Ann Hutchinson, Carol Meale and Lesley Johnson (eds), *Medieval Women: Texts and Contexts in Late-Medieval Britain* (Turnhout: Brepols, 2000).

Zadnikar, Marijan, with Adam Wienand (eds), *Die Kartäuser: Der Orden der schweigenden Mönche* (Cologne: Wienand Verlag, 1983).

Electronic sources

Copsey, Richard, Chronology of the Medieval Carmelite Priory at York (*http://www.carmelite.org/chronology/york.htm*)

Index

Abelard, Peter 128
abjection 16, 104–5, 107–11, 117, 121–2, 126
Adam 48
Addyman, P. V. 87
Aelfwald of East Anglia, king 45
Aelred of Rivaulx
    Institutione Inclusarum, de 3, 16, 23, 30, 31, 32, 33–5, 95–101, 132, 133, 136, 153, 155–6, 159, 160
    'Rule of a Recluse, The' (fifteenth-century translation) 30–1
    'Rule of Life for a Recluse, A' (trans. by Macpherson) 37, 101, 108, 140, 159
    '*Sermones*', in *Opera Omnia* 164
Alan of Lynn 82, 186
Albert Avogadro 78
Aldhelmi Malmesbiriensis Prosa de Virginitate 43, 45
Alexander, St 61
Alfonso de Jaen 193
Allen, Hope Emily 89, 141, 192
Althusser, Louis 26
Ambrose, St 50
'anchorite', meaning of 13, 56, 103
Ancrene Wisse 3, 4, 10, 13, 21, 23, 30, 31, 32–3, 35, 63, 103–4, 112, 113, 132, 133–4, 135, 136, 138, 172–3, 175, 178, 179, 183, 184, 185, 188, 189, 190
    asceticism of 19, 145–57
    and lay piety 20, 145, 146–7, 161–7
    versions of 165–7

angels 41
animals 46
anointing 33, 34, 177
Anselm of Canterbury
    Prayers and Meditations 50
anti-Semitism 119
Antony, St 12, 43, 44, 46, 56, 58, 60, 64
Apocrypha
    Ecclesiasticus 154
Arsenius 159
artes predicandi 168
Arundel, Thomas, Archbishop of Canterbury
    Constitutions 82
asceticism 55, 109, 118
    anchoritic 19, 132–3, 145–57, 189, 191
Athanasius, St
    Life of St Antony, The 43, 44, 46, 56, 64
Athelbald of Mercia, king 45
Auberger, Jean-Baptiste 74, 75
August, Marilyn 114
Aylesford (Kent), Carmelite community in 78
Ayto, John 37, 101
Azarias (on the Song of the Three Children in the Furnace) 52

Bale, John 84, 85, 90
baptism 34, 106, 181
Barnes, W. R. 62
Barratt, Alexandra 10–11, 14, 23, 37, 101, 173, 180
Barron, Caroline M. 180